WITHDRAWN

ORSON WELLES, SHAKESPEARE, AND POPULAR CULTURE

FILM AND CULTURE

John Belton, General Editor

FILM AND CULTURE

A series of Columbia University Press, edited by John Belton

—

ORSON WELLES

—

SHAKESPEARE

—

AND POPULAR CULTURE

Michael Anderegg

COLUMBIA UNIVERSITY PRESS

NEW YORK

Columbia University Press
Publishers Since 1893
New York   Chichester, West Sussex
Copyright © 1999 by Columbia University Press
All rights reserved
Library of Congress Cataloging-in-Publication Data
Anderegg, Michael A.
Orson Welles, Shakespeare, and popular culture / Michael Anderegg.
p.   cm.
Includes bibliographical references and index.
ISBN 0–231–11228-9 (cloth : alk. paper).
ISBN 0–231–11229-7 (pbk : alk. paper).
1. Shakespeare, William, 1564–1616—Film and video adaptations.
2. Shakespeare, William, 1564–1616—Appreciation—United States.
3. Popular culture—United States—History—20th century.
4. English drama—Film and video adaptations.
5. Welles, Orson, 1915–   .   I. Title.
PR3093.A53   1999
791.43'00233'092—dc21   98–24770

Casebound editions of Columbia University Press books are
printed on permanent and durable acid-free paper.
Printed in the United States of America

c 10 9 8 7 6 5 4 3 2 1
p 10 9 8 7 6 5 4 3 2 1

To Laurence Goldstein

—

Poet, Critic, Friend

CONTENTS

I feel obliged to begin by paraphrasing the kind of sentence that inaugurates many a study of Shakespeare's plays: "Why," a reader may ask, "do we need another book on Orson Welles?" A great deal has been written, particularly in recent years, on Welles. In the last decade or so, from around the time of his death in 1985, five long biographies (one of which is the first volume of a projected two), totaling some 2,500 printed pages, have been published. What more is there to say? One answer to that question could be that what the world now needs is a short book on Orson Welles. This, at least, I feel confident of having provided—and something more as well. Neither a biography, on the one hand, nor a study of Welles as film auteur (of which several excellent examples already exist), on the other, my study of Welles adopts an approach that might be thought analogous to the activity of a geologist who, unable to examine the earth's crust as a totality, drills a hole in the ground and extracts a core sample for closer study. My core sample has as its focus Welles as popularizer of Shakespeare, and my thesis is that Welles holds an unparalleled place in American life as a mediator between high and low culture, between the culture of the printed word and the electronic culture of the modern era. Welles, I will argue, was at once a classicist, a modernist, and a postmodernist, and in attempting to work out the tensions among these modes and cultural stances, he, perhaps inevitably, fashioned a body of work that intensified as much as it resolved those tensions.

Employing archival materials of various kinds, I consider selected aspects of Welles's activities as actor, producer, director, and writer in theater, radio, film, television, and sound recordings. I place particular emphasis on Welles's function and "image" as a Shakespearean actor-director-popularizer within the context of American culture from the 1930s to the 1960s and beyond. Following up on some observations by the cultural historian Lawrence Levine in his book *Highbrow/Lowbrow: The Emergence of Cultural Hierarchy in America*, I will show how Welles attempted to reverse the process whereby Shakespeare had, by the end of the nineteenth-century, ceased to be perceived as a "lowbrow" popular entertainer and had become transformed into an icon of "highbrow" elitist culture. More generally, I look at Welles's own complex role, much of it self-constructed, as a cultural artifact in his own right, someone who was simultaneously an icon of popular and elite culture.

Although this study has a single primary focus—Welles's Shakespearean projects—each chapter approaches its particular topic in a somewhat different manner. Chapter 1, cast in the form of an introduction and overview, triangulates Welles, Shakespeare, and the mass audience of twentieth-century America. My objective here is to suggest something of the complex of attitudes Welles's role as cultural arbiter and public figure generated throughout his career. In chapter 2, I present a survey of Welles as Shakespearean, conceiving of his activities as both distinctive recastings of Shakespearean texts and barometers of popular cultural interest in Shakespeare from the 1930s to the end of the 1950s. Chapter 3 takes a detailed look at an early Shakespearean project, one that could be said to symbolize a transition from book culture to electronic culture: *Everybody's Shakespeare* and the Mercury Text Records. Here my intent is to gauge the nature of Welles's achievement and, more broadly, to show the relationship between culture and commodity as it emerges in the age of mass-produced cultural artifacts.

The main body of my study, however, treats Welles's trio of Shakespearean films, in part because they represent Welles's most ambitious attempt to popularize and disseminate his views of Shakespeare and in part because, unlike stage productions, they exist in a more or less permanent form and thus allow us to better evaluate the relationship between a text and its reception. Chapter 4 previews Welles's trilogy by placing it in the context of the Shakespeare film as genre: I outline some of the issues involved in filming Shakespeare and suggest as well the nature of the critical discourses Shakespeare films have generated in recent times. Chapter 5, on *Macbeth*, strives to explain, among other things, both the film's complex production history and its almost equally complex reception. My discussion of *Othello* (chapter 6), though also concerned with production and reception, discusses as well Welles's modernist approach to Shakespeare's play as he cuts himself off from Hollywood filmmaking. With *Chimes at Midnight/Falstaff*, the subject of chapter 7, my focus shifts to Welles's interpretive strategies and, in general, the ways Welles takes Shakespeare's most political plays and relates them to issues of language and power as these were emerging in the discourse of the 1960s.

Finally, in chapter 8, I step back somewhat from my specifically Shakespearean theme in order to consider Orson Welles as performer. To put the matter in another way, I take the liberty of expanding the connotative possibilities of the term "Shakespearean" so as to include within it Welles's acting personality. My twin guides here are Shakespeare and Brecht, and my purpose is to show how Welles encompassed within himself a plenitude of identities and personae—King and Clown, Sage and Buffoon, Artist and Magician, Hero and Villain, Star and Supernumerary—that made him a kind of amalgamation of Shakespearean types.

All too often, Orson Welles has been regarded primarily as a failed artist, a man who scattered his talents in too many directions at once, who lacked discipline, focus, and perseverance. Without directly concerning myself with these charges, I hope to have revealed here a very different Orson Welles, a man whose many talents and energies were, for more than half a century, dedicated to re-creating what he saw as the essence of Shakespeare's works for a twentieth-century audience and by twentieth-century means. His desire to transcend the barriers separating the classics, the avant-garde, and popular culture remains, I believe, his most enduring legacy.

ACKNOWLEDGMENTS

I n completing a project that has engaged me for a good number of years,
I am particularly sensible of the debts I have accumulated at the same
time that I despair of recalling each and every one of them. The University of North Dakota has assisted my work through a faculty development
leave and several research grants. Ev Albers and the North Dakota Human-
ities Council provided an important impetus for this work in granting me
a Larry Remele Memorial Fellowship in 1990–91. I am grateful to a number of librarians and archivists: Rebecca Campbell Cape at the Lilly
Library, Bloomington, Indiana; Pat Sheehan at the Library of Congress
Motion Picture Division; and the staffs of the New York Public Library at
Lincoln Center, the Folger Shakespeare Library, the Federal Theatre
Archive at George Mason University, the Special Collections at the University of California at Los Angeles, the Special Collections at Northwestern University, the Wisconsin Center for Film and Theatre Research, the
Margaret Herrick Library of the Academy of Motion Picture Arts and Sci-
ences, the Doheny Library at the University of Southern California, and
the Chester Fritz Library at the University of North Dakota.

Two Welles scholars, Jonathan Rosenbaum and James Naremore, not
only helped me by the example of their own work but also read portions
of the manuscript and provided valuable advice. William Paul helped, at
just the right moment, to bring this work to the attention of Columbia
University Press, where Jennifer Crewe, John Belton, and Roy Thomas
offered useful advice and editorial talents. Bill Archibald, Jack Coldeweigh,
Thomas Doherty, Neil Helgeson, Christopher P. Jacobs, Frank Manchel,
James McKenzie, Randy Rasmussen, Laura Shea, and William Simon all

shared with me advice, references, illustrations, clippings, videos, and a variety of other items.

I am especially grateful, once again, to my wife Jeanne for her loving support and for several sensitive and unfailingly helpful readings of each chapter, and to my sons Timothy and Niles for cheering me on and putting up with some inconveniences along the way.

Portions of chapters 7 and 8 originally appeared in, respectively, *Film Quarterly* and *Persistence of Vision*.

I dedicate this work to Laurence Goldstein, whose interest in Orson Welles goes back at least as far as mine, and with whom I began to think about the relationship between popular culture and Shakespeare while enduring elementary school in Culver City, California. He has encouraged my work in many ways, not least by publishing an earlier version of chapter 8 in the *Michigan Quarterly Review*.

Orson Welles, Shakespeare, and Popular Culture

ONE

Shakespeare in Las Vegas

—

Welles and American Culture

W hen I was around twelve years old, I had, like most kids, a nearly insatiable desire for narrative pleasure, for stories of virtually any kind, and I was able to satisfy that desire in a great variety of ways: not only did I have access to books (including comic books), but movies, radio, and, increasingly, television all contributed to the primarily imaginary world in which I spent so much of my time. For the period in question was the early to mid-1950s, a time before television would almost simultaneously eliminate radio as a narrative medium and absorb into itself much of the narrative function of the movies. It was possible, at this time, to read a story in the afternoon, listen to an episode of "The Lone Ranger" or "The Cisco Kid" or "Inner Sanctum" or "The Whistler" on radio after dinner, watch one or another of these very same programs on television later in the evening, and spend much of the following Saturday afternoon at the movies, enjoying an episode of, say, a Superman serial, in addition to four or five cartoons, a "B" western, and the featured "major motion picture" of that week.

It was also possible to experience simultaneously, in various media, "high" and "low" culture, Shakespeare as well as Milton Berle. To be more specific, and more personal, I can remember clearly my attachment both to the much maligned "horror" comics and to "Classics Illustrated," both to *Space Patrol* and to *Omnibus*, both to Joseph Mankiewicz's adaptation of Shakespeare's *Julius Caesar* and to Samuel Fuller's Cold War thriller *Pickup on South Street* (both released in 1953), although I would not have known who Mankiewicz and Fuller were. If my reading interests ranged from the Hardy Boys to Sherlock Holmes to *The Three Musketeers* to *Hamlet*, this was in part because of what I experienced at the movies and on radio and tele-vision. "Culture," in my childhood, was a complex interweaving of high, middle, and low, all uneasily brought together through the enormous reach of mass media.

This is where Orson Welles comes in. He was very much a part of this nexus of media and cultures at the same time that he was not truly central to it. In my case, an understanding of who Orson Welles was was largely a matter of happenstance. When I became interested in Shakespeare, pri-marily through television and Classics Illustrated comic books, the first Shakespeare text I owned—picked up in a used bookstore where I spent a lot of time—was an old copy of *The Mercury Shakespeare*, edited by Orson Welles and Roger Hill, a volume originally published in 1939. One of my favorite radio programs was "The Third Man: The Adventures of Harry Lime," starring Orson Welles. (I hadn't seen the 1949 movie *The Third Man* and hence could not know that the amoral villain Welles played in that film had here been transformed into a relatively benign rascal.) I can also remember seeing Welles on television, playing King Lear on *Omnibus* and reciting Shakespeare on the *Steve Allen Show*, a program my family partic-ularly enjoyed.

The one place where I cannot recall seeing Welles very often was, iron-ically, in the movies. Welles did not direct any films in Hollywood from 1948 to 1958, and his European films—notably *Othello* (1952), which I would have tried to see had I known about it—were virtually invisible in the United States. The only film I can be sure I saw Welles in during most of the 1950s was *Moby Dick* (1956), in which he appears in a single, albeit memorable, scene. Near the end of the fifties, Welles appeared in several important or highly publicized movies for Twentieth Century Fox that I did see, notably *The Long Hot Summer* (1958), *The Roots of Heaven* (1958), and *Compulsion* (1959), though I missed the only one he directed in Hol-lywood, *Touch of Evil* (1958). It wasn't necessary to see Welles at the movies, however, to be vaguely aware that he was a significant force there, too.

In short, Welles, who had virtually dominated the cultural landscape of the late thirties and early forties, continued, albeit in a subterranean way, to be a presence in 1950s culture. Though no longer a seemingly omnipotent figure, he was, at least, omnipresent, difficult to avoid. At the same time, he was an enigma: what, exactly, did Welles represent in the culture to which he contributed? What was the connection between *King Lear* and Harry Lime, Shakespeare and Steve Allen? One way of gauging the nature of

Welles's reputation as it might have been understood at about the midpoint of his career would be to look at his appearance on the *I Love Lucy* show on the evening of October 15, 1956. As he was to do on many subsequent television appearances, Welles, the "guest star," here plays one of his favorite roles—himself. The premise is that the famous Mr. Welles has been invited to perform at Ricky Ricardo's club, and his act, we are informed early in the broadcast, is to be "the same one he did in Las Vegas," namely, "some Shakespeare and, of course, his magic routine."[1] Shakespeare and ("of course") a magic act: the juxtaposition suggests that Orson Welles was generally perceived as a performer who moved comfortably between "highbrow" culture and "lowbrow" entertainment. The balance in this instance may lie somewhat more on the low than the high side of the line; after all, this is an act Welles had been doing in Las Vegas, the capital of lowbrow culture if ever there was one. On the other hand, Welles's act is billed as a benefit, a small detail that erases purely commercial considerations (benefit for what, we are never told) as well as providing the opportunity for some verbal humor at Lucy's expense—"when Lucy gets into the act, nobody benefits."

Much of the evening centers on Lucy's desire to participate in Welles's act: she wants to join him in performing some scenes from Shakespeare. Ricky, as usual, does not want Lucy to have anything to do with an act at his club. Welles, however, needs an assistant; not, it turns out, for Shakespeare—he only plans to recite soliloquies—but for his magic tricks, and in this he is happy to oblige Lucy. The conflict here allows for several scenes that play off of Welles's personality and public image as it would have been available to the viewing audience of the time. Lucy, for example, begs Welles to let her act with him. "I think you're the greatest Shakespearean actor in the whole world," she tells him. "I think you're better than John Gielgud, I think you're better than Maurice Evans, I think you're better than, than Sir Ralph Richardson . . ." A slight pause, and then Welles responds, "You left out Laurence Olivier." At another point, Ricky is telling Welles how disruptive and unreliable Lucy is. "You mean she did all those things in Europe and Hollywood?" Welles comments, referring to the previous season of *I Love Lucy*. "Every one of them," Ricky answers. To which Welles responds, "And they call *me* a character." Welles is thus allowed to undercut himself, to play off of his image as egoist and cranky "genius." Whatever pretensions Welles has to highbrow culture is thereby brought under control in much the same way that "Shakespeare" is removed from the realm of the elite by being associated with Las Vegas and magic tricks.

In the end, Lucy does not get the opportunity to do Shakespeare with Orson Welles at Ricky's club; instead, she becomes the central prop in his levitation act. The scriptwriters, however, do allow both Lucy and Welles to act out, in a rehearsal session, a few moments from *Romeo and Juliet*. Poor Lucy, who had played Juliet in high school, forgets her lines; Welles nonetheless goes on to do what he claims is his favorite scene from the play—Romeo's speech over the body of the supposedly dead Juliet. The joke is, as usual, on Lucy, but it is notable that we never see the full Shakespeare portion of Welles's nightclub act; there are, perhaps, limits to what can be presented on an enormously popular, prime-time U.S. television program in the mid-1950s. The episode ends with Welles levitating Lucy and then forgetting to bring her back down. This sets up the final Shakespeare joke, as the deserted Lucy, floating above the stage, can only cry out "O, Romeo, Romeo, wherefore art thou Romeo!"[2] This gag, it is worth noting, is based on a popular misreading of the line from Shakespeare: Juliet is *not* asking Romeo where he is but rather why his name is Romeo, the name of a family enemy. Shakespeare has here been appropriated and (I assume) deliberately misread, so that he may contribute to popular culture. Welles presumably would not have complained about this: he himself made a career of appropriating Shakespeare for his own ends, of mediating between a view of Shakespeare as high art and a view of Shakespeare as popular entertainment.

Orson Welles, in short, was a presence in the American culture of the 1950s, though one of a particular and peculiar sort. His reputation associated him with highbrow culture, especially Shakespeare, but his activities, as distinct from his reputation, were of the popular culture variety. The paradox here might be expressed another way if we consider that Welles spent much of his life upholding values usually associated with highbrow culture but doing so through media that were by definition irredeemably lowbrow. To appear on television and recite Shakespeare is an act that can be regarded from quite different viewpoints, either as a worthy attempt to stress the popular roots of Shakespeare's art and thus reclaim his works for the kind of audience for whom they were intended or as an equally worthy attempt to lift the cultural level of television viewers by presenting them with high culture not normally to be found on the "boob tube." Both of these views can be said to have their negative shadows, however: on the one hand, a mistaken notion of what popular culture is or ought to be; on the other hand, a condescending, elitist understanding of cultural consumption.

That Welles was simultaneously associated with Shakespeare and with popular entertainment suggests something about America's need to negotiate the gap between high and low culture in the postwar era. A minor brouhaha in the pages of *Saturday Review of Literature* at the beginning of the fifties indicates something of the dimensions of the problem. John Mason Brown, a regular contributor to the magazine and a well-known man of letters, wrote a column decrying the publication of a comic book version (not the Classics Illustrated) of Shakespeare's *Macbeth*. Brown's review is light in tone and mildly whimsical, but there is no denying the seriousness of his concerns. Not surprisingly, he hated the whole thing:

> The mystery of darkness, the supernatural terrors of the heath, the agonies of introspection, the drive and depth of the drama, indeed its greatness which in the theatre or in the library is its excuse and glory—all these are pitifully missing. What is left is not a tragedy. It is trashcan stuff.[3]

"Let us have comics which are comics," he urges, "leave the masterpieces unraped." The rape analogy is picked up in a subsequent letter to the editor, one of three devoted to the topic: "If young people demand comic books and the like, I suppose they must have them," writes a "retired teacher of literature," "[but] in heaven's name let us keep Shakespeare, and keep him undefiled."[4] The "middlebrow" position, one supposes, could not be better articulated.

The other two letters take a rather different tack, however, and each is written by figures who had or would soon gain some cultural weight of their own. The notorious Frederic Werthem, not yet the author of *Seduction of the Innocent*, a passionately misguided attack on comic book culture, but already known for his writings (in the *Saturday Review* and elsewhere) decrying the cultural trash corrupting the morals of teenagers, begins his letter unequivocally: "This is just another crime comic book, this time done up as Shakespeare." On the very first page of the comic, Werthem complains, Lady Macbeth "says 'Smear the sleeping servants with BLOOD!'—Is this the keynote of 'Macbeth'—or of the typical crime comic book?"[5] The third letter, in contrast, lambastes Brown and warmly defends the comic book *Macbeth*, concluding that "Shakespeare's plays originally were produced for masses of people. That this is not true today is due solely to the pedagogical, nose-in-air approach of quasi-scholars who, like Mr. Brown, feel that to share their literary property with others will mean spoilage."[6] The author of this letter, one Herschell Gordon

Lewis, of Coatesville, Pa., then only a young man dreaming of glory, would in the 1960s establish himself as schlockmeister extraordinaire ("The Grandfather of Gore") with such revolutionary blood-and-guts B movies as *Blood Feast* (1963) and *2,000 Maniacs* (1964).

A *Saturday Review* reader might assume that the good Dr. Werthem, though he is attacking comics, was not terribly happy with Shakespeare's influence on the young either. For guardians of public morals, Shakespeare has always presented something of a problem. Given the significant amounts of sex and violence in some of the most popular of his plays, the Thomas Bowlders and Anthony Comstocks of the world frequently found themselves in the uncomfortable position of protecting the innocent from the "World's Greatest Poet."[7] Filmmakers and publishers of comic books became adept at throwing "culture" at the critics of popular entertainment and daring them to do anything about it, as Hugh Hefner and his Playboy Enterprises were quite aware when they financed Roman Polanski's *Macbeth* in the early 1970s. In the fifties, furthermore, purveyors of commodified culture were increasingly interested in attracting the young— teenagers, it was just then being discovered, had considerable buying power on their own.[8] A publicist for Republic Pictures, trying to market Welles's 1948 film version of *Macbeth*, claimed that the film, "with proper promotion . . . can draw not only the regular movie fans and lovers of Shakespeare, but the teen-agers as well." "In terms of modern cycles," the writer adds, " 'Macbeth' combines the thrills of Dick Tracy, Hopalong Cassidy, Roy Rogers, Dracula and Frankenstein."[9]

The Republic publicist clearly hopes to package Shakespeare as popular entertainment, a task that had been somewhat easier a century before. As Lawrence Levine has convincingly argued, Shakespeare's plays had been enormously popular in America throughout much of the nineteenth-century: "From the large and often opulent theaters of major cities to the makeshift stages in halls, saloons, and churches of small towns and mining camps, wherever there was an audience for the theater, there Shakespeare's plays were performed prominently and frequently."[10] Furthermore, Levine notes, "Shakespeare was presented as part of the same milieu inhabited by magicians, dancers, singers, acrobats, minstrels, and comics," appearing "on the same playbills and . . . advertised in the same spirit."[11] Here a key text might be Mark Twain's *Huckleberry Finn*, published in 1884, which presents us with a couple of con artists, the King and the Duke, who, among their mixed bag of activities, plan to present garbled versions of Shakespeare to a gullible public, billing themselves as David Garrick the Younger and

Edmund Kean the Elder. (We might note here that when Welles adapted *Huckleberry Finn* for radio in the late 1930s, he cast himself as the Duke.) Shakespeare, Twain clearly tells us, was a crowd pleaser, a draw (at least potentially) even in the small Mississippi river towns visited by Huck and company.[12]

But this situation, according to Levine, no longer obtained by the turn of the twentieth century. By mid-century, certainly, "the nature of [Shakespeare's] relationship to the American people had changed: he was no longer their familiar, no longer part of their culture, no longer at home in their theaters or on the movie and television screens that had become the twentieth-century equivalents of the stage."[13] As early as 1905, an observer of the cultural scene could write that Shakespeare and other famous writers were "infinite bores to every-day people."[14] Levine and others have provided a number of tentative explanations for this change in Shakespeare's cultural status, though these tend to be causes that themselves need explaining. Among these would be the decline of oratory, the rise of naturalistic acting, the influence of Romanticism, which redefined Shakespeare as a poet rather than a dramatist, and, perhaps most significantly, the intensification of class differences which led, among other things, to a distinction between theater as entertainment for the mob and as culture for the well-to-do. As Levine writes, "From the time of their formulation, such cultural categories as highbrow and lowbrow were hardly meant to be neutral descriptive terms; they were openly associated with and designed to preserve, nurture, and extend the cultural history and values of a particular group of peoples in a specific historical context."[15] The main point to bear in mind here, in any case, is that Shakespeare, in the nineteenth century, had been simultaneously popular and elite, and that by the early years of the twentieth century he had become more and more associated with elite culture and less and less with popular culture.

What Levine's study makes clear is that Shakespeare, in nineteenth-century America (as is evident from *Huckleberry Finn*), could simultaneously be an object of awe and admiration and the butt of jokes—jokes that ranged from the affectionate to the malicious, from high spirits to defensive resentment. By a kind of transference, thus, much the same mixed response came to those associated with Shakespeare, so that by the middle of the twentieth century, to be labeled as "America's greatest Shakespearean actor" is to be both admired and ridiculed (to be "Poland's greatest Shakespearean actor," a title Jack Benny claims in Ernst Lubitsch's *To Be or Not to Be* [1942], invites nothing but ridicule). In John Ford's *My Darling Clementine*

(1946), which brings a twentieth-century perspective to a nineteenth-century world, we have a clearly divided attitude toward Shakespeare. The Shakespearean actor Granville Thorndyke (Alan Mowbray) is both a pretentious drunk and a dignified victim of cruel treatment by the villainous Clanton boys. Wyatt Earp (Henry Fonda) protects and defends him: he represents civilization and culture ("Shakespeare in Tombstone," Earp says in awed tones); the townspeople, on the other hand, are ready to ride him out of town on a rail: he's unreliable and he doesn't pay his bills. Ford, like Earp, clearly values him, however unable he may be to present him without a good deal of—mostly good-natured—kidding.[16]

My Darling Clementine, whatever its shortcomings as history, does get one thing right: from almost the earliest days of the Republic, American culture had been primed to regard Shakespearean actors with a mixture of awe and suspicion. Almost simultaneously, in the early nineteenth century, three visiting British Shakespeareans caught the imagination of American theatergoers: George Frederick Cooke, Edmund Kean, and Junius Brutus Booth were all three dynamic and passionate performers, and two of the three, Cooke and Booth, remained in America until the end of their careers. Booth toured in Shakespearean roles all over the United States. All three were also, in the words of theater historian Charles Shattuck, "quite mad at times."

> If their best stage performances provided the greatest thrills and deepest revelations that American audiences had ever known, their worst performances and extratheatrical carryings-on stirred up excitements of another kind. Their brawling or boozing or whoring amused some observers, disgusted others, but could not go unnoticed. . . . They were the Wild Ones.[17]

Booth had three sons who followed in his footsteps. One, Edwin, would become the premier Shakespearean of his time and beyond; another, John Wilkes, a part-time Shakespearean and all-around matinee idol, would assassinate Abraham Lincoln. To be a Shakespearean actor in America was, in the popular imagination, nearly the same as being a Shakespearean character. At the very least, a larger-than-life flamboyance, an attachment to the bottle, and a general aura of physical self-indulgence appear to have become prerequisites for inheriting the mantle of American Shakespearean. John Barrymore, who would insert jigs and comic byplay between scenes in his performance as Hamlet in the 1920s, fits the mold; Welles does too, though his varied achievements tended to both detract from and at the same time set off in a peculiar light his Shakespearean identity.

Welles inherits as well another tradition of Shakespearean performance, one that may be considered at once marvelous and silly: he is one in a "long line of Young Rosciuses and Infant Wonders"[18] who, ranging in ages from four to twelve, played Richard III, Hamlet, Shylock, and Portia, among other roles, on the English-speaking stages in the nineteenth century. In fact, the actor who is often referred to as America's first Hamlet, the native-born John Howard Payne, essayed that role in New York at the age of ten. Welles's childhood accomplishments were comparatively modest, and much of what has been written of his earliest Shakespearean activities belongs more to the realm of myth than to verifiable fact. Infant prodigies, in any case, are invariably irritating, as Welles was himself the first to acknowledge,[19] and a Shakespearean prodigy might be considered doubly so. It is not entirely to Welles's credit that, according to one account, "[he] was presenting his own versions of Shakespeare before he knew his ABC's," especially when we learn from the same source that Welles was mixing highballs for himself at age "eight or nine" and "started on cigars at about ten."[20] Welles's guest appearances on radio, especially with Jack Benny, would often center on his prodigy reputation. "Why, when he was seven," Benny jokes in a 1940 program, "he [Welles] played Uncle Tom, Little Eva, Simon Legree, and the Cabin in *Uncle Tom's Cabin*."[21] However much this "information" is presented either tongue in cheek or as outright kidding, the conjunction of precocious Shakespeare with premature decadence is one that once again serves to mark off the Shakespearean actor as a bizarre and eccentric individual.

The ambivalence with which both Shakespeare and Welles are so frequently surrounded can be glimpsed in the appearance Welles made as "special guest star" on the long-running Rudy Vallee radio program on December 19, 1940. The other guest that evening (actually, a semiregular) was John Barrymore. Barrymore was, by 1940, a longtime alcoholic near the end of his life (he died two years later at the age of sixty) and well past the end of his career as one of the great stars of American theater and film; his final years, nonetheless, revealed a fine talent for self-mockery and for slogging through with courage and something like dignity in spite of the odds. What, in 1940, tied the twenty-five-year-old boy wonder and the fifty-eight-year-old near has-been was their status as Shakespearean actors and, simultaneously, as egotistical "hams." Barrymore, who provides a direct link to nineteenth-century theatrical traditions through his uncle John Drew and his father Maurice Barrymore, had done for American Shakespeare in the 1920s what Welles did in the 1930s: turned him into a box office success and made him a cultural commodity of some note. Barry-more's success in *Hamlet* and *Richard III* placed him at the pinnacle of fame and led to a remarkably generous Hollywood contract as the major male star at Warner Brothers at the end of the twenties.[22]

The Vallee program is structured as a duel between egos (much of radio seems to have been built around feuds of one kind or another), with Vallee as referee. Although Barrymore is in some ways the main butt of the jokes, a number of them cruelly aimed at his "advanced" age, Welles comes in for a good deal of ribbing as well. Barrymore, who comes on first, chafes at having to perform with Welles. "Why," Barrymore sputters, "he's an exhi-bitionist, a publicity seeker, a headline hunter, a cheap sensationalist, why, why, he's another John Barrymore." "John, I believe you're jealous," Vallee retorts, "jealous because Orson Welles is the greatest living Shakespearean actor." Introduced as a "night of thespian delight," the program, like many radio variety shows of the period, turns into vaudeville—a few jokes by Barrymore, some jokes by Welles, a song by Vallee, a skit with Welles and Barrymore, another song by Vallee, a "soft shoe" routine, and so forth, con-cluding with some "real Shakespeare." Real Shakespeare as opposed to what? Presumably as opposed to the shenanigans Barrymore and Welles have been engaging in for most of the program: two Shakespearean actors fooling around can be regarded, in this light, as "fake Shakespeare."

Given the vaudeville-like structure of the program, the closing bit of what Vallee terms "real" Shakespeare becomes simultaneously a change of pace, a cap on the evening, and a throwaway. Barrymore and Welles per-form a portion of the Tent Scene from *Julius Caesar*, Welles playing Brutus, Barrymore Cassius. Welles's reading is authoritative—he knew this scene backwards and forwards, having played it on Broadway in his own pro-duction of *Julius Caesar*—but it is Barrymore's performance as the seem-ingly wronged Cassius that provides a moving note to what is essentially a declamatory exercise, though his delivery lacks the crispness that we know he was capable of from early recordings. That these few moments of Shake-speare turn out to be rather poignant may or may not be an accident, depending as it does on our knowledge, listening to the program today, that Welles had arrived at what would be perceived by many as the high-water mark of his career while Barrymore was at the end of his. Barrymore and Welles, furthermore, would turn out to resemble each other as bywords for squandered talent and self-destructive behavior, which adds yet another note of irony to the proceedings, even if we want to insist that the parallel is not really that convincing.

What the Vallee show most clearly suggests, however, is that though Welles was never regarded only or even primarily as a Shakespearean, his various projects—in this instance, the forthcoming *Citizen Kane*—could not help but be tinged with his Shakespearean identity, if only for purposes of comic deflation. Shakespeare, in other words, was part of the "mix" that defined Orson Welles. With very little encouragement, Welles would present himself as a commentator—an often commonsensical and insightful one—on Shakespeare's plays. Given that his formal education ended at the age of sixteen, his intellectual self-confidence was particularly impressive. When the British *South Bank Show* presented a program on *Hamlet* in the 1980s, Welles, via black-and-white BBC videotape from the 1960s, became, along with Peter Brook, Michael Pennington, and others, an expert on the play. Welles was then (c. 1963) in his "sleek" years, clean-shaven, well-fed, and cherubic, and his remarks are made with that combination of spontaneity, light self-mockery, and self-assurance that were his trademarks as raconteur. Of course Hamlet was not mad, he tells us, but only "sick." "I don't think any madman ever said 'Why, what an ass am I,' "Welles comments, adding, "I think that is a divinely sane remark."[23] Welles here becomes the television entertainer as Shakespearean scholar.

Just such a wedding of entertainment and scholarship informed both Welles's Shakespearean activities and his career as a whole. Though he did not precisely fit in with the primarily Eastern academics and intellectuals who were responsible for such phenomena as the Book-of-the-Month Club (1921—), the Great Books seminars (1920s), and the use of media— notably radio—as a means of disseminating cultural information, Welles can be associated with the movement to popularize culture which developed in the first half of the century; this is very much the atmosphere to which he was exposed and to which he made his own contribution. Welles, of course, did not have a Ph.D. (prodigies, presumably, do not need university degrees). He was not an academic, and, as an intellectual, he was almost entirely self-taught. He could, nonetheless, more than hold his own as a guest on the popular middlebrow radio quiz show, "Information Please." If he did not play a direct role in the discourse of middlebrow culture as that phenomenon became established in the first half of the twentieth century, and if he seems to have not been aware of the complex of motives that underpinned the movement, his cultural interests largely coincided with the goals of those who more directly formulated middlebrow culture.

As Joan Shelly Rubin has shown,[24] some of the promptings for middlebrow culture were reactionary and antimodern in nature; in other instances, progressive visionaries were ready and willing to embrace modernity while at the same time wishing to ameliorate its dangers. Some of these intellectuals wanted primarily to preserve culture, others wanted to disseminate it as broadly as possible. Welles, perhaps because he was not a traditional intellectual with ties to the academy, was far more open to viewing "culture" as a wide spectrum: as much as he may have honored Shakespeare, he was by instinct and interest equally drawn to Conan Doyle and Dashiell Hammett, as his "Mercury Theatre on the Air" programs demonstrate. In other words, it was not necessary for Welles to "discover" popular culture or to accommodate it to elite culture.

One way of suggesting the impulses guiding Welles's cultural interests would be to look at the two projects he considered seriously during his first months at RKO studios before finally turning to the original screenplay for *Citizen Kane*. The first of these, Joseph Conrad's *Heart of Darkness*, is one of the founding texts of high modernism; the second, Nicholas Blake's *Smiler with a Knife*, is a country-house detective novel in the Agatha Christie–Dorothy Sayers school of popular entertainment (albeit it was written pseudonymously by England's future poet-laureate C. Day Lewis). All that connects these two projects is the presence of a central character who represents or embodies—indirectly in one instance, directly in the other—the impulse to fascism. One could argue from this and other incidents in Welles's career that the division between art and entertainment is not one Welles took very seriously. Such a distinction did not, in any case, govern either his choice of material or his methods of production. In the event, Welles's first Hollywood film turned out to be neither highbrow nor lowbrow but rather an amalgam of the two impulses—an ambitious, modernist foray into film style wedded to a tale of detection, a kaleidoscopic, nonlinear, fragmented meditation on the human condition easily unraveled, reassembled, and reconstituted into a straightforward tale of a journalist's quest for the big scoop.

These dichotomies continue throughout Welles's life: on the one hand, *Macbeth, Othello, The Trial* (1962), *Chimes at Midnight* (1967), *F for Fake* (1973); on the other, *Journey into Fear* (1942), *The Stranger* (1946), *Lady from Shanghai* (1948), *Touch of Evil*.[25] Classic, modern, postmodern, popular—everything was grist for his mill. As an actor, if he is not playing Tiresias in *Oedipus the King*, he is playing Laffiche in *Casino Royale* (1967). On television, he is King Lear on *Omnibus* and engaged in slapstick on *I Love Lucy*. He played Brutus in *Julius Caesar* late evenings on Broadway after rushing over from the studios of CBS radio where, an hour earlier, he had been "The Shadow." In practice, Welles's cultural interventions were inevitably viewed as either too high or too low or in some way compromised by a quirky, individual vision to fit comfortably into any niche available to him. Both *Touch of Evil*, clearly lowbrow material, drive-in theater fodder, and *The Trial*, modernist, elite, "European," failed to please their natural audiences and at the same time could not find a middle ground. *Touch of Evil* was too perverse, too stylistically abnormal, to work as mass entertainment; *The Trial* was too much of a gangster movie, too "American," to please the art cinema audience. But neither film had crossover potential: the elite audience could not get past the pulp fiction elements of the former and the general audience had little patience for the sound-image dislocations of the latter. Welles was uncompromising at both ends of the spectrum, either unwilling or unable to gauge the nature of his potential viewers.

The perceived wedding of lowbrow with highbrow in Welles's career did not necessarily work to his advantage. Though he might reasonably be thought of as something of an icon of mass culture, Welles nevertheless tended to identify himself, and was frequently identified by others, as an artist firmly positioned within an elite, avant-garde tradition. Just as there are two Charles Foster Kanes, warring with each other—one a robber baron, the other a trustbuster—so there are two Orson Welleses, one an eccentric, difficult genius, the other a huckster and eternal television personality. The precipitous "decline" of Welles from Shakespeare and high seriousness in general to Paul Masson wines, from classical and modernist art to postmodern commodification of self, becomes the favored scenario for those wishing to lament Welles's fate. The "genius" label was a very sharp two-edged sword, attached to Welles's name as much to denigrate his person as to recognize his achievement. Welles was aware of this quite early on: in a 1937 newspaper interview he is quoted as commenting, "I'm either the genius they say I am or the world's godawfullest ham. It's a fifty-fifty split."[26] Given the anti-intellectual strain in American culture, it can fairly be supposed that Welles suffered more than he benefited from being perceived as a highbrow. So much so, indeed, that even the obvious evidence of his attraction to lowbrow material worked against him: such projects were inevitably depicted as falls from on high, evidence of declined powers, "comeuppances" of one kind or another. That Welles was never able to find a comfortable cultural niche for himself can partly be attributed to issues of personality and temperament, but it has almost as much to do with his chameleon-like refusal to be pinned down at any particular point on a scale from "high" to "low." When, by the end of the 1940s, Welles had, for all practical purposes, moved to Europe, this too fueled resentment in some quarters, especially when the move was attributed to tax problems as well as a failure on his part to work successfully within the Hollywood studio system.

What such an interpretation of Welles's career overlooks, however, is that the two Welleses always existed side by side. Welles established himself professionally on the radio in the mid-1930s by helping to sell Goodrich tires ("The Shadow") and Campbell's cream of tomato soup ("Mercury Theatre on the Air" becomes "Campbell Playhouse"). His working life was inextricably bound up with commercial sponsorship; even when he was not the on-the-air spokesman for this or that product, his activities functioned in the same way. The movement from a situation where Welles's dependence on tires and soup was buffered by the use of announcers who sold the product for Welles to a situation where Welles sold the product for himself (i.e., was his own announcer-pitchman) can be regarded simply as a gradual demystification of the relationship between art and commerce in the twentieth century. The major difference needs to be stated in another fashion, however. In the 1930s Welles was selling soup by creating a product—radio drama—that involved him in an aesthetic activity, or series of activities, as writer, producer, director, actor. When, however, Welles sold Paul Masson's wine, he was not creating a product: he *was* the product. Which is another way of saying that Welles was as much engaged in selling himself, keeping himself alive as a commodity, as he was in pushing his sponsor's creation.

As promoted by Welles, Shakespeare too becomes, as does "culture" in general, a commodity, something that can be sold, but also, and perhaps more significantly, a product that lends luster to that greater product, the one who sponsors these cultural activities. As Michael Bristol puts it, referring to a magazine ad of the 1980s which promoted the decision of a realty company to offer buyers subscriptions to the Alabama Shakespeare Festival, "In the world of practical affairs, Shakespeare has real importance, for he is, among other things, the greatest apartment salesman of our time."[27] To the question, "How is tomato soup like Shakespeare?" an obvious answer presents itself: they are both excellent of their kind. Such is the aura of "culture" that the sponsor of culture necessarily becomes "classy" in its presence. When Welles produced a radio version of *King Lear* on his "Mercury Summer Theatre" program, the announcer proudly told his listeners that the makers of Pabst "Blue Ribbon" beer, in honor of the occasion,

"have omitted their usual commercial message between acts."[28] This obei-
sance in the direction of high art no doubt redounded to the sponsor's
credit, perhaps compensating for the decision to present Shakespeare's
most complex tragedy in less than thirty minutes.

The commercialization of Welles's media activities, the process whereby his image became associated primarily or even exclusively with brand-
name products—American Airlines, Paul Masson wines—parallels the
commercialization of American media. Just as the percentage of commercially sponsored programs (as opposed to unsponsored, "sustaining" programs) grew, on NBC radio, from 23.6 percent to 49.9 percent from 1933
to 1944, and from 22.7 to 47.8 percent during the same period on CBS,[29]
to such an extent that, by the beginning of the 1940s, radio programming
was the creation of advertising agencies, so Welles's cultural activities necessarily became gradually more enmeshed with commercial sponsorship.
Welles's "Campbell Playhouse" did not answer primarily to CBS but to
Ward Wheelock, whose ad agency represented Campbell Soup. When
Welles deviated from the desires of the agency, he heard about it.[30] Welles's
independence was, from the beginning, something he had to fight for, not
something guaranteed to him.

Welles's relationship to commercialization was multilayered and complex. At one end of the scale, he was simply a professional announcer, the
possessor of a voice and delivery particularly suitable to the medium of
radio and, later, television. The timbre of his voice and his "mid-Atlantic"
accent made him especially appropriate as narrator for "class" projects like
the *National Geographic Specials*. (For similar reasons, the voice of Alexander
Scourby, an actor virtually unknown to the public at large, was used in the
same way by a number of sponsors and organizations, including the
National Geographic Society.) At the other end of the scale, Welles was a
celebrity in his own right, and his identifiable voice or on-camera appearances were in the nature of celebrity endorsements. Most of Welles's
commercial activities fell somewhere in between these extremes or, more
accurately, combined the two functions. As a celebrity, Welles projected an
aura partly constructed from his association with Shakespeare and high
culture; and the celebrity testimonial had long been a part of the American advertising world in which Welles had found his earliest success.

The general American ambivalence toward highbrow culture was one
that, to a certain extent, Welles himself may have shared. The attempt to
detach Shakespeare from his rarefied cultural ghetto is one indication of
this. Another indication is the way the discourse of "opera" functions in the

narrative of *Citizen Kane*.[31] From Kane's point of view as well as, to a lesser extent, from the point of view of his protegée Susan Alexander (Dorothy Comingore), opera equals "real" singing, the highest reach of a musician's art. At the same time, opera signifies Kane's pretensions to culture and his tyranny over Susan. We are meant to assume that Jed Leland (Joseph Cotten), Kane's friend and employee, cuts out paper dolls and falls asleep during Susan's debut because she is such a bad actress–singer, but, of course, this doesn't really make much sense: first, would Jed necessarily know the difference? and second, there is more to an opera than the performance of the soprano. Equally likely, Jed is bored by opera itself. His response, in other words, might be thought to stand in for the response of the average filmgoer watching *Citizen Kane*. A more tellingly ambivalent moment, perhaps, is the famous upwardly vertical camera movement that comes to a stop on stagehands standing far up in the flies, one of whom holds his nose as Susan seemingly fails to come to terms with the difficulties of her opening aria. He may be a working man, the shot tells us, but even he knows his high "C's." Or does he? Is it not simply opera that stinks? Again, the moment is nicely ambiguous.

Or consider the scene in *Lady from Shanghai* where Michael O'Hara (Orson Welles), escaping through San Francisco's Chinatown from both the police and, although he may not know it yet, Rita Hayworth, stumbles into a theater where a performance by the Mandarin Theatre Troupe is in progress. The film nearly comes to a halt at this point in order that we, the viewers, may take in a bit of incomprehensible, if intriguing, highly formalized mummery. Here, in the midst of a film *policier*, Welles introduces a few moments of high art of the most rarefied kind. The film's attitude toward this is not easy to gauge. Welles seems admiring of the act he is presenting at the same time that he uses the actors' reactions in part for comic effect. The meta-theatricality of the episode no doubt reflects, as Barbara Leaming points out,[32] Welles's interest in Brecht at this time, but the conjunction of "high" art with a "low" context is characteristically Wellesian. *Mr. Arkadin* (aka *Confidential Report*, 1955), too, juxtaposes high and low in ambivalent fashion.[33] At other times, the relationship is one of text to mode of production—so Welles films Shakespeare's *Macbeth* on the B western sets of Republic Pictures. Or the tension is between form and content. *Touch of Evil*, another *policier*, has something of the structure and thematic resonance of Greek tragedy. Similarly, Welles as actor teeters uncertainly from "old-fashioned" actor-manager barnstorming to Brechtian distantiation (see chapter 8).

The elite/popular dichotomy in Welles's films can exist in a form where the elements are, at first sight, extremely difficult to separate out. Why, for example, should *The Magnificent Ambersons* (1942), adapted from a novel by a popular American regionalist, have been received as somehow "high hat"? Members of the preview audiences, both those who liked the film and those who did not, used such words and phrases as "fine art," "artistic," "too deep for the average stupid person," and "*artistic* trash."[34] Presumably, something in Welles's (and RKO's?) handling of the material called forth such reactions. Welles had, in fact, taken the oedipal subtext of Booth Tarkington's novel and intensified it; here, the "elite" element could be seen as a matter of "attitude" and emotional force. Tarkington was himself aware of a connection between his protagonist's excessive attachment to his mother and Hamlet (and this before Freud); he includes a chapter making the parallel explicit. If the film of *Ambersons* is at all "high brow," it is so in the sense that Welles refuses the more obvious melodramatic and linear elements of his source for the sake of complex character development, atmospheric detail, and ambiguous actions. With *Ambersons* he was making a film in which what does not happen seems as important as what does. The majority of the preview audiences in Pomona and Pasadena, at least, was not quite open to that kind of experience.

Highbrow, middlebrow, lowbrow: Welles's relationship to these cultural tags was in constant flux throughout his career, and nowhere is this more evident than in the various ways he interacted with the plays of William Shakespeare. For well over half a century, Welles contributed to a remarkable miscellany of Shakespearean activities. Some of these projects could be characterized as central to his interests and of significance for American culture, while others were marginal to or accidental by-products of activities not primarily Shakespearean in nature. In virtually every media open to him—including but not limited to books, stage, radio, recordings, film, and television—Welles turned again and again to Shakespeare's plays with an energy and enthusiasm that suggests a paramount need both to express himself through Shakespeare and to make Shakespeare's plays and characters, themes and motifs, available to a wide popular audience.

Many of Welles's Shakespearean projects were highly publicized and have subsequently received a good deal of attention: the "voodoo" *Macbeth* for the Federal Theatre in 1936, the "fascist" *Julius Caesar* on Broadway in 1937; the films, *Macbeth*, *Othello*, and *Chimes at Midnight*. But these are only among the better known of Welles's Shakespearean activities. He also produced and starred in *King Lear* at New York's City Center in the 1950s, and he played the title role in that play for Peter Brook on television in 1953. On radio he directed and starred in a production of *Hamlet* in 1936,[35] and did the same for *Julius Caesar* in 1938. In the late 1960s he filmed a so-far-unreleased (and seemingly uncompleted) version of *The Merchant of Venice*.[36] In the 1970s he produced a documentary for West German television on *Filming Othello*. And not long before his death in 1985, he prepared a screenplay for a projected film version of *King Lear*. Perhaps most visibly, he appeared a number of times on television variety shows to perform a Shakespearean "turn." This list, which could easily be supplemented, provides some indication of the variety and extent of Orson Welles's interactions with Shakespeare.

Welles both promoted Shakespeare as a cultural value and employed Shakespeare's plays, more often than not, as pegs on which to hang his own product, as the means toward transforming or promoting his own career and his distinctive image. Shakespeare, furthermore, can be seen as an element in all of Welles's work, an influence that comes to suffuse the approaches and methods he employs in a variety of media, particularly as a performer and a personality. More broadly, a close look at a few of the more significant of his Shakespearean projects can tell us something not only about Welles but as well about how Shakespeare functioned in twentieth-century American culture. What does it mean to be a "Shakespearean" in the United States? What are the cultural advantages and disadvantages of promoting Shakespeare and his work? Can Shakespeare be reconciled to modern popular taste? And to what extent does Welles himself "become" Shakespeare in the process?

TWO

"Raise Hell with Everything"

—

Shakespeare as Event

Welles's lifelong alliance with Shakespeare's plays, which simultaneously reached backward to the nineteenth century and forward to the world of the postmodern, presented itself under a variety of guises—Shakespeare as Star Vehicle, Shakespeare as Culture, Shakespeare as Commodity, Shakespeare as Romantic, Shakespeare as Subversive, and even Shakespeare as Welles. In sum, what Welles almost always produced was "Shakespeare as Event." Many and varied as his Shakespearean activities were, however, Welles seldom strayed very far from a focus on the plays that had become established as the standard Shakespeare repertoire as early as the 1810s and '20s, and which remain so (with some modifications) to this day: *Julius Caesar*, *Macbeth*, *Othello*, *King Lear*, *Hamlet*, and *The Merchant of Venice*. In part, this reflects the essentially nineteenth-century theatrical tradition in which Welles came of age; as we will see in the next chapter, however, it reflects as well his awareness of what constituted the secondary school curriculum, which would have suggested a potential market ripe for exploitation.

At the same time, Welles's choice of particular plays and the manner in which he reconstructed them can be seen as an expression of his politics and social beliefs. His Shakespeare productions were, to a degree at least, potentially subversive: the all-black *Macbeth* in Harlem and the antifascist *Julius Caesar* on Broadway pretty much speak for themselves. As Michael Denning observes, "For Welles, the Elizabethan tragedies and histories of Shakespeare and Marlowe offered a critique of fascism's worship of power, and their giant protagonists paralleled the 'great dictators' of modern times."[1] But *Othello*, with its emphasis on the love between a black man and a white woman, and *Chimes at Midnight*, which thoroughly under-mines traditional authority, were also projects that highlight and bring into play a Shakespeare who cannot be too readily allied with middle-class comforts and conventional pieties.

That Welles's Shakespearean scope was largely limited to specific texts—*Macbeth, King Lear, Othello, Twelfth Night, Julius Caesar, The Merchant of Venice*, the "Falstaff" plays—reflects as well a compulsion to repeat that characterizes all his work. Welles was early on enamored of certain narra-tives and certain characters, including, in addition to Shakespeare, Oscar Wilde's *The Happy Prince*, Joseph Conrad's *Heart of Darkness*, and *Don Quixote*. *Julius Caesar*, for example, is the subject of a textbook, a stage pro-duction, two audio recordings, a radio adaptation, and at least three pro-jected films. Lear was a role Welles played on radio, on stage, and on tele-vision, and a *Lear* film was the project he was working on at the end of his life. In each instance, Welles both repeats himself, by adapting central con-cepts or just bits of business to which he has become attached, and at the same time does it differently. Perhaps only too aware of this tendency, he rather disingenuously informed Peter Bogdanovich that the only connec-tion between his "voodoo" *Macbeth* of 1936 and the Republic film of 1948 was that "when Macbeth goes up to Duncan's bedchamber, for me—I don't know why—he simply has to move stage right to left. That's all [*laughs*]."[2] Actually, as can be easily shown, there are a great number of con-nections, large and small, between the two productions, and between them and the Salt Lake City staging of the play which immediately preceded the film. Welles always went back, and he was always impatient with what he had done in the past; he wanted to do it again, but with a difference: a dif-ferent medium, a rethought setting, an altered context, a reconceived adap-tation, a new role. These dual impulses, to return and to change, provided Welles with a productive tension throughout his career.

One principle Welles learned early on and nearly always adhered to was that Shakespeare needs to be treated, insofar as possible, as an event, and preferably an event in which Welles himself could also be an event of at least equal interest. This is not entirely a matter of ego, though ego unde-niably plays a part; it is also to some extent an instinct for showmanship, for selling—selling himself was one way to sell Shakespeare. As early as his high school years, Welles was packaging Shakespeare in an eye-catching fashion, putting plays together and taking them apart as best suited his purposes. Staging Shakespeare's history plays as "Winter of Our Discontent" and playing both Richard Crookback and Falstaff, as he did while still a student at the Todd School for Boys, was a way of making Shakespeare stand forth in a distinctive fashion while at the same time calling attention to his own virtuosity and nerve, albeit in the safe, protected environment of a secondary school. At the Gate Theatre in Dublin, where Welles ended up after a painting tour of Ireland, he talked Hilton Edwards and Michael MacLiammoir, the codirectors, into allowing him to play the Ghost of Hamlet's father and Fortinbras, not, perhaps, the most obvious casting for a sixteen-year-old—Laertes, one might suppose, would have been more appropriate. But playing the Ghost, in particular, garnered attention; it was a piece of casting and a performance to be remarked upon, singled out, noted even if only in passing. Who pays any attention to Laertes?

His stay at the innovative Gate Theatre taught Welles a good deal about Shakespeare and about the modern theater. In becoming acquainted with Edwards and MacLiammoir, he plugged into a rich, significant theatrical tradition. Edwards had been a member of Charles Doran's Shakespeare Company as well as, later, the Old Vic, and now acted, directed, and designed the lighting at the Gate. MacLiammoir had been a child actor in Sir Herbert Beerbohm-Tree's company at His Majesty's Theatre in London, and, in addition to being an actor, was a set and costume designer. Both were strongly influenced by the "new stagecraft" which had developed at the end of the nineteenth century and came to dominate staging and design in the first decade of the twentieth century.[3] The new stagecraft was not all one thing; its principles and practitioners pulled in two directions at once. On the one hand, the movement championed the highly decorative or concept-oriented work of designers like Edward Gordon Craig, Adolphe Appia, Leonid Bakst, and Norman Bel Geddes and of directors like André Antoine, George Pitöeff, and Fyodor Komisarjevsky. On the other side, and especially with reference to Shakespeare production, the new stagecraft, at least in Great Britain, meant the work of William Poel and Harley Granville-Barker, whose aim it was to re-create, insofar as possible, the simplicity, speed, and intimacy of Elizabethan staging, as well as such singular but influential experiments as Barry Jackson's modern dress Shakespeare at the Birmingham Repertory Theatre.[4] Both tendencies would characterize Welles's own approach to Shakespeare staging.

When Welles returned to the United States, however, his first professional association with Shakespeare, as a member of Katharine Cornell's troupe, was at some remove from the new stagecraft. Welles found himself involved in what was both something of an anachronism and very likely the last of its kind: a touring repertory company, playing Shakespeare (among other offerings), composed around a major Broadway star and performing one- and two-day engagements as well as numerous one-night stands through the whole length and breadth of the country—all told, the company traveled over 16,000 miles, giving 225 performances over some twenty-nine weeks.[5] Nothing remotely like it would be seen again. For a comparable event, one would need to go back to the Edwin Booth–Lawrence Barrett tour of 1887–88. They traveled for thirty-five weeks, visiting seventy-three cities (covering, like Cornell, about 16,000 miles) with an all-Shakespeare repertory.[6] The scope and nature of their tour goes some way in confirming Lawrence Levine's thesis about the popularity of Shakespeare in the nineteenth century. Booth and Barrett, however, were, by the late 1880s, themselves becoming anachronisms. The magical aura surrounding Booth's name sustained the tour, but his and Barrett's success at the end of the nineteenth century marked the conclusion of a period when such a heavy dose of Shakespeare would be acceptable to audiences far and wide. By the time Orson Welles was born (1915), Shakespeare was no longer the surefire draw he had been some two decades earlier. Although he did not do it alone, it would be Welles's mission to rekindle, at least in part, that interest, and he would do it, if not entirely successfully, for a far wider audience than even Booth and Barrett, or Katharine Cornell, could have imagined.

Welles, in other words, as part of Cornell's entourage found himself participating in what was essentially a nineteenth-century version of bringing culture to the masses. True, only one play was Shakespeare's, and *Romeo and Juliet* was given only thirty-nine times, whereas *The Barretts of Wimpole Street*, probably Cornell's best-known starring vehicle, was given 144 times. The tour as a whole, nonetheless, would have suggested to Welles some idea of how Shakespeare—in this case, fairly traditionally mounted Shakespeare—would play to varied audiences. His immediate response to the tour was ambivalent: "Miss Cornell's tour was a great and gracious gesture," he wrote in a small notebook sometime around his twentieth birthday, "but there is something a bit insulting in its implication."[7] Welles, presumably, is commenting on the air of noblesse oblige that the tour might have signified to some. Whatever his private reservations, Welles, in a circumstance where he had no control over any part of the productions in which he appeared, was nonetheless able to use Shakespeare to his advantage. Cast as Mercutio in *Romeo and Juliet*, he was effective in a showy, highly rhetorical role, one that took full advantage of his voice and his propensity for bombast. (No one commented very much on his other roles on tour—his Octavius Moulton-Barrett in *The Barretts of Wimpole Street* and Marchbanks in *Candida*.) Even when, no doubt to his chagrin, he was "demoted" (Brian Aherne took over as Mercutio) for the Broadway run of *Romeo and Juliet*, he continued to make an impact in the dual roles of Tybalt and the Chorus. It was while playing Tybalt that he memorably came to the attention of John Houseman,[8] and, in consequence, was given the opportunity to mount a major production of Shakespeare himself.

Before that occasion, however, Welles, during the hiatus between the end of the Cornell tour and the opening of *Romeo and Juliet* on Broadway, retreated to the comforts of Todd School, where, joined by his Gate friends MacLiammoir and Edwards, he and the school's headmaster, Roger Hill, created something called the Todd Summer Theatre Festival and School. Among the plays chosen for the summer repertory was *Hamlet*, and Welles, trumpeted in both the local and the Chicago papers as "The Boy actor from Racine [*sic*]" and "the only foreign artist ever to have been starred in the Irish Abbey [*sic*]," now cast himself as both Claudius and the Ghost. As Claudius, according to one reviewer, Welles

> thumbed a flat nose at convention, achieving a make up somewhere between an obscene old woman and the mask of Lechery that visits 'Doctor Faustus' at the Old Globe. Decadence here is a thicket of curls hung from a bald pate, with voluptuous mouth confirming the evil glimpsed in heavy-lidded eyes. Almost a caricature, this face, but rescued from absurdity by the command of the rich voice that is Mr. Welles' passport to stardom.[9]

Another reviewer commented that Welles "plays the king much as Charles Laughton played Nero, lasciviously, swinishly."[10] For Welles, clearly, Claudius becomes an excuse, at least in part, for showing off, and showcasing, his own presence and performance. As Simon Callow comments, "It is clear from this description that his performance was a melodramatic one, again: he created an ogre, a nightmare figure. It is hard to imagine what else, at his age, he could do—other than play safe and dull."[11]

It is also clear that for Welles Shakespeare was never far removed from Grand Guignol and melodrama, or, to put it another way, that his access to Shakespeare was through those "low" forms of popular theater. Of course, Shakespeare's plays themselves are always balanced on a thin line between dignity and farce, tragedy and bathos, high seriousness and play. It is just that Welles was seldom content to stand poised on that line for very long.

—

Here, however, his practice was consonant with a specifically American approach to Shakespeare. The Mercury Text Records (which will receive fuller discussion in chapter 3) represent Welles's attempt to wed Shakespeare and education, revealing in him a pedagogic impulse that was a central element in his artistic life. But the Shakespeare activities that brought Welles the greatest fame, and initiated his claim to be a premiere American Shakespearean,[12] were his New York productions of *Macbeth* and *Julius Caesar* in 1936 and 1937, respectively.[13]

The story of the WPA–Negro Theatre *Macbeth* has been often and well told, and its general importance and effect carefully analyzed.[14] Here I want to place it in the context of Welles's theory and practice of Shakespeare production. Certainly, this was "Shakespeare as Event" with a vengeance. In mounting a production of *Macbeth* in Harlem, Welles had the opportunity to carry into practice his theories on the accessibility and commercial viability of Shakespeare's plays; he can hardly be said, however, to have lived up to his claim, expressed in *Everybody's Shakespeare* (see chapter 3), that "one of the wisest ways to play Shakespeare is the way he wrote it."[15] It is not even clear, apart from problems of syntax, just what that statement means, though Welles is presumably thinking of the seeming simplicity of the Elizabethan theater. At first sight, at least, Welles's "voodoo" or "Haitian" or "Negro" Macbeth, as it came variously to be called, seems far removed from anything Shakespeare might have imagined or intended. Cast entirely with black actors and set in nineteenth-century Haiti, Welles's production was—given financial and other constraints—an elaborately staged spectacle, a wedding of Shakespeare and magic, full of "thrills and sudden shocks."[16] In designing the production, Welles was influenced by the historical accounts of Henri Christophe and the slave revolts against the French in the early nineteenth century as well as by Eugene O'Neill's recasting of these events in *The Emperor Jones* (1920). The voodoo elements, in any case, suffused all parts of the production and, in Welles's interpretation, *Macbeth* became almost entirely "a suspense thriller about a man who is manipulated by the forces of darkness."[17]

In spite of what might seem a rather drastic alteration in setting and focus, however, Welles did not abandon Shakespeare's text—allowing, that is, for the transpositions, cutting, and other changes typical of nearly all Shakespeare productions. The actors speak, for the most part, the playwright's verse, and the references to thanes and heaths and other specific Scottishisms remain pretty much unchanged (although "Pale" Hecate becomes, necessarily, "Dark" Hecate). However transformed the play, the resulting production was still recognizably Shakespeare, albeit Shakespeare adorned and amplified by a whole series of effects—choirs, voodoo drums, music—appropriate to the new time and setting. A promptbook now at the Lilly Library in Indiana gives some idea of the tone of the production.[18] As Macbeth prepares to visit the witches, for example, "a low wind starts building." "Build tympani," we read, "thunder drums and sheet and wind, build up and up . . . Cellophane rain (Big), gong—2 flashes of lighting—Rain—all voodoo drums (very loud)." Whoever wrote these cues into the manuscript got sufficiently carried away, at one point, to draw, in red block capitals, "RAISE HELL WITH EVERYTHING."[19] The achievement of spectacle for its own sake clearly became a major aim of all involved in the production.

Of the many controversies that surrounded and continue to surround the Harlem *Macbeth*, perhaps the most sensitive and complex remains that of the Negro Theatre's—and, in particular, Orson Welles's—racial politics. From one point of view, the Haitian setting and the parallels with the career of Henri Christophe can be considered demeaning to black sensibilities, insofar as they point to a historical moment which finds black people first supplanting and then, somewhat fantastically, imitating their former white oppressors. On the other hand, Welles's production, by giving the black actors a specific historical texture drawn from black experience—and a revolutionary one at that—supports and enforces an attempt to take black history and culture seriously. Whether the wedding of Shakespeare and blackness was or was not successful depends, in the 1936 context, on where you are standing ideologically, even within the black community. Those who want to see the whole project as taking black American performers seriously by giving a number of them a rare opportunity to interpret a classic of the larger Western culture for which, as Americans, they have a claim, will find here evidence for that point of view.[20] The Negro press, it should be noted, was generally favorable to the production; its reviewers did not seem to find it condescending or in any way preposterous. If, on the other hand, you are inclined to see the combination of Negroes and Shakespeare as ludicrous, either from racist impulses or from liberal discomfort, the voodoo *Macbeth* provides plenty of ammunition for those on this side of the controversy as well.[21]

Some of these issues were addressed, directly and indirectly, in the reviews. A strong undercurrent of racism can be detected in the critical reception to Welles's *Macbeth*: the tone is frequently condescending, even in favorable comments. Several reviewers expressed the wish that Welles had jettisoned Shakespeare's language (to be replaced by what, one wonders—Negro dialect?), had somehow made the production more consistent, more of a piece. "It might have been a better idea to forget 'Macbeth' altogether," Robert Garland wrote. He then went on to praise the production as "colorful, exciting, and a good colored show."[22] Another newspaper critic wrote that the actors "play Shakespeare as if they were apt children who had just discovered him and adored the old man."[23] Conservative observers were quick to dismiss the whole project principally because it was government-sponsored: Percy Hammond of the *New York Herald Tribune* described it as "de-luxe boondoggling";[24] he spends a good part of his review merely listing the number of people involved (137, including both cast and crew). From the government's perspective, of course, to employ as many people as possible was precisely the point, and Welles, by staging an elaborate Shakespearean play, complete with crowd scenes and chorus, had found one especially effective way of meeting this challenge.

However we wish to gauge the social impact, the cultural significance, or the aesthetic merits of Welles's production, it was undoubtedly a popular success, running for seven months in New York and subsequently going on tour. We can see, in retrospect, that the voodoo *Macbeth* made a number of contributions to the American theater: it participated in a reinvigoration of Shakespeare on the New York stage at a time when Elizabethan drama and the classics in general were box office poison, thus paving the way for Welles's even more successful *Julius Caesar* on Broadway the following year; it demonstrated that government-sponsored art need not be safe and dull; it encouraged other experiments in nontraditional casting by the Federal Theatre, including all-black productions of *Lysistrata*, *The Mikado*, and Shaw's *Androcles and the Lion*; and it connected Shakespeare with the immediate social and political issues of the day. Perhaps most significant of all in the present context, however, Welles's *Macbeth*, conceived, mounted, and publicized in a manner that would have pleased P.T. Barnum himself, transformed Shakespeare into a special "event" and associated him with popular culture to an extent not seen in the American theater since the mid-nineteenth century.[25]

With *Julius Caesar* the following season, Welles was now able to combine his Shakespearean activities in a manner reminiscent of nineteenth-century actor-managers like Edwin Booth, Henry Irving, and Herbert Beerbohm-Tree. Given the specific circumstances surrounding the project, the Harlem *Macbeth* had given Welles no acting opportunity.[26] Now, with his own theater company, the Mercury, Welles was able to adapt, direct, and play a leading role in a Broadway Shakespeare production. The success of *Caesar* (as it was renamed) was all the more remarkable because it took place at a time when the New York theater had not been especially welcoming to Shakespeare. (Cornell's *Romeo and Juliet* had been a modest harbinger of a possible revival of interest.) Though Welles once again packaged his production in an attention-grabbing fashion, his methods were in many ways diametrically opposed to those employed in mounting *Macbeth*, in part, no doubt, for very practical, commercial reasons. Without the generous government support that had made an elaborate *Macbeth* possible, Welles fell back on ideas he had absorbed at the Gate. *Caesar* depended for its effects primarily on lighting and the conceptual clarity that made such a dependence possible.

Drawing in part on his Gate experience, Welles had suggested, in *Everybody's Shakespeare*, that scenery per se was not essential for the staging of Shakespeare, and he followed his own advice, at least to a point, with *Caesar*. In presenting the play on a nearly bare stage, with a minimum of props and a relatively small cast, Welles was, in one way, going with the flow: his friend and mentor, Thornton Wilder, was preparing to do precisely the same thing with his own play *Our Town*. In fact, even the modern dress, and in this case "fascist," costuming was not original with Welles, though he made it seem as if it were. Shakespeare in contemporary clothing had made a splash in the late twenties with Barry Jackson's productions of *Hamlet* and, less successfully, *Macbeth*, at the Birmingham Repertory Theatre. More to the point, *Julius Caesar* with fascist trappings had been staged months before the Mercury production by the Delaware Federal Theatre, a fact of which Welles and company could not have been ignorant.[27] (The playwright Sidney Howard, furthermore, had suggested precisely such an approach in a letter to Houseman dated February 9, 1937.)[28] The point here is not to take credit away from Welles, but to suggest instead the extent to which, quite apart from the very real virtues of the production, sheer showmanship once again played a crucial role in exciting interest in the Mercury *Caesar* and in sustaining that interest over the long haul.

One notable aspect of Welles's *Caesar* seldom commented on was its pedagogic dimension. As with another of his Shakespearean projects at the time, the Mercury Text Records (discussed in the following chapter), Welles was concerned to involve the educational establishment. He hired (at fifty dollars a month) a stagestruck graduate of Dartmouth and the Yale Drama School by the name of Harold J. Kennedy (later to become a minor movie actor and major summer theater impresario) to lecture to school groups. Kennedy, in fact, claims that this was his own idea, but if so it was an idea that clearly fit in with Welles's interest in pedagogy. Among his other activities, Kennedy preceded *Caesar* when it went on tour. "By the end of the second week of the tour," Kennedy later recalled, "well over one third of the tickets being sold at the box office were in huge blocks of seats purchased by the various schools and colleges where I had lectured."[29] A brochure entitled "The Student and *Julius Caesar*" was prepared for the Chicago run, emphasizing the extent to which the production, if not entirely true to Shakespeare, was true to Shakespeare's "methods."

In the same brochure, Kennedy, billed as "Lecturer, Modern Shakespearean Drama" (an intriguing concept, certainly), is quoted as saying: "To me it seems there is more triumph for Shakespeare in four students talking intelligently about 'Julius Caesar' over doughnuts and coffee than there has ever been in all the Shakespearean discussions which have gone on at pink teas for centuries." "Students," we are told, "are invited to visit backstage at matinees, chat with the cast, and study the technical and lighting set-up of the production at the Erlanger Theater."[30] Student interest, presumably, was excited as well by the production of one-sheet tabloid papers with headlines like "Dictator Slain, Rome Revolts" and "Cleopatra Dons Widow's Weeds; Ogles Antony?" In a press release, we read that "Welles believes that it is time for a new deal in the academic approach to Shakespeare." Welles "would introduce Shakespeare to students in the fifth and sixth years of school, not as an academic subject but as an entertainment."[31] The educational "angle" no doubt helped the box office and sustained the run of the play, but the emphasis Welles placed on school groups was part of an interest that, the evidence suggests, was quite genuine.

The Harlem *Macbeth* and the "fascist" *Julius Caesar* were, nonetheless, opportunistic projects, and though they were perhaps Welles's most successful Shakespeare productions, their popular appeal has been somewhat exaggerated. *Macbeth*, though no doubt a succès de scandale, was achieved completely outside the commercial theater: it was, with Uncle Sam as angel, very probably the most heavily subsidized production of Shakespeare in American theatrical history. With *Julius Caesar* Welles drew on the headlines of the moment, packaged his production in a melodramatic and sensational fashion ("Death of a Dictator"), virtually eliminated two of Shakespeare's five acts, and created a more or less modern play on the bare skeletal outline of his original. Both productions, though reasonably "pure" Shakespeare by Broadway standards, found an audience by means somewhat marginal to the essential qualities of their respective texts. Both reveal Welles as showman and magician: like the strippers in *Gypsy*, he adopted the policy that, with Shakespeare at least, "you gotta have a gimmick."

Welles's final Shakespeare project before going to Hollywood was *Five Kings*, later to be discussed in relation to *Chimes at Midnight* (see chapter 7). Cosponsored by the Mercury and the Theatre Guild, it was not a successful production: it closed without reaching New York after brief tryouts in Boston, Washington, D.C., and Philadelphia. In constructing what was to be another Shakespeare event, Welles's reach seems to have exceeded his grasp: the gimmicks, in this instance, may have simply overwhelmed the play. Welles perhaps forgot the lesson he learned with *Julius Caesar*: less is more. The aim, Welles's partner John Houseman told a reporter at the time, "will be to combine the immediate quality of the Elizabethan with all the devices and techniques possible in the modern theatre,"[32] and *Five Kings* was consequently dependent on elaborate stage machinery that not only tended to overshadow the actors but never even worked properly. Though Shakespeare would continue to absorb Welles's interest as a filmmaker, he did not return to the stage with Shakespeare until the mid-1950s.

Although Welles's career as a filmmaker would engage the greater part of his energies over the next several decades, he continued in his role as American Shakespearean not only by completing and releasing three cinematic adaptations of Shakespeare's plays (to be discussed in subsequent chapters), but also, among a miscellany of activities, through his first foray into the relatively new medium of television and his subsequent return to the New York stage, in both instances with productions of *King Lear*. In the first *Lear*, a 1953 broadcast of *Omnibus* on the CBS television network, Welles's contribution, at least officially, was as actor only. The adaptation and staging was by a young Peter Brook, who would mount a more famous stage production of the play a decade later (and, about a decade after that, a film version as well). The other *Lear* was Welles's own staging at New York's City Center, a production remembered most vividly for Welles having played the title role in a wheelchair. Both productions can be said to have had a populist bent. The presentation of Shakespeare on television, engaged in by both NBC and CBS in the early 1950s, invites a discussion of the relationship between high- and lowbrow culture, not to mention a discussion (one that is neverending) of the commercial nature of television versus its social and cultural responsibility. But even the stage production of *Lear* was aimed at a more or less "popular" audience. The municipally operated City Center prided itself on its "popular prices," its actors working for the equity minimum (eighty-five dollars a week, in Welles's case, was the salary reported in the press). Both *Lears*, albeit in different ways, center on Welles as performer: in each, the phenomenon of "Shakespeare as Welles" becomes especially apparent.

The "live" television *Lear*, though not a Welles project as such, was thought of at the time—and continues to be referred to—as the Orson Welles *King Lear*. It is certainly difficult to imagine that Welles would have entirely kept himself out of production decisions, especially when one of his favorite Shakespeare plays was involved. The program, after all, marked Welles's first appearance on television, a medium for which he evidenced a continuing fascination, but one that included a good deal of ambivalence and that never engaged his primary creative energies, although he would become, in the last several decades of his life, a notable television "personality" as well as a familiar "pitchman," sometimes only as a voice but also, notoriously, as the visible spokesman for Paul Masson wines and other products.

Omnibus, sponsored initially by the Ford Foundation as well as commercial sponsors like Greyhound Bus, hearkened back to the various workshops and sustaining programs of 1930s radio, including Welles's own "Mercury Theatre on the Air." Broadcast on Sunday afternoons, well out of prime time, *Omnibus* generally presented a mix of original drama, theatrical adaptations, musical segments from jazz to opera, as well as filmed documentaries and short subjects. The audience was clearly drawn from educated, upper-middle-class households with a preexisting interest in "culture." Viewers—some fifteen million of them, according to Frank Brady[33]—tuning in to *Omnibus* did so with certain presuppositions as to the nature and content of the programming they would be experiencing,[34] though it was not the norm for the show to devote its entire ninety-minute time slot to a single item. A fairly typical menu was the one from April 5, 1953: first, an adaptation of *Everyman* starring Burgess Meredith, followed by a documentary entitled "Grandma Moses at Home," and closing with a telecast of Georges Méliès's 1902 film, *A Trip to the Moon*. In short, solid middlebrow fare with highbrow pretensions.

We may suppose, nonetheless, that many of those tuning in to *King Lear* would have some knowledge of or interest in Shakespeare. We know that they would have chosen not to watch NBC's *Hallmark Hall of Fame* (which was, at that time, not quite the "class act" it would later become—the program for that particular Sunday afternoon was something called "McCoy of Abilene," starring George Nader) or ABC's "Super Circus" or any of the local programming available. We don't know how many of them might have switched over at 6:00 P.M. to *Meet the Press* (NBC) or *Captain Midnight* (ABC), thereby missing the final half hour of *Omnibus*. Regarded in this light, the *Omnibus Lear* does not precisely represent bringing Shakespeare to the masses. It represents, instead, a somewhat different phenomenon: giving a receptive audience outside the New York–Chicago theater nexus (Los Angeles and San Francisco hardly counted as theater cities in the 1950s) the opportunity to experience something like the cultural variety available to similarly minded audiences in the urban centers of American culture.

Alistair Cooke's introduction to the *Lear* broadcast deftly balances that combination of reverence and flippancy so characteristic of a 1950s attitude to Shakespeare. Cooke, a transplanted Briton who interpreted British culture (as, among other things, host of the Public Broadcasting System's *Masterpiece Theatre*) to a whole generation of Americans, tells us that this is to be "a very special *Omnibus*." "We have only one item," he continues, "but it is the noblest item in English dramatic literature, Shakespeare's *King Lear*." After a commercial for Greyhound Bus—much was made, as with Welles's radio *Lear* of 1946, of the sponsor's willingness to limit its commercial messages to the "bookend" portions of the program—Cooke returns to inform us that Peter Brook has taken the subplot, the bane of all schoolboys, "invented to rest the chief actors," and thrown it "out the window." Cooke also points to the relevance of Shakespeare's play for a modern audience, or "at least those of us who've been lucky to survive the violence and the barbarities of the twentieth century." "Maybe," he suggests, "we're a little better qualified to look at this work with a little more humility." He concludes with the hope that "you may learn more from Shakespeare's pessimism than from the optimism of lesser men."

The production itself, looked at today in the existing, slightly murky video copies of a kinescope of the live production, remains striking both for the modesty and pathos of Welles's performance and for the evidence of Brook's struggle to adapt essentially theatrical techniques to the requirements of live television broadcasting. Up to three video cameras are employed to provide the effect of something like a cinematic editing pattern. The actors are at times awkwardly arranged, having been blocked to fit into various compositions that will facilitate the switch from one camera to another while at the same time having been positioned uncomfortably into the shallow-focused, tightly framed video image. The effect, at times, is, one imagines, something like the completely pragmatic blocking of a nineteenth-century company of actors who have been told to stand ten feet to the left and well downstage of a touring star with whom they have never properly rehearsed; the star, in this case, however, is television itself.

Brook, following his theatrical training, frequently tries to create a mise-en-scène rather too elaborate or detailed for the small screen, and the frame consequently becomes somewhat cluttered. His regular employment of triangular compositions, though appropriate for the exchanges between Lear and his daughters, becomes, at times, overly symmetrical and self-conscious. The most effective scenes are those involving the fewest characters: the meeting of Lear and Gloucester, for example, suffers little from the constricted scope of the production. At its best, Brook's *Lear* becomes a chamber work, intimate and domestic—what is lost in terms of scope and large dramatic effects is balanced by a gain in careful observation of emotional detail. Welles's performance perfectly coheres with Brook's strategy. Hampered initially by a costume that might have reminded a fifties audience of the wicked queen from Disney's *Snow White* (a large ruff collar and an especially vertical, pointy crown), he nonetheless demonstrates how well qualified he was to play Lear. He finds ways throughout of underplaying, of giving us a sense that Lear, if only he could, would be larger than he is able to be. The effect is of a powerful man holding himself in check, struggling desperately not to give way to the full range and force of his emotions. Welles speaks with careful deliberateness, providing the television audience the opportunity to understand and follow what is going on.

But if Welles's performance puts up easily read guideposts to Lear's character and actions, the production as a whole is not nearly as coherent. Much like a Classics Illustrated comic book, Brook's adaptation provides the bones of Shakespeare's play but little of the connecting tissue. The heath scenes, in particular, are powerfully realized but almost impossible to follow. A television viewer unfamiliar with *King Lear* would have had great difficulty making sense of the action in these sequences. Full of sound and fury they are, but what do they signify? Where, for one thing, did "Poor Tom" come from? Or, more to the point, *who* is he? With no Edgar in the play, he comes from nowhere at all. Though well-played by Michael MacLiammoir, who seems to know that he is, or ought to be, Edgar, he nonetheless becomes one extra, babbling mad person too many. Some of Shakespeare's "deliberate" absurdities, controlled and channeled by context and structure, become absurdities pure and simple when presented without sufficient linking material. In such moments, the popularization of

Shakespeare turns, without quite intending it, into the mystification of Shakespeare.

Furthermore, some of Brook's ideas about the play, ideas he would carry out more fully in his Royal Shakespeare Company production with Paul Scofield in the early 1960s, interfere with rather than contribute to a clear apprehension of the abridged text. For a historian of the theater, it is certainly interesting to note that Brook, long before he could have read Jan Kott's essay "*King Lear* as *Endgame*"—often cited as Brook's inspiration—(written in Polish, it was translated into French in 1962 and into English in 1966), played up the more nihilistic moments of the play.[35] He here introduces, tentatively, the conceit of having Lear's knights behave riotously, thereby partly justifying Goneril's bitter denunciation. The blinding of Gloucester, done in painful detail, is undeniably powerful and disturbing, but it is also especially nihilistic: without the subplot and the consequent revelation of Gloucester's metaphoric blindness, the physical blinding is entirely gratuitous, having neither thematic nor symbolic significance. It is pure Grand Guignol, sensational in the extreme. A difficult scene in any production—difficult, indeed, in the reading—its presentation is almost impossible to justify ripped out of context.

In spite of its various problems and shortcomings, the production, and Welles's performance in particular, were generally well received, more so by the trade and periodical reviewers (one clear exception was the *New Yorker's* Philip Hamburger, who found the whole project amusing: it is not entirely clear from reading his review if he is condescending primarily to Welles, to television, or to Shakespeare) than by the more highbrow Shakespeare professors and scholars. The reviewer for *Variety* could barely contain his enthusiasm: "Measured in terms of any show biz media, including the legitimate theatre and films, this 'Omnibus' production can hold its head high as superlative entertainment." Welles himself, *Variety* believed, "scored a notable triumph."[36] Jack Gould, in the *New York Times*, though less taken with the production as a whole ("For the last half-hour or so . . . it was almost incomprehensible"),[37] praised Welles for a performance of "true excitement, restraint and feeling." John Crosby, in the *Herald Tribune*, found Welles "enormously impressive": "You can hardly give a restrained performance of Lear," Crosby elaborates, "but Welles kept himself decently reined in, even in the storm scene, where the language is as wild as the elements."[38]

The academic critics were far less taken with this televised *Lear*. Even someone as sensitive to performance-based criticism of Shakespeare as

Marvin Rosenberg seemed to have wanted a more or less "faithful" ren-
dering of the text in what was clearly presented as a limited experiment of
a little over seventy minutes. He described the project as "a stern lesson in
what not to do with Shakespeare on TV," objecting to the "visual confusion" and clutter of Brook's staging and terming the blinding of Gloucester "an exercise in sadism."[39] He found Welles's performance promising but
overwhelmed by an inadequate production. Alice Griffin, in *Shakespeare
Quarterly*, described Brook's adaptation as "unforgivably bad," but she too
praised Welles's acting, at least in the scene of the meeting with Gloucester. Griffin was clearly more welcoming of the *Hallmark Hall of Fame*'s far
more conventional *Hamlet*, with Maurice Evans, that had been broadcast
the preceding April. The television critics, it would seem, were happy to
accept Shakespeare on the small screen, as long as he was mounted with
some panache; the Shakespeare scholars were not quite ready to accept the
kinds of liberties television appeared to demand, particularly when those
liberties were taken in a seemingly high-handed fashion.

His experience with *King Lear* in the cramped space and small scope
required by television may have inspired Welles to mount his own production of the play in New York's cavernous City Center. If the reviewers
can be trusted, Welles provided a very different interpretation of at least his
own role from the one he had given on *Omnibus*. No doubt the theater
itself demanded a larger, broader performance style, but it must have been
so much larger and broader than necessary to call so much attention to
itself. Welles, who avoided the trap of hamminess on television, was now
accused of precisely this fault by some of the reviewers. That he managed
to break both of his ankles immediately before opening night, and thus had
to play the entire run in a wheelchair, added a "sideshow" feel to the production. Welles, hampered in his movements, had to rely primarily on his
voice for characterization. In any case, the production had about it much
of a carnival atmosphere, and Shakespeare, more than ever, became background and setting rather than the focus of critical interest.

The City Center *Lear* turned into an occasion for assessing—or, more
accurately, reassessing—Welles's position in the American theater. The
reviews, which range so wildly in attitude and specific critical analysis,
become barometers for measuring the critics' attitude toward Shakespeare
and toward Welles as much as they are analyses of a specific production of
a particular play. Welles's decision to play Lear on Broadway was an act
filled with hubris to start out with. The title role may be the most challenging in the Shakespeare repertoire, and completely successful produc-

tions of the play are few and far between. At the same time, however, the play—in one version or another—has traditionally been central to the repertoire of outsized, barnstorming "star" actors like Junius Brutus Booth, Edwin Forrest, and, more recently, one of the last of the great touring actors, Sir Donald Wolfit (the model for "Sir" in Ronald Harwood's play *The Dresser*), actors for whom the play was as much as anything a vehicle for the exhibition of physical stamina and vocal power. *Lear* has been considered a great poetic masterpiece, too large and complex for mere theater to encompass; it is, simultaneously, an inevitable choice for any Shakespearean actor claiming star status. For a classical actor, playing Lear can be seen as the summit of his art, but the role can appear as a ham's delight, and audiences can find, in a less than adequate production, evidence for maintaining a view of a Shakespeare play as something loud, incomprehensible, violent, and absurd.

As a choice for Welles himself, *King Lear* is full of pitfalls. For those wishing to think of him as an overactor, almost any performance he gives will confirm the prejudice—the play virtually demands an outsized deployment of gesture, voice, and emotion: as the *Theatre Arts* reviewer noted, "Lear, of course, is a tremendously taxing role for any actor, and its more extreme moments might reasonably be calculated to bring out the, let us say, more florid aspects of a performer whose style never has run to understatement."[40] (That Welles was able to *underplay* the role on television has much to do both with the nature of the medium and with Peter Brook's developing vision of the play.) For those inclined to accept the view of Welles as a man of once enormous talents now in sad decline ("self-destructive in the grand manner of the Jazz Age"),[41] the role of a great king brought low invites uncomfortable parallels. If Welles's ego, a topic of discussion from the outset of his career, is in question, what more egotistical act can there be than to both stage and play the starring role in Shakespeare's most complex and demanding play? And if one is inclined to look at *King Lear* itself with some suspicion, as a play somehow too remote and old-fashioned for contemporary concerns, too outsized for a sophisticated Broadway audience in the age of "the Method" (the *Time* magazine cutline for its review of Welles's production, "Old Play in Manhattan," perhaps reflects this attitude), then Welles becomes, by association, something of a throwback and a pretentious one at that. Welles and *Lear*, taken together, reinforce the notion that both are old-fashioned, bizarre, melodramatic, and marginal.

Perhaps inevitably, too, the production was reviewed as if it were a contest between Welles and Shakespeare, a tremendous agon in which Shakespeare is, mainly, the loser. "[It] is easy to appreciate the robustness of his [Welles's] attack on the problems of staging a fiery, Elizabethan drama," Brooks Atkinson commented, but the attack "has left Shakespeare prostrate."[42] Or, in *Newsweek*'s flippant "Summing Up": "Welles up, Shakespeare on deck."[43] Implicitly, Welles's *Lear* emerged as well as a contest between Welles and the preconceptions of the critics with regard to how Shakespeare should be spoken and staged, preconceptions that seem to have been molded by British Shakespeare and the example of Maurice Evans, a transplanted Englishman who was considered by many the "premiere" American Shakespearean actor from the late thirties to the fifties. Henry Hewes, in the *Saturday Review*, finds that "Mr. Welles speaks Shakespeare's verse not as the torrents of emotion and word music it is, but in fitful splashes like a faulty spigot when a bit of air has got into the plumbing."[44] Atkinson, similarly, complained about the verse-speaking, claiming that Welles "breaks the lines whimsically, as if he were not much interested in their meaning."[45] On the other hand (such are the pitfalls of depending on the observations of reviewers), Richard Hayes, writing in *Commonweal*, found Welles "vocally elegant, with inward moments of some beauty and depth."[46] Although one cannot precisely reconstruct just how Welles did speak the verse in this production, the comments of critics suggest that he was employing a more matter-of-fact approach to verse-speaking than was then customary on the New York stage. Interestingly, Paul Scofield, in Peter Brook's 1971 film adaptation of *King Lear*, speaks in "a broken, prosaic idiom, in which individual words stand out like pebbles in sand,"[47] and is praised for doing so.

Welles himself was clearly disappointed by the circumstances surrounding the production. In a letter to Marc Blitzstein, who was in charge of the music, he claims to have been "brought to America to stage and star in a repertory of two plays in the commercial theatre. . . . Eight weeks later I find myself whittled down to a single play at City Center."[48] For Welles, the opportunity to play Lear was partly a matter of personal satisfaction and ambition. "I'm not getting any younger," the forty-year-old Welles wrote in the *New York Times*, "and if Lear must wear long white whiskers, by a grim paradox, few actors capable of growing such a beard are still physically capable of getting through the role."[49] Welles, like so many before and after him, had hoped to help found "a classical repertory theatre on Broadway." The other play Welles had planned to stage, Ben Jonson's *Volpone*, was dropped before *Lear* opened. Welles had considered casting the popular comedian and television star Jackie Gleason as Mosca to his Volpone: they had discussed the matter over drinks at Toots Shoors.[50] Though nothing came of the project, Welles's bold casting idea here antic-ipates the production of *Volpone*, adapted as *The Fox*, that played success-fully on Broadway some years later, with "straight" actor George C. Scott as Volpone and borscht-belt comedian Jack Gilford as Mosca.

As with his film of *Macbeth* (1948), discussed in chapter 5, Welles, in attempting *Lear*, was once again in at least implicit competition with Lau-rence Olivier, whose film of *Richard III* was in the final stages of produc-tion at about the same time. The issue of *Theatre Arts* in which a brief (two-paragraph) review of *Lear* appeared contained as well a three-page, nicely designed, and heavily illustrated story entitled "At Home and Abroad with *Richard III*," which made much of the forthcoming television broad-cast/American premiere of Olivier's film and included, as a "service to its readers," a detailed listing of cast and production credits. The same issue of *Theatre Arts*, perhaps not coincidentally, carried a full-page ad for the com-plete RCA Victor recording of the *Richard III* soundtrack. *Saturday Review*, which had given short shrift to *King Lear* in January, put Olivier on the cover of its March 10, 1956, issue and devoted no less than three separate reviews to *Richard III*, representing its film, theater, and television depart-ments.[51] Certainly, a limited run of a stage production in New York could hardly be expected to compete for attention with a spectacular Technicolor film, and one set to appear on television (in color, for those with color receivers) at that. In the "Shakespeare as Event" sweepstakes, Olivier, not surprisingly, won hands down.

That Welles, nonetheless, received the attention he did is partly due to the position of fascinating object he continued to hold in the American imagination and partly to the peculiarities of the production itself and the attendant publicity that peculiarity attracted. Though it would probably be unfair to suggest that Welles broke both of his ankles on purpose (Eric Bentley more than hints as much when he writes that if Welles "had had three legs, he would have tripped three times"),[52] playing Lear in a wheel-chair may have suited him just fine. Once again, he had managed to turn a production of Shakespeare into an event, an event that centered squarely on himself. Welles, furthermore, was given the opportunity to indulge his pedagogic and anecdotal talents when, on the second night of the run, hav-ing broken his other ankle (he had played the first night on crutches), he found himself unable to go on and so presented instead an "Evening with Orson Welles." (Appropriately enough, and perhaps partly as a result of this experience, it was soon after that that Welles went to Las Vegas with his magic act cum Shakespeare recitation, in the course of which he included, along with excerpts from *Julius Caesar* and *The Merchant of Venice*, passages from *King Lear*). For Welles, sitting in a wheelchair and reciting as well as talking about Shakespeare may have been as satisfying as actually playing Shakespeare's king. Here and elsewhere, he was able to function in a dual role, actor and teacher, performer and commentator. It is this pedagogic dimension in Welles's activities, in particular, that I want to look at in the next chapter.

THREE

"Cashing in on the Classics"

—

Everybody's Shakespeare and the Mercury Text Records

O rson Welles's ambition to serve Shakespeare and at the same time promote himself can already be detected in one of his earliest Shakespeare projects. While still in his late teens, Welles collaborated with Roger Hill, his teacher, mentor, and friend, on a series of play-texts entitled *Everybody's Shakespeare*; three volumes were initially produced, *Julius Caesar, The Merchant of Venice,* and *Twelfth Night.* They were printed and published in 1934 at the Todd School for Boys in Woodstock, Illinois, where Hill was headmaster and where Welles, several years earlier, had completed his formal education. These texts were revised and reissued in the late thirties as *The Mercury Shakespeare,* in conjunction with sound recordings of each play, the Mercury Text Records. An additional, final Shakespeare recording, of *Macbeth,* together with a printed text, was produced in 1941. Welles's recordings were pioneer efforts; no one before had attempted to record full-length audio versions of Shakespeare. Taken together, *Everybody's Shakespeare* and the Mercury Text Records contributed to the popularization of Shakespeare in a manner at once pedagogic, innovative, and commercial.

In its combination of biographical, textual, historical, and theatrical materials, the Roger Hill–Orson Welles *Everybody's Shakespeare* is quite unlike any previous edition of Shakespeare's plays. The most popular school editions of Shakespeare in America at the time were those edited by W. J. Rolfe (from 1881 to 1902) and, especially, H. N. Hudson (from 1890 to 1903): so popular were they that volumes of both can be found today in almost any store with a decent collection of secondhand books. Rolfe stressed the philological approach to the plays—a stress on grammar and on the meaning of words—that had become established in colleges and universities in the nineteenth century; Hudson, who edited more of the plays and whose editions were revised after his death as the *New Hudson Shakespeare* (1908–1910), steered teachers and students away from an exclusive emphasis on "word-mongering" toward something like aesthetic appreciation of the plays.[1] Neither, however, showed much interest in Shakespeare as performance texts. It was only in the 1920s that the idea of acting out selected portions of the plays in the classroom began to gain some currency, though students were almost never encouraged to actually see a play performed.[2]

In contrast, though *Everybody's Shakespeare* was clearly designed to be used in secondary schools and colleges (*The Merchant of Venice* and *Julius Caesar* were the two most frequently taught literary texts in American high schools in the first decades of the twentieth century),[3] the primary emphasis throughout is on theater, on realizing Shakespeare on the stage. Hill and Welles divided up the editorial labors: Hill wrote the biographical-historical-textual portion of the introduction, Welles the theatrical portion; Hill edited the text, while Welles (probably) wrote the stage business and (certainly) created the drawings that adorn virtually every page. But the volumes are of a piece, and quite professional both in content and in physical appearance. One would hardly guess that the whole project had been carried out through the talents and facilities of a relatively obscure midwestern prep school. When the volumes were republished by Harper & Brothers in 1939, the original plates were used for much of the text, and the result was not notably more attractive than the Todd School Press editions.

The suggestion of bricolage, of cobbling things together, characteristic of so many of Welles's activities over the years, affects the Shakespeare texts as well. Welles's biographers identify two separate editions of the plays, *Everybody's Shakespeare* (1934), published at the Todd (School) Press and edited, so the title page tells us, by "Roger Hill and Orson Welles" (these were published both as individual play texts and as a single volume containing all three plays), and *The Mercury Shakespeare* (1939), essentially a reprint, we are usually told, of *Everybody's Shakespeare*, published by Harper and Brothers, but now edited by "Orson Welles and Roger Hill." *The Mercury Shakespeare* is not, however, a mere reprint of the 1934 Todd texts. Although the introductory materials, the text of the plays, and the illustrations are nearly identical in both cases, the stage directions have been thoroughly rewritten and rearranged to incorporate the spoken narration and other added materials from the Mercury recordings. In addition, many of the sketches have been moved around, sometimes placed on different pages of the text.

We can, in addition, identify an "interim" text of at least one of the plays, *The Merchant of Venice*. This volume, dated 1938, was evidently published at Todd and is in nearly every way identical to the original 1934 edition, except that the title page reads "Edited by Orson Welles and Roger Hill," as it will in the 1939 edition. Presumably, texts were needed to accompany the Columbia/Mercury recording of *Merchant of Venice* at a point in time before the Harper editions were ready for distribution; a label, pasted on the cover of the 1938 *Merchant*, reads "With the Complete Recorded Play by the Mercury Theatre." The text, however, is not identical to the text of the recording, since the added narration is not included. To further complicate this publication history, another separate edition of *The Merchant of Venice* can be identified; published by McGraw-Hill, and keyed to the Mercury recording, it bears the same publication date as the Harper edition and presumably succeeded it. So we have, in effect, at least three versions of even this modest enterprise. The development of the Hill/Welles Shakespeare editions in part reflects the changing fortunes and remarkable success of Orson Welles himself. At the same time, what happens to these volumes underlines a key aspect of Welles's artistic personality—the desire never to let anything go, but on the contrary to recycle, revise, and reshape the same materials in new forms, a tendency particularly evident in his interactions with Shakespeare.

Roger Hill's biographical and textual introduction to *Everybody's Shakespeare* displays a mastery of the available scholarly sources, circa 1934 (these, however, were notable: E. K. Chambers's magisterial—and still indispensable—*William Shakespeare: A Study of the Facts and Problems* had been published in 1930),[4] presented in an attractive and unfussy manner. Very little has become dated in these materials. The occasional reference to, for example, "these duly Winchellized blessed events"[5] would certainly require a footnote today, Walter Winchell's fame having pretty much evaporated, and only research can tell most of us who or what "the Juke family" or "Darius Green" were. But in nearly every other way, Hill's essay is up-to-date both in content and in tone. The somewhat disproportionate amount of space devoted to the authorship controversy, though Hill handles it with humor and common sense, does suggest that the issue had more resonance in the 1930s than it does today. The urge to prove that, say, Francis Bacon or Edward de Vere, seventeenth Earl of Oxford, wrote Shakespeare's plays, an effort which had intensified in the latter half of the nineteenth century, was related to the construction of Shakespeare as a highbrow artist—the middle class, ill-educated actor gives way to the titled philosopher or the university-educated aristocrat. The ridicule Hill heaps on the anti-Stratfordians becomes another weapon in the rehabilitation of Shakespeare as a popular artist.

Hill's tone and style aim at disarming his readers from the outset: his introduction begins with the heading "On Studying Shakespeare's Plays," immediately followed by the one-word paragraph "*Don't!*" "Read them. *Enjoy them.* Act them" (3), he urges. "Put Shakespeare where he belongs—on the stage" (3), he insists a bit later. Although an occasional note of bardolatry creeps in from time to time—as when Hill writes that merely to handle the First Folio "is to some way touch the hem of the garment—to burn away the mists of separation and stand bathed in the aura of [Shakespeare's] very presence" (15)—the overall tone is straightforward and commonsensical. Hill forges throughout an easy intimacy between writer and reader. Discussing the legend that Shakespeare's wife was something of a shrew, for instance, Hill notes that "great genius is seldom appreciated at such close perspective." "Witness the fact," he adds, "that at this moment my wife is suggesting I lay aside scrivening and put up the screens on the cottage porch" (7).

Welles adopts a rather different tone, at least initially, for his portion of the introduction, into which he plunges with highly wrought vigor: "Shakespeare said everything. Brain to belly; every mood and minute of a man's season. His language is starlight and fireflies and the sun and moon. He wrote it with tears and blood and beer, and his words march like heartbeats" (22). It is perhaps well to remember that the author was nineteen when these words were published. In any case, the young enthusiast soon settles down to some sensible observations. In discussing the changes in theatrical space since Shakespeare's time, Welles notes that "before the Restoration, theatres were court-yards around platforms where you went to hear and to be heard. Since then they've been birthday cakes in front of picture-frames where you go to see and be seen" (26). He argues for simplicity in staging: "I entreat you who are going to use this book for producing these plays to try at least one of them utterly without impediment. Fix up a platform in a class-room, a gymnasium, a dance-hall or a backyard and give Shakespeare a chance" (26–27). Welles is no purist, however; he does not insist on a single way of staging Shakespeare. The keynote, rather, is flexibility and a call for improvisation.

Writing of Elizabethan staging, Welles notes: "If you think the Elizabethans had a pretty primitive way of putting on a play, I don't blame you. The show/business [*sic*] has been certain of it for two hundreds [*sic*] years but lately it is beginning to wonder" (24). Welles here alludes to the innovations in staging that were making themselves felt in the early decades of the twentieth century. Along with the pioneer work of William Poel, Harley Granville-Barker, and Edward Gordon Craig—who all, in their quite different ways, had rethought the staging of Shakespeare's plays,[6] Welles, as we have seen, could draw on his own experience several years earlier with Dublin's Gate Theatre. The Gate's *Hamlet*, in which Welles had appeared as the Ghost, had been a production "of the most extreme severity and simplicity necessitating the use of the absolute minimum of scenery and properties and depending upon effects that can be achieved with the speed of light."[7] Though Welles himself would never be quite so Spartan in his own productions of Shakespeare, his *Julius Caesar* in 1937 comes very close to this ideal.

Throughout his essay, Welles reveals a tension between scholarship and theatricality, a respect for Shakespeare on the one hand and a desire to experiment on the other, which is quite nicely expressed at the conclusion of his introduction:

> This book is a popular presentation of three plays from the players' and producer's viewpoint. We have adapted it from the prompt-books of the great actors and from other sources, and arranged it into a sort of simplified composite of that whole unpublished literature. . . . Our business has been with the more respectful actors' versions and our reverence for the original has helped us in again adapting them, this time to star Shakespeare. (28)

"Reverence for the original," evidently, does not conflict with "again adapting them." In the very next paragraph we learn that "certain scenes and many lines are unnecessary and sometimes even dull, and in this direction Mr. Hill has blazoned away with a discreet and scholarly blue pencil" (28). The spirit of the whole enterprise shines forth in Welles's concluding words: "The actor-half of this editorship believes in this book's platform and urges the study of these plays by acting them. This is because he thinks the theatre the pleasantest, speediest and safest way to that zealous and jealous love which most intelligent people, once exposed to him, must inevitably feel for Shakespeare" (28).

What is perhaps most notable about *Everybody's Shakespeare* at first glance, however, is not so much the text as Welles's dozens of drawings, examples of which appear on every page of the text proper as well as scattered throughout the introductory material. These sketches complement and enforce the highly theatrical bias of the whole project, a bias that is revealed as well in the sometimes detailed and elaborate verbal character sketches and stage directions that supplement Shakespeare's text. Welles's sketches—and they are, for the most part, just that, sketches, not finished drawings, some in pen and ink, some in charcoal—lend an aura of incompletion and tentativeness appropriate to a presentation of Shakespeare that eschews solemnity and stresses spontaneity and fun. Some of the sketches for *Twelfth Night*, for instance, depict a close sequence of events in a comic strip or flip-card fashion. The pen-and-ink drawings of famous actors in costume, usually derived from photographs and prints, which adorn the texts of both *Twelfth Night* and *The Merchant of Venice*, are rendered in considerably more detail than the rough sketches of imagined scenes and stage pictures. These latter show the strong influence of the famous designers and producers of Shakespeare, especially Gordon Craig and William Poel—Craig in the monumental simplicity of some of the set designs, Poel in the boxlike, highly balanced, almost childlike look of some of the renderings of the stage picture.

Welles and Hill were evidently quite familiar with the stage histories of each play they chose to edit, though they had had significant firsthand experience only with *Twelfth Night*, having codirected the play two years earlier at Todd School for the Chicago Drama League competition.[8] (This production, of which some photos and a short film survive, had been based on a 1930 New York production by Kenneth McGowan.) *Twelfth Night*, in any case, is of the three plays the most fully annotated with stage business,[9] although *The Merchant of Venice* owes perhaps more to theatrical tradition, both in the written stage directions and in the illustrations, which reproduce a good number of existing stage designs; *Julius Caesar*, by contrast, is lightly annotated and illustrated entirely with original sketches. The stage directions and drawings for *The Merchant of Venice* are of particular interest in demonstrating the warring impulses, the conflict in Welles between austerity and simplicity on the one hand and a desire for the big effect on the other. So Welles suggests the need for a bridge on stage for act I, scene iii, "because it has been found tremendously effective in stage business."[10] And he is not above borrowing from the nineteenth-century actor-manager Sir Henry Irving when he describes the business that closes II.iv: "Sneering, [Shylock] listens to the tumult of song and laughter as it grows dim in the distance. After a moment he descends and crosses slowly to his house. At the door he stops, raises his hand and knocks twice, very deliberately. Motionless, he stands there—waiting—waiting—" (31).[11] Welles reproduces a drawing of an elaborate David Belasco set for the trial scene, but he also provides smaller sketches of less complex alternatives. Overall, Welles has attempted with all three plays to fulfill the program outlined in his introductory comments: "We have tried, without getting technical, to present three plays as interestingly and with as many ideas as we could. We hope that where tradition and we are inadequate, you will jump in and fill the holes with ideas of your own."[12]

As my examples suggest, Welles frequently wedded the verbal stage directions to the drawings, and both the descriptions of stage business and the illustrations aim at openendedness and flexibility. Sometimes Welles writes a note next to a sketch: "Andrew might wear a night gown like this—as though Toby had dragged him out of bed for a carouse."[13] For *Julius Caesar* he sketches, as one staging possibility, a permanent set which in its simplicity and flexibility prefigures his New York production of the play: a minimalist combination of steps and platforms on an otherwise bare stage. But in other places in the same play, he provides several options: the first sketch of Brutus's orchard (I.ii), for instance, is stylized but nevertheless "realistic" and detailed. On the next page, he sketches four more versions of the orchard set. These are small, very roughly drawn, highly impressionistic alternatives, ranging in style from austere to quite busy. At the beginning of *Twelfth Night* (I.vi), he writes that the set "can be a painted drop, plain curtains, or as elaborate as the facilities of your stage will permit."[14] The overall effect perhaps suggests that Welles was himself uncertain as to the best means for presenting Shakespeare's plays. In his introduction, he hints at this ambivalence: "Scenery belongs with many plays; it's an interesting study, a worthy art, and it's fun, but I don't think there ever was a production of a play by Shakespeare, however expensively authentic, where and whenever that was entirely worthy of its play."[15] The ambivalence hinted at here would be reflected in Welles's first two professional Shakespearean productions: the elaborate and colorful "voodoo" *Macbeth* and the bare stage, "fascist" *Julius Caesar*.

It was during the run of *Julius Caesar* in 1937–38 that Welles convinced Columbia Records to issue an audio recording of selections from the play with the original cast. This experiment led to a more ambitious project—a complete recorded collection of Shakespeare's plays. In the event, only five recordings of four Shakespearean plays were made by Welles and his

Mercury players: *Julius Caesar* (which was recorded a second time in 1938 with some changes in casting and a different text), *Twelfth Night*, *The Merchant of Venice*, and *Macbeth*. Not coincidentally, the first three of these were the plays included in *Everybody's Shakespeare* in 1934. The texts used for the second version of *Julius Caesar*, as well as for *The Merchant of Venice* and *Twelfth Night*, were those prepared by Welles and Hill, copies of which— later published as *The Mercury Shakespeare* by Harper and Brothers—were included with each set of 78 rpm recordings. When *Macbeth* was recorded in 1940, a playscript was prepared to accompany the recordings. The resulting package provides us with what was the most obviously pedagogical of Welles's Shakespearean activities, and the whole project can fairly be considered a distinctive contribution to the teaching and general appreciation of Shakespeare in America.

The Mercury Text Records, as the series of recordings was somewhat awkwardly called, were designed to contribute to a developing interest in audiovisual aids for the teaching of literature, and especially Shakespeare, in the American public schools. Welles was himself quick to associate his project with education. Together with Roger Hill, he wrote a brief article, somewhat grandly titled "On the Teaching of Shakespeare and Other Great Literature," for *English Journal* ("The Official Organ of the National Council of Teachers of English"), wherein he decries a perceived trend aimed at making the study of literature "scientific and analytical" and, consequently, dull. As they had in *Everybody's Shakespeare*, Welles and Hill stress the vigor and freshness of Shakespeare by noting that "only those folks whose blood courses hot through their veins can understand [Shakespeare's] tingling lines."[16] A major hindrance to the successful teaching of Shakespeare, Welles and Hill write, is that too many teachers "are incapable of reading Shakespeare aloud or instructing their charges in adequately reading Shakespeare aloud" so that "classroom renditions are doomed before they start." The solution to this difficulty, they somewhat disingenuously assert, lies in the use of the "growing library of phonograph recordings which are tremendously helpful" in bringing Shakespeare dramatically to life.[17] Although they do mention the first *Julius Caesar* recording, they make no reference to the Mercury Text Records, then in active preparation.

Self-serving though this article may have been, the issues Welles and Hill address must have been of genuine concern to educators; certainly, once the recordings were issued, the educational community responded with enthusiasm. The inaugural issue of *College English*, for example, included an essay on teaching Shakespeare with the aid of recordings in which the

Mercury productions are cited along with previous recordings of brief excerpts from Shakespeare's plays.[18] One thing the article makes clear is that, before Welles, no full-length recordings of Shakespeare were available. Teachers wishing to employ such aids had to depend on isolated passages recorded by E. H. Sothern and Julia Marlowe, Herbert Beerbohm-Tree, John Barrymore, John Gielgud, and a few others. These recordings existed almost entirely for the purpose of preserving a famous actor's reading of a set speech: Sothern recites "Hath not a Jew eyes" from *Merchant of Venice*, Barrymore interprets "O, what a rogue and peasant slave am I" from *Hamlet*. The custom of recording speeches and brief duologues by great actors, although partly a matter of technology and packaging (a speech can fill one side of a 78 rpm disk), reflects a cultural reality as well, an attitude toward Shakespeare that sees his plays as predominantly a collection of purple passages and wise saws.[19] As a look at textbooks used in nineteenth-century classrooms will reveal, although Shakespeare figured significantly in the curriculum, he was represented almost exclusively by a series of excerpts. William Endfield's *The Speaker*, first published in London but reprinted in Philadelphia in 1799, includes eighty-eight passages from Shakespeare. But, as was true of other early textbooks, no context was provided for the quoted passages and even the names of the plays from which they had been extracted were not indicated. Thus, though it can be fairly said that "Shakespeare became fixed in the educational curriculum by 1850,"[20] his was an ambiguous position.

Gradually, however, longer passages were excerpted. The "tent scene" from *Julius Caesar* (a scene, interestingly, that Welles himself would often excerpt when a brief performance of Shakespeare was called for, as he did on radio on separate occasions with John Barrymore and Charles Laughton), which was included in William Scott's *Lessons in Elocution* (London, 1808), reappeared in the first purely American school reader to use Shakespeare, John Pierpont's *American First Class Book* (Boston, 1823), and it was used once more in McGuffin's sixth *Reader*, published in 1853. As we can gather from some of these textbook titles, the Shakespeare excerpts were used for oratory and to teach moral principles primarily. For these purposes, at least, Shylock's "Hath not a Jew eyes" and Portia's "the quality of mercy," the speeches that constitute the two sides of one 78 rpm recording by E. H. Sothern and Julia Marlowe, provides listeners with the essence of *The Merchant of Venice*. The production of complete—or, at least, coherently abridged—versions of the plays places the emphasis on theater rather than oratory. Belatedly, Shakespeare recordings reflect the changes in theatrical history that, in the 'teens and twenties, saw a movement away from Shakespeare as star vehicle to an integrated, concept-orientated view of the plays in which the overall design means more than the specific interpretation of one role by a notable actor.

The Mercury Text Records thus offered something new—Shakespeare's plays themselves, cut somewhat, of course, but nevertheless plays rather than turns. Not that Welles is a shrinking violet in these productions: he plays both Cassius and Mark Antony in *Julius Caesar*, both Shylock and the Prince of Morocco in *Merchant of Venice*, and, though he only plays one character, Malvolio, in *Twelfth Night*, he portrays the Elizabethan actor Richard Burbage in a prologue written especially for the recording. Additionally, he narrates the stage directions for the initial three plays. Only in *Macbeth* is he satisfied with simply playing the title role. Nevertheless, it remains fair to say that, in these Mercury recordings, the play's (more or less) the thing. Inevitably, the recordings are variable in both scope and quality of interpretation. The acting is uneven, which is not surprising given Welles's peculiar habit—which continued into his film career—of casting nonacting members of his production staff in minor roles. Furthermore, the decision to have invented stage directions read along with Shakespeare's text, though it makes for greater ease of understanding, tends to detract from the fluidity of the pacing. Welles reads the stage directions in an interesting manner, very much like someone in the wings, intimately communicating with the audience and not noticed by the players. Nevertheless, these stage directions are often distracting; producers of subsequent Shakespeare recordings would not follow Welles's lead in this regard. For the most part, however, the Mercury Text Records represent a valuable experiment in recorded sound. Welles's radio background served him well: he was able to present Shakespeare as an intimate experience between speaker and listener; each of these recordings gives us a sense that we are overhearing, rather than being talked at by, the actors.

The *Twelfth Night* album is the most elaborate and unusual of the Mercury Text Records. Welles wrote and recorded a prologue to the play which purports to be a conversation between Richard Burbage (played by Welles) and Shakespeare (George Coulouris), and which wittily sets forth the play's (imaginary) genesis. Welles added an epilogue as well, stringing together various comments on *Twelfth Night* made by critics and playgoers over the centuries, from John Manningham to George Brandes. The prologue is especially well done, employing music, multiple narration, layered voices, and evocative repetition, in a manner that demonstrates Welles's radio tech-

Orson Welles as Macbeth (*Macbeth*, 1948). (Photo courtesy of Christopher P. Jacobs)

Lucy is miffed: instead of playing Juliet, she becomes a prop in Welles's magic act (*I Love Lucy*, October 15, 1956). (Photo courtesy of Jerry Ohlinger's Movie Material Store)

STAGE
After Dark

Orson Welles as *Brutus*
in the Mercury Theatre
production of *Julius Caesar*

In this issue
STAGE Awards
the Palms

JUNE 1938 · THIRTY-FIVE CENT

The Shakespearean actor as matinee idol: Orson Welles as Brutus in *Caesar* on the cover of *Stage* (June 1938).

THE MERCHANT OF VENICE

ACT I

Scene I

VENICE—A Street

Some producers have opened the play with music, peopling the stage with peddlars and vendors of sweets and folk of every degree walking up and down in pursuit of their business, a colorful and interesting picture of Venetian street life in the age of Shakespeare. With the entrance of Antonio and his friends the crowd melts away and the play is permitted to begin. For most productions a simple setting is the best. It needn't take up much of the space on the stage nor need it be elaborately pictorial. Center and side entrances seem to be called for and a piece center, a bench or steps or something to sit on. (Sketches here are suggestions.)

As the play opens Antonio, a prosperous merchant, a dignified, quiet, well-dressed gentleman of middle-age, enters chatting with friends of his, two gentlemen of Venice: Salarino and Salanio. They come downstage and pause; talking—

Antonio. In sooth, I know not why I am so sad:
 It wearies me—You say it wearies you;
 But how I caught it, found it, or came by it,
 What stuff 'tis made of, whereof it is born,
 I am to learn. *(Sighs)*
 And such a want-wit sadness makes of me,
 That I have much ado to know myself.

Salarino. *(Wisely)* Your mind is tossing on the ocean.

Salanio. *(Nodding)* Believe me, sir, had *I* such venture forth,
 The better part of my affections would
 Be with my hopes abroad. I know Antonio
 Is sad to think upon his merchandise.

Antonio. Believe me, no. I thank my fortune for it,
 My ventures are not in one bottom trusted,
 Nor to one place; nor is my whole estate

Some sky – Some drapes and a well for Antonio to sit on

Curtain and the suggestion of an arch cut out of heaven. Braced for an extremely small stage

Two flats angled against a glowing sky – Poles in the distance and in the foreground a long ledge

---

Everybody's Shakespeare: The Merchant of Venice: Welles's sketches offer a variety of set design possibilities for act I, scene i.

Sam Brown belts and trench coats: Orson Welles as Brutus, Martin Gabel as Cassius in the 1937 production of *Caesar*. (Author's collection)

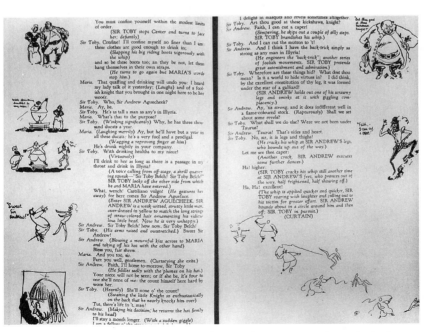

Everybody's Shakespeare: Twelfth Night: Welles supplies an animated strip in the lower right-hand corner.

MURGER!

Orson Welles doth foully slaughter Shakespeare in a dialect version of his "Tragedy of Macbeth"

The scene opposite is not, as you might think, taken from a musical-comedy skit laid in an alcoholics' ward. It is Orson Welles's movie version of Act III, Scene 1 of Shakespeare's *Macbeth*. It shows Macbeth, criminally crowned king of Scotland, plotting with two hired murderers the assassination of his faithful friend Banquo.

Faces and costumes like these, striking as they are, are not the most unusual feature of this production. Mr. Welles has had the idea that 11th Century Scotsmen appearing in a 17th Century play should express themselves in the accents of Sir Harry Lauder on the vaudeville stage of the 20th. Thus we have the witches promising to meet again "when the hoorly-boorly's done" and Lady Macbeth swooping down an endless stone staircase shrieking, "Oot, damn'd spot, oot, I say."

People who are familiar with the original play may have some difficulty in placing the individual lines. Scenes have been ruthlessly juggled, characters interchange their lines freely, a brand-new character named A Holy Father has been added to the cast. To add excitement to Shakespeare's text, Lady Macbeth is made to jump off a cliff instead of dying inside the castle. The movie ends with a line from Act I: "Peace, the charm's wound up!" which means, despite what Mr. Welles may think, not "over and done with" but "ready to work."

Such rearrangements and mutilations are not much more than what Sir Laurence Olivier did in his great production of *Hamlet* (LIFE, March 15), and they are much less than what Shakespeare did to the old chronicle of bloody dynastic feuding from which he got his story. The difference is that Olivier slashed the play to make a consistent and harmonious movie, just as Shakespeare shuffled the scenes of history to make a tragedy of human ambition and crime and retribution. Welles, on the other hand, has gone back to the senseless violence of all the generations of hams who have hacked and gesticulated their way through *Macbeth* for out-of-town audiences. It is such a jumble of gallopings and sweaty close-ups and fog and bubbling cauldrons that the spectator can only stagger from the theater howling with Macduff, "Confusion now hath made his masterpiece."

Welles (who a few sad years ago was the Boy Wonder of Hollywood) made *Macbeth* in 21 days on the Republic lot. Two westerns were in production at the same time on neighboring sets and may have influenced his style. He brought the finished product to the Venice film festival in August but withdrew it when he heard that the first prize was likely to go to *Hamlet*, a film he considers far inferior to his. He showed it to the Italian film critics and they all panned it. An English critic suggested it might be all right with English subtitles. Welles, however, says, "For the first time in my life I got what I aimed for." And the film has been extravagantly praised by international Gossip Columnist Elsa Maxwell.

"ALL HAIL, MACBETH, THAT SHALT BE KING HEREAFTER!"

WITCHES APPEAR and "prophesy in accents terrible" against a bleak Scottish sky to Macbeth and Banquo (*above*). Macbeth communes with his wife on the ramparts of his castle after the murder of Duncan (*below*). Both scenes might be impressive if the sound track broke down.

"I AM AFRAID TO THINK WHAT I HAVE DONE"

TO SAVE MONEY, cameraman wearing a mask on the back of his head to look like an extra was sent into the busy throng of spear-carrying Scottish soldiery to get close-ups while crowd scenes were being shot from behind him.

"MURDER!" *Life* magazine (October 11, 1948) ridicules Welles's *Macbeth* . . .

. . . and *Life*'s very different treatment of Laurence Olivier's *Hamlet* (1948).

Orson Welles as Macbeth, Jeanette Nolan as Lady Macbeth, and some Republic Pictures papier-mâché rocks. (Photo courtesy of Larry Edmunds Bookshop, Inc.)

nique at its best. Welles manages, in this added material, to stuff in a great deal of information, supplemented, in the printed transcript included in the revised Harper text of the play, by no less than fifty-one footnotes, which identify the likes of Christopher Marlowe, William Prynne, Samuel Johnson, and many others mentioned in the dialogue. For someone listening to the recording, of course, the notes are irrelevant, unless the listener is following along with the text in hand—in which case there would be no leisure to read them. In his introduction to the text of the prologue and epilogue, Welles writes: "While certain dangers in this type of representation are recognized, it offers a means of introducing a great mass of scholarship to the layman or student in an unusually palatable form."[21] Welles here reveals a peculiar tension between popularization and pedagogy, a tension which, in different ways, informs nearly all his Shakespearean activities.

Twelfth Night itself is not produced quite as entertainingly or performed as vividly as are Welles's prologue and epilogue. The actresses playing Viola and Olivia are less than adequate; Viola is unnecessarily high-strung and speaks the verse flatly, while Olivia maintains throughout a dignity that completely eliminates the character's romantic side. The pacing, furthermore, is often too rapid. Here the influence of radio aesthetics seems to work against the play: Welles and company clearly abhor a sound vacuum. Consequently, the actors at times pick up each other's cues with a misjudged alacrity that sacrifices the sense of the words and the dynamic interplay between and among the characters for a bright manner and clear diction. Welles's reading of Malvolio is problematic as well. He does not strive for subtlety; this is no tragic Malvolio, but simply—perhaps too simply—a pompous ass. Welles is content to nasalize his voice and project it from somewhere behind his neck, giving the impression that Malvolio speaks through some innate constipation of character. The low comedy scenes, on the other hand, are nicely rendered, especially the byplay between Sir Toby (Eustace Wyatt) and Sir Andrew (Will Geer); here, vocal characterizations, for which an aural medium is ideally suited, are sufficient to create the needed comic sense and texture.

If the Mercury Text *Julius Caesar* seems the most unified and coherent of the recordings, this may be in part because the play, consisting as it does of oratory of one kind or another, does not need to be seen to be understood and in part because Welles and most of the other participants had been involved with the New York production. Welles, however, in his somewhat perverse fashion, scrambles the casting. Having played Brutus on the stage, he switches to Marc Antony and Cassius for the recording. We can get a sense of his performance as Brutus, and of what the Broadway production in general might have sounded like, by listening to the abridgment of *Caesar* he presented on his "Mercury Theatre on the Air" (September 11, 1938). Although much of what made his modern dress production memorable on stage—costuming and lighting especially—could not, of course, be reproduced on the radio, Welles nonetheless found an ingenious way of modernizing *Caesar* by employing a narration by CBS news reporter H. V. Kaltenborn. Kaltenborn, who provides a running commentary drawn from Shakespeare's source, Plutarch, was associated, for millions of radio listeners, with German aggression in Europe: at the same time that he was participating in *Caesar*, he was constantly on the radio reporting on the Czechoslovakian crisis. (Frank Capra used Kaltenborn to similar effect in his 1939 film, *Mr. Smith Goes to Washington.*) Marc Blitzstein's modernist score, adapted from the stage production, and appropriate sound effects (marching feet, crowd noises, etc.) completed the illusion of immediacy Welles was after.

The scene of Marc Antony's oration uses choreographed voices in a particularly effective manner. On the line "Look you here./Here is himself, marred, as you see with traitors," one voice from the crowd shouts "O, villains," another voice, "O, traitors." And then, after a moment of total silence, a voice whispers, "revenge." Several voices repeat the word, quietly but urgently, with a few variations: "we'll be revenged, vengeance." The next voice cries out "vengeance," and is immediately cut off by Antony's "stay, good countrymen." Near the conclusion of Antony's speech, we hear a whispered "we'll mutiny." Then, in a normal speaking voice, "we'll burn the house of Brutus," followed by a series of quietly spoken imperatives, "about, seek, burn, kill, slay," until Antony, once again, picks up the thread, certain now that he has the crowd completely under his control. All in all, a chilling demonstration of demagoguery and mass hysteria.

In the Mercury Text Records version of *Julius Caesar*, which makes no attempt to re-create the Broadway production, Welles's performances as Cassius and, especially, Antony, are extremely effective: more so than his radio Brutus. Having introduced the broadcast as "the personal tragedy of a great liberal," he went on to give a diffident, low-key reading of Brutus ("a little soporific," Simon Callow suggests).[22] He is, throughout, tentative and self-conscious, in sharp contrast to the forceful, bitter, insinuating manner of Martin Gabel's Cassius. In the "tent scene," which features a fierce argument between Brutus and Cassius, Welles sounds pompous, giving the impression that Brutus, not Cassius, is in the wrong. One suspects that play-ing "a great liberal" did not, as a performer, interest him all that much, and that Brutus is not nearly as compelling or as accessible to him as the manip-ulator Cassius or the opportunist Mark Antony.

On the Mercury Text recording, the slightly heightened naturalism that characterizes Welles's delivery seems both very modern and entirely appro-priate to Shakespeare. He speaks Antony's funeral oration, which gives an actor the opportunity to indulge in a highly declamatory style, in an understated but nevertheless powerful manner, more in sorrow than in anger. The passage beginning "If you have tears, prepare to shed them now" (III.ii.169) is quietly spoken: Antony seems to be musing aloud, bringing forth very personal memories which are only incidentally for public consumption. In spite of his two roles, however, Welles does not hog the microphone—of all the recordings, this is the one that projects the greatest sense of ensemble playing. Edgar Barrier, as Caesar, and George Colouris, who now plays Brutus, both provide sharp, intelligent readings; they sound a bit dated only because they exhibit a theatrical diction that suggests an older acting tradition. The only real flaw in this recording lies, ironically, in Welles's handling of crowd noises, which here frequently seem amateurish and obtrusive. Regrettably, Welles did not follow his own stage direction for act I, scene i of the play in the *Everybody's Shakespeare* text: "They [the crowd] regard the Tribunes in respectful silence."[23] "Respect-ful silence," of course, is tricky to get across on a sound recording.

The Mercury *Merchant of Venice* contains perhaps the most powerful dra-matic moments of the three recordings, with Welles providing a strong focal point as Shylock. Surprisingly, given his reputation for overacting, he underplays Shylock, at least initially. In the first scene in which he appears (I.iii) he is very low key; he seems, as will Laurence Olivier in Jonathan Miller's much later National Theatre production (1970; televised, 1973), almost casual, distracted: not at all the vengeful figure, cunning or angry, that had become more or less traditional since Kean. Even in the "Hath not a Jew eyes" speech (III.i.51f.), Welles maintains tight control, his delivery seething but quiet. Unlike, for example, E. H. Sothern, whose recording of the speech was available to him, Welles does not build to a climactic "Why, *revenge!*" He begins slowly, almost matter-of-factly. Anger only comes to the fore in the greater emphasis he puts on each succeeding word in the catalogue "hands, organs, dimensions, senses, affections, passions." But on "And if you wrong us, shall we not revenge," Welles "comes down," so to speak; Shylock is not so much vengeful as stating an obvious fact, a logical

proposition. The remainder of the speech is spoken in a reasonable, subdued, albeit threatening manner. When he arrives at "Why, revenge," the
second word is almost whispered.

In the trial scene, however, Welles raises the ante, giving us the right-
eous, implacable Shylock we expect. Here, "The Voice" comes into its own,
Welles using its range and modulation in timbre to trace the varying fortunes of Shylock's suit. The most powerful moment on the recording
comes when Shylock, holding his knife—so we are told—high in the air,
speaks, with force and deliberation, the words "*Come . . . prepare!*" What
"ham" there is in Welles is reserved for his other role, the Prince of
Morocco. Here the bombast and declamatory style with which he is often
associated are given full rein. As Shylock, Welles uses the intimate manner
he learned working in radio: he is subtle and subdued, and always appears
to be thinking; he maintains Shylock's dignity throughout. As Morocco, on
the other hand, Welles gives full scope to his theatrical training and instinct,
delivering his lines in a large, orotund, and highly artificial manner—a
manner quite appropriate, it must be added, to the character he is playing.
Thus on one recording we have, not for the first or last time, two Orson
Welleses, one serious, one comic, one dignified, moving, highly disciplined,
one a rather foolish, if likable, buffoon.

But if Welles seems to dominate this recording, it is not because he plays
two parts, but because Shylock nearly always dominates productions of *The
Merchant of Venice*. Actually, the production as a whole is quite good. Brenda
Forbes makes a very attractive Portia; her reading combines intelligence
with sprightliness, and if she does not sound particularly young, she nevertheless gives her lines a light, bright, slightly humorous, very appealing
tone. Edgar Barrier as Bassanio and Joseph Holland (Welles's Caesar on
Broadway) as Antonio acquit themselves about as well as these roles,
reduced to voices only, allow. Once again, the comic characters—
Launcelot (Norman Lloyd) and Old Gobbo (Erskine Sanford)—suffer
perhaps the least among the secondary figures in being reduced to words
and voices: the wordplay, the accents, the comic rhythm are preserved even
if the physical humor is pretty much lost.

The plan to issue recordings of each of Shakespeare's plays, like so many
of Welles's ambitious projects, was not carried out. (London Records, in
conjunction with the Cambridge Shakespeare Society, would accomplish
this task for the first time in the mid-1960s.) A final album and playtext, of
Macbeth, were produced in 1940 and issued in 1941. By that time, of course,
Welles was deeply involved in fulfilling his RKO contract: he had been

working on an adaptation of *Heart of Darkness* in the late summer and early fall of 1939; after this and several other projects were abandoned, he turned to *Citizen Kane*, which went before the cameras in June 1940. The Mercury *Macbeth* bears all the signs of having been cobbled together in haste. This is particularly evident with the printed text. In the other three playscripts, for one example, when they were prepared for republication to accompany the recordings, Welles kept a variety of introductory material to certain scenes that were not part of the phonographic versions, including further elaborate stage directions, character description, discussions of historical stage business, and so forth. With *Macbeth*, passages directly quoted from Shakespeare's primary source, Holinshed's *Chronicles of England, Scotland, and Ireland*, now make up some 90 per cent of this "extra" material. A similar perfunctoriness characterizes the artwork, which Welles did not have time or inclination to do himself. The *Macbeth* drawings have none of the variety in style and content evident in the *Everybody's Shakespeare* playscripts. Gone are the elaborate reproductions of stage pictures, the suggestions for staging, the costume designs, and the carefully finished portraits of actors that we find in, especially, the *Merchant of Venice* and *Twelfth Night* volumes. The visual style adopted by the anonymous artist owes little or nothing to the "voodoo" *Macbeth* of 1936. The primary inspiration, rather, seems to have been photographs of late nineteenth and early twentieth-century "archaeological" productions of the play, especially Sir Herbert Beerbohm-Tree's at His Majesty's Theatre in 1911.

Welles's Harlem production of 1936 did, however, influence the text of the Mercury *Macbeth*, in a sense reversing the process whereby the *Julius Caesar* of *Everybody's Shakespeare* served as a kind of blueprint for the 1937 Broadway production. In a number of details, including verbal echoes in stage direction, as well as in some broad structural alterations, the *Macbeth* texts are quite similar. In both versions, for instance, act I, scene ii is omitted, so that Macbeth and Banquo greet the witches immediately after the opening incantations. Lady Macbeth, in both versions, is present when, at the entrance to Macbeth's castle, Duncan settles the royal succession, and it is Lady Macbeth, not Macbeth, who, with the appropriate change in pronoun, speaks the line "The Prince of Cumberland! That is a step/On which you must fall down, or else o'er leap,/For in your way it lies" (I.iv.48–50). In both versions, Banquo addresses the lines beginning "Thou hast it now: King, Cawdor, Glamis, all/As the weird women promised" (III.i.1–2) directly to Macbeth rather than as an aside. These examples, which could easily be multiplied, indicates that Welles had a copy of the 1936 promptbook in front of him as he prepared the Mercury Text.

The overall interpretation of the play, insofar as it can be reconstructed from the book and the records, is in harmony with both the Harlem production and the later (1948) Republic film in the prominence it gives to the supernatural. In part, this may simply be a matter of the way in which a recorded medium takes advantage of and thereby heightens those moments which seem to demand music and sound effects; Bernard Herrmann's musical score, which includes variations on the "power theme" from *Citizen Kane*, is particularly effective in the witch scenes. Welles's performance, on the other hand, does not here exhibit the haunted, nearly zombielike qualities evident in the film; he plays Macbeth as a blunt, straightforward soldier; and he gives to the major soliloquies greater intensity and emotional variety than he will in the film. The dagger speech is particularly well modulated: Macbeth is a relative innocent at this point, whereas in the film, he is already damned. In general, the brute villainy that essentially characterizes Macbeth in the Republic production is only intermittently present in the Mercury recording. Fay Bainter, as Lady Macbeth, exhibits a forceful single-mindedness; she becomes vulnerable and moving only in the sleepwalking scene, where her changes in mood and vocal quality compares favorably with Jeanette Nolan's relatively flat performance in the film. The balance of the cast is adequate, though so many roles are doubled, tripled, or even quadrupled—George Colouris, for example, plays Macduff, Angus, and the Doctor; Erskine Sanford is heard as Duncan, the Porter, Siward, and Seyton—that overall vocal variety is sacrificed to the demands of a tight budget and brief recording schedule.

Welles's Shakespeare playtexts and recordings, whatever final judgment we might reach on their aesthetic qualities, were well-received by those who made the greatest use of them—teachers and students of Shakespeare. In an age that has available to it what might be considered an overload of audiovisual aids for the teaching of literature, it takes an act of the imagination to reconstruct the excitement the Mercury Text Records generated. In the April 1940 issue of *English Journal*, Walter Ginsberg presents the findings of a survey, sponsored by something called the National Research Council's Committee on Scientific Aids to Learning, evaluating the use of Welles's recordings in the classroom. "Many of the boys realized for the first time," one participating teacher is quoted as saying, "that Shakespeare was a dramatist whose plays were and are actually produced on the stage."[24] "All types of scenes and speeches seemed to be sharpened and rendered much more vital and realistic for [all] the students by the playing of the records," another teacher reported; "Students seemed delighted by the whole procedure." "For the first time," wrote a third, "I felt that I made a Shakespeare play live for Sophomores in high school. . . I think these records enabled them to see . . . why Shakespeare's plays are famous." Ginsberg concludes that "the general results are overwhelmingly favorable to the use of the recordings."[25] A similar enthusiasm is evident in an article entitled "Recordings and the English Classroom," published in *High Points*, a publication of the New York City Board of Education. "It is a lost soul, indeed," the authors write, "who will not somehow be stirred, stimulated, moved and excited by this material so thoroughly scholarly and yet so utterly real and human." "These Mercury recordings," they add, "present a whole experience to the pupil, in a form that he will never forget."[26]

The Mercury Text Shakespeare, though it may be credited, in some small way, with having made a contribution to American secondary education,[27] was prepared and packaged very much as a commercial enterprise. In practice, of course, the conflict between these seemingly distinct motives—education and commerce—may not, perhaps, be as absolute as it might first appear. In line with what might be considered the peculiarly American view that anything that is any good should make money[28] (i.e., "if you're so smart, why aren't you rich?"), the publicity material for the Mercury Text Records stressed the commercial viability of Shakespeare himself:

> It is well to emphasize . . . the fact that Shakespeare's plays are today bringing money to producers, fame to actors, and enjoyment to audiences throughout the world. Any classroom conception that Shakespeare is still read simply because some graybeards say "it is good for you" should be dissipated. His books sell, his plays attract audiences simply because there are great delights to be found in them.[29]

A rather less subtle, internal document was prepared by Columbia Records outlining a promotional campaign aimed at record distributors. The overall rubric for this document was "Cashing in on the Classics." "This whole deal," we are assured, "will have behind it more publicity and more angles of sales promotion than any records ever brought out by any company." (Even allowing for the pardonable overstatement of marketing departments, this seems a large claim.) The sales strategy involved a series of letters to distributors, the first of which was to be on the topic "Orson Welles—his commercial value." A subsequent letter is headed "Cashing in on Orson Welles." A third letter makes clear that the record distributor "must [be] thoroughly familiar with the advantages of these records in class-room teaching." A primary advantage is outlined in telegraphic prose: "Greatest dramatic classics. Students can't escape them. Might as well be made interesting."[30]

We could, if we wished, find in this material a microcosm of the way highbrow culture becomes grist for the mill of what are essentially carnival sideshow hucksters; like Mark Twain's King and Duke, the Columbia/Mercury publicity flacks could claim that Shakespeare "always fetches the house."[31] "There is a ready market for this type of stuff," letter no. 4 informs us. "Every play to be done by Mercury Text Records has been produced for profit in the entertainment world."[32] In spite, or perhaps because, of this vulgar, energetic hucksterism, "Cashing in on the Classics" begins to sound, depending on the context, like a respectable enterprise. Consider, for example, the following passage from letter no. 1: "*Welles believes in cashing in on the classics*" (emphasis in the original). "To him," we are assured, "the great works of dramatic literature were not made to be swathed in layers of cotton to protect them from the light of day . . . not to be dissected by pedagogues as if they were so many cadavers . . . but to be *enjoyed*."[33] What we have here, in other words, is two different definitions of cashing in: in one sense, the phrase means "to make a lot of money," but it can also mean "to take advantage of," even, perhaps, "to find value in."

Throughout his career Welles would find ways to "cash in" on the classics, at least in the sense of making the classics, and especially Shakespeare, a central part of his professional life. In the *I Love Lucy* episode discussed in chapter 1, Welles at one point runs into Lucy in a department store where he has come to autograph what someone describes as "these new Shakespeare albums." The albums in question are, in fact, the Mercury Text Records from the 1930s, reissued in the Long Play format that had, by the mid-1950s, completely supplanted 78 rpm recordings. Welles, it would seem, is getting in a free plug in partial return for guest-starring on *I Love Lucy*. But what Welles is really selling here, I suggest, is Shakespeare, a place for Shakespeare in American culture, a place where Shakespeare and the classics can appear on the same bill with Lucy Ricardo and magic tricks. The three film adaptations of Shakespeare Welles was able to complete would carry on, in a somewhat different form, the experiments in wedding Shakespeare with technology represented by *Everybody's Shakespeare* and the Mercury Text Records.

FOUR

Welles/Shakespeare/Film

—

An Overview

Commenting on the proliferation of officially sanctioned cultural festivals in postwar Europe, Theodor Adorno found that culture itself, "in an effort to preserve a feeling of contrast to contemporary streamlining, . . . is still permitted to drive about in a type of gypsy wagon; the gypsy wagons, however, roll about secretly in a monstrous hall, a fact which they do not themselves notice."[1] It could be said of Orson Welles's Shakespearean films—indeed, of most of his post-*Citizen Kane* films—that they were attempts on his part to drive his gypsy wagon outside of the great hall of the culture industry. *Macbeth* (1948), from this point of view, was the last project he worked on that still remained within the hall, however much it strained to get out of it. *Othello* (1952), *Mr. Arkadin* (aka *Confidential Report*, 1955), *The Trial* (1962), *Chimes at Midnight* (1967), and *F for Fake* (1973) were, to a greater or lesser extent, compromises, at once inside and outside the hall, though Adorno would undoubtedly claim that it was no longer possible to find the "outside." Welles had in fact planned to present *Othello* on stage at the Edinburgh Festival and to produce the film under the auspices of the American National Theatre Association (ANTA), both significant manifestations of the phenomena Adorno was describing. Though neither of these plans was carried out, they indicate how aware Welles was, in the late forties and early fifties, of the limited options for producing Shakespeare films—or, for that matter, any films—now at his disposal.

The three Shakespearean films Welles completed—*Macbeth*, *Othello*, and *Chimes at Midnight*—appear at first sight to be less dependent on "gimmicks," more "faithful" to the plays on which they were based, than either of Welles's famous theatrical productions of the 1930s, the "voodoo" *Mac-*

beth and the "fascist" *Julius Caesar*. In spite of their reputations as eccentric films, each can be described as a fairly straightforward return to traditional Shakespeare performance in terms of language, period setting, and thematic emphasis. Their distinctiveness—on which I will elaborate in subsequent chapters—lies in a different direction from the popularizing and sensationalist impulses that lay behind Welles's stage productions. The Shakespeare films reveal an aspect of Welles in some ways diametrically opposed to his democratic, populist tendencies: they exhibit an emphasis on self-expression that results in a radicalization of style, in a singular, uncompromising personal cinematic practice. Starting with *Lady from Shanghai* (1948)—some might say with *Citizen Kane* (1941)—Welles made films that, in their violation of the basic norms of Hollywood filmmaking practice, were always dangerously on the edge of putting off audiences rather than inviting them in.

That film versions of Shakespeare's plays could draw on audiences of sufficient size to justify their production seems to have been an article of faith for filmmakers from almost the beginnings of the cinema, but it was a faith sorely and continuously tested. Paradoxically, perhaps, the most active period of film/Shakespeare collaboration was the silent era: Shakespeare without words—or, at least, without spoken words—did not seem to be a contradiction in terms. But why should the movies have been interested in Shakespeare at all? In the very earliest days of film, one might argue, again following Lawrence Levine,[2] Shakespeare was still positioned at a cultural crossroads, or at least could still be claimed as disputed territory, no longer truly popular as he seems to have been in the nineteenth century, but not yet fully co-opted for highbrow culture. At the turn of the century, as Pearson and Uricchio have observed, "Shakespeare may have been far more accessible to a diverse spectrum of viewers than may be apparent from a late twentieth-century perspective."[3] Furthermore, Shakespeare's plays could be reduced, by what might be called a process of "retro-adaptation," to the relatively simple tales and brief narratives from which many of them had been initially drawn: stripped of most of its language, a Shakespeare adaptation frequently reverts, intentionally or not, to an adaptation of Shakespeare's source. A one-reel (approximately twelve-minute) or two-reel version of a Shakespeare play is thus perhaps not as ludicrous as it sounds. Indeed, such a film would naturally be congruent with the "key phrase, key scene, key image approach to Shakespeare"[4] that seems to have been popular during the early part of the century.

With the advent of sound in the late 1920s, at least one more reason for Hollywood's interest in Shakespeare, one already implicit in the silent era, becomes paramount: cultural respectability for a medium under increasing attack from censors and moral arbiters of various stripes. As Graham Holderness remarks, "The repute of cinema art and of the film industry can be enhanced by their capacity to incorporate Shakespeare; the institution of Shakespeare itself benefits from that transaction by a confirmation of its persistent universality."[5] Warner Brothers' *A Midsummer Night's Dream* (1935)—the first major Shakespeare film of the sound era—can be seen, at least in part, as a response to the controversies leading to the establishment of the Production Code Administration, whose edicts were formulated in 1930 but did not become enforceable until 1934.[6] Another impulse, of course, was simply the presence of the famous German stage director Max Reinhardt in Hollywood, itself a consequence of Hitler's rise to power in Germany: Warner's film was a refurbishing of Reinhardt's frequently revived, peripatetic stage production, which had most recently been mounted, with Mickey Rooney as Puck and Olivia de Havilland as Hermia, in the Hollywood Bowl, an outdoor amphitheater. The casting strategies of the film—Rooney once again as Puck and de Havilland as Hermia, James Cagney as Bottom, Joe E. Brown as Flute, Dick Powell as Lysander— together with Mendelssohn's music and Vera Zorina's choreography, as well as the two credited directors, Reinhardt and William Dieterle, suggests that Shakespeare was still seen as somehow balanced between popularity and propriety; or perhaps the filmmakers believed they were reproducing the original conditions of the theater as a social institution in Shakespeare's time: something for the groundlings and something for the "better sort." The film was, in any case, promoted as a "class act" at the same time that Warner undoubtedly hoped for a popular success.

With MGM's *Romeo and Juliet* the following year, "class" seems to have taken over almost entirely, the casting of Andy Devine as the Nurse's servant, Peter, being one of the few remnants of the Warner's approach. Interestingly, it was in part the recent Broadway (and national tour) success of the Katharine Cornell *Romeo and Juliet*, in which Welles had notably participated, that may have given MGM the impetus for a film version:[7] Shakespeare, after a long dry spell, was once again box office, at least in New York, as Welles's "voodoo" *Macbeth* and "fascist" *Julius Caesar* would continue to demonstrate. (Ironically, Basil Rathbone, Cornell's Romeo, appears as Tybalt in the film, the role Welles had been "demoted" to, in his case from Mercutio, when the Cornell production had opened on Broad-

way at the end of its national tour.) Fully conscious of the cultural significance of its production, MGM sponsored an elaborate and attractive tie-
in book to accompany the film's release. In spite of the publicity—much
of it free—both *A Midsummer Night's Dream* and *Romeo and Juliet* generated, however, neither film enjoyed the kind of commercial success that
would encourage further experiments along the same line, and Hollywood
pretty much ignored Shakespeare for the next decade or so. The Shakespeare films of Welles and Laurence Olivier would initiate another round
of interest in Shakespeare adaptation, an interest that would speak to the
international film culture that came to the fore in the late fifties and early
sixties, with Italian, Soviet, and Japanese filmmakers bringing a new and
distinctive approach to filmed Shakespeare.

In addition to these social and cultural considerations, filmmakers
seem to have believed—as numerous commentators have subsequently
asserted—that Shakespeare's plays are in some essential way "cinematic."
Unlike the modern drama, so the argument goes, Shakespeare, like other
Elizabethan playwrights, builds up his actions in brief scenes, and organizes
both time and space in an extremely fluid fashion: *Antony and Cleopatra*, for
one notable instance, has over forty scenes and its action covers some ten
years. Shakespeare is thus naturally suited to the cinema.[8] Actually, of course,
the analogy is not really apropos, for it emphasizes what are in fact only inci-
dental properties of both Shakespeare and the film medium. The essence of
Shakespeare's dramaturgy can have only a tangential relationship to these
rather obvious dramatic conventions. Besides, many of Shakespeare's plays
involve very few locations and take place in a quite short period of time:
Twelfth Night, *Othello*, and *The Tempest* quickly come to mind. More to the
point, Shakespeare's plays actually unfold in no specific place at all, at least
in no place that needs to be specified or particularized. *Antony and Cleopatra* can move from Egypt to Rome and back quite easily because those
places are defined metaphorically rather than materially.[9] Shakespeare's
plays are set, literally and figuratively, on an essentially bare, abstract performing area, far removed from the concrete, detailed "realism" the cinema
very early on discovered to be one of its major resources and attractions.

The analogy between Shakespeare and film also lacks conviction when
considered from the film side as well. Although it is a popularly held conviction that film depends on rapid movement from place to place together
with a unique ability to expand, compress, or in a variety of ways distort
time, neither of these factors is necessary to film. The error comes from
confusing what is possible to a given medium with what is essential to it.

All that can truly be said to be essential to the cinema is its mechanism: the camera, lights, projector, celluloid, and all the other paraphernalia required to produce that which we finally see projected in front of us. The supposed affinity between Shakespeare and film simply does not hold up, which may at least help us to understand why Shakespearean films have always fallen short of the theory that would make such a film inevitably successful.

In one of the first important studies of Shakespeare and film, Jack Jorgens described some of the traditional ways Shakespeare adaptations have been categorized in terms of stylistic modes and approaches: the "theatrical," the "realistic," and the "filmic." The theatrical mode "uses film as a transparent medium" to "capture the essence of a theatrical performance"; the realistic mode " 'takes advantage of the camera's unique ability to show us *things*— great, sweeping landscapes or the corner of a friar's cell, a teeming market-place or the intimacy of a boudoir, all in the flash of a moment' ";[10] and the filmic mode demonstrates what he calls the work of the "film poet, whose works bear the same relation to the surfaces of reality that poems do to ordinary conversation."[11] Immediate objections can be raised to this scheme, of course: no medium is transparent; realism cannot be so easily defined; all films are, by definition, filmic. Jorgens, who presents these categories without embracing them, is the first to admit that "good Shakespeare films often move fluidly between modes and styles, merge several simultaneously, so that it is not possible to make simple judgments."[12] These categories, nonetheless, can help point to distinct elements in each of Welles's films: *Macbeth* as "theatrical," *Chimes at Midnight* as "realistic," and *Othello* as "filmic."

These primarily formal strategies are closely related to the distinct production histories of each of Welles's Shakespeare films. With *Macbeth*, the unlikely sponsor (Republic Pictures, known primarily for its cliffhanger serials and B westerns), the modest budget, and the brief (three-week) production schedule, all encouraged Welles to adopt an enclosed, claustrophobic, highly set-oriented, long-take method of filming. The look and mood of this film—the papier-mâché sets, the tackily inconsistent costumes, the wide-angle and deep-focus photography, the wildly variable quality of style and performance—can be seen to have had their origin in the means of production even while they serve to express Welles's vision of Shakespeare's play. In adapting *Macbeth*, Welles, in the words of Lorne Buchman, "shortened the play by two-thirds, cut entire scenes, excised characters, added others, [and] rearranged what remained of the play."[13] Welles constructed a deliberately deglamorized world for Macbeth; the whole production has a lean and hungry look. The film's style, rightly described as "expressionistic,"[14] has analogues to films like Edgar G. Ulmer's *Detour* (1945) and William Cameron Menzies' *Invaders from Mars* (1953), both of which employ expressionist techniques in part as a defense against minimal budgets. Although *Macbeth* was not, like *Detour*, a bottom-drawer production, Welles employed a B picture approach in order to keep what would have been a potentially expensive film within reasonable bounds.

The very different style evident in *Othello* in part derives from a very different production context. Rather than working within a preset, clearly defined budget, and within the institutional constraints of a specific studio or production organization, Welles had at his disposal varying amounts of money over several years. Reflecting Welles's peripatetic existence as a Hollywood outsider and exile from America, *Othello* exhibits evidence of having been filmed in different locations at different times, even within a single scene. In contrast to the claustrophobic unity of *Macbeth*, *Othello* appears open and fundamentally fragmented in terms of both time and space. Welles, once again, drastically cuts and rearranges Shakespeare's text, eliminating, for example, virtually all of Iago's self-justifying soliloquies. He creates a sound design that has the effect of making what dialogue remains difficult to follow. His methods result in an "opening up" of one of Shakespeare's most tightly constructed plays. If the visual style of *Macbeth* has affinities with the Hollywood B movie, the visual style of *Othello* finds its affinities in the European art cinema tradition.

With *Chimes at Midnight*, we have a production history that can be conceived of as a kind of composite of those of the other two films. As with *Macbeth*, Welles was working within a reasonably firm, limited budget and a precisely delineated, albeit more generous, time frame. The filming itself was restricted in terms of space as well: a few Spanish locations and an equally restricted number of studio sets. And, as he had with *Macbeth*, Welles had at his disposal, and drew on, a recent theatrical production of the same material. As with *Othello*, on the other hand, Welles was working outside the dominant Anglo-American traditions of Shakespearean production. The entire film was produced in Spain, and the casting included Spanish, French, and other European performers, along with the established Shakespeareans like John Gielgud (Henry IV) and Ralph Richardson (narrator). As with *Othello*, Welles therefore relied heavily on dubbing non-English-speaking actors with, frequently, his own voice. Even more drastically than with *Othello*, Welles also chose to de-emphasize the linguistic dimension of Shakespeare and to rely more on visual equivalents to the written text.

In both *Othello* and *Chimes at Midnight*, Welles's effectual destabilization of narrative form, thematic consistency, and unity of character is carried out to an extent that it can resemble incoherence. On the one hand, Welles restructures Shakespeare's plays so as to present us with the ending at the beginning—particularly in *Othello*, which opens with the funerals of Othello and Desdemona, but also with the opening of *Chimes*, where we can see and hear the aged Shallow and Falstaff speaking lines from the fourth act of *Henry IV, Part II*; he then proceeds, on the other hand, to construct in each film a narrative which precisely fails to explain what the initial scene has shown us. The need for explication is much stronger in *Othello*, and in both films an implicit, intricate act of closure is gradually revealed by the end of the narrative not to be closure at all. Welles in these late Shakespearean films (perhaps in all his films) resists the sense of inevitability, of the already done, that critics of mass culture like Adorno have sometimes identified as the essence of cinema.[15]

Another way of understanding the differences between Welles's three films would be to suggest that each reproduces in formal terms the central thematics of the Shakespeare text upon which it is founded. In *Macbeth* the mise-en-scène and photography combine to re-create the self-enclosed and self-referential world of its protagonists. *Othello*, filmed with off-kilter camera angles, discontinuous editing, elliptical sound bridges, and vertiginous compositions, plays out the growing disorientation that becomes the focus of Othello's experience in Cyprus. *Chimes at Midnight* articulates the essential dynamics of the Hal/Falstaff relationship through a style that emphasizes the physicality of the body and at the same time separates out distinctly opposed spaces through a mise-en-scène that contrasts the court and tavern worlds. Eschewing both the artificially "theatrical" space of *Macbeth* and the essentially naturalistic and geographically identifiable world of *Othello*, *Chimes* opts for a style less dependent on either the manipulation of obvious artifice or on the foregrounding of formal cinematic techniques than its predecessors.

As an alternative to Jorgens's primarily stylistic distinctions, Shakespeare films in general could be categorized by pointing to the material circumstances of their production. To simplify matters somewhat, we could identify two basic types: those made from the center and those made at the margins. The former merge the cultural authority of Shakespeare with institutional support, whether commercial (major studio), governmental (Kosintsev's *Hamlet* and *King Lear*, for instance), or both (Olivier's

Henry V). In these works, the cultural authority is both assumed and reinforced: the performance of Shakespeare's text is simultaneously an affirmation of the value and status of that text. The marginal films, among which
Welles's figure prominently, challenge, or at least qualify, the cultural
supremacy of Shakespeare by, to one extent or another, pushing the source
text toward its own margins or by revealing, through the film's low-budget strategies and absence of gloss and finish, the fragmentary and tentative
authority of the original. As we have been relearning in the past few
decades, Shakespeare's plays themselves, as they have come down to us, can
be defined as extremely unstable texts, never entirely "finished," works in
progress, playhouse documents, even sketchy blueprints for an edifice that
we can never satisfactorily reconstruct. But this, needless to say, is not the
image of Shakespeare as he is understood in the larger culture. When Kenneth Branagh's *Hamlet* (1996) is publicized as including the full, original
text, what is ignored is that we have no way of knowing precisely what the
original text is. Branagh's film, for all its virtues, presents a Shakespeare in
full high-Victorian garb—a Shakespeare that Sir Henry Irving and Sir
Herbert Beerbohm-Tree would have been proud to produce. Welles, on
the other hand, presents a Shakespeare from hunger, what we might term,
paraphrasing Jerzy Grotowski, a "poor" Shakespeare.

No film in commercial release, one must concede, could ever be as
"poor" as a theater presentation can be: Welles's Shakespeare films were
not precisely cheap (though they were cheaper than most): I am referring, rather, to certain stylistic considerations and production circumstances that give us a "poverty effect" (just as, in Roland Barthes' terms,
specific narrative devices and techniques can give us a "reality effect").[16]
Although a long take, as with the ten-minute-plus of the murder of Duncan in Welles's *Macbeth*, may serve a variety of useful purposes, it registers
as an effect of minimal resources: Welles filmed the scene that way, some
viewers will assume, in order to save money. Actually, long-take filming
can be just as time-consuming, and hence expensive, as breaking the
scene down into numerous setups, but the impression of cheapness and
speed is what I am getting at here. The obvious absence of synchronous
sound in so much of *Othello* and *Chimes at Midnight* provides the viewer
with a similar projection of "poverty effect." And Welles, as the record
clearly shows, did cut corners in his Shakespeare films, employing, for
example, stand-ins for reverse shots simply because he could only afford
to hold on to his actors for brief periods of time. My point is simply that
Welles's Shakespeare films, as marginal products, are not surrounded by

the same aura of class and respectability that surrounds most Shakespeare adaptations.

Welles's Shakespearean trilogy is comparable in ambition if not in effect to the trilogies of Laurence Olivier, Franco Zeffirelli, and Kenneth Branagh. In contrast to Welles, however, Olivier and Branagh project, in different ways, issues of national purpose and national identity: "Britishness" of one sort or another. Olivier's films—especially *Henry V*—are intimately linked to Shakespeare's unmatched place in English history and culture as well as his high value as a cultural export. Branagh, although—as a Belfast boy—ostensibly reacting against the very English, respectful, traditional attitude Olivier supposedly brings to Shakespeare, nevertheless falls rather easily into what Harold Bloom would term the "Anxiety of Influence." He surrounds himself with paternal and maternal figures drawn from the great tradition of British Shakespeare—John Gielgud, Paul Scofield, Derek Jacobi, Judi Dench—while he makes a gesture toward a more international Shakespeare by casting, usually in minor roles, such Americans as Denzel Washington, Keanu Reeves (in *Much Ado About Nothing*, 1993), Jack Lemmon, Billy Crystal, and Robin Williams (in *Hamlet*). Both Olivier and Branagh provide, albeit in somewhat different ways, an official Shakespeare. As John Collick notes, "Most people have been brought up to equate Shakespeare with great British actresses and actors dressed in period costumes and speaking in mellifluous accents."[17] The films of Olivier and Branagh, though they reveal specific and distinctive cultural and formal strategies and styles of their own (Olivier draws from art-historical design in *Henry V*, Freudian theory in *Hamlet*, televisual staging in *Richard III*; Branagh associates King Henry V with Tim Burton's *Batman*), are also intimately associated with the establishment British Shakespeare of the Old Vic (Olivier) and the Royal Shakespeare Company (Branagh) insofar as the genesis of their films comes from previous stage productions and from the iconography of the classical British acting fraternity.

Zeffirelli's Shakespeare films would seem to offer a specifically European approach in that the Italian director's style inherits simultaneously from a neorealist film aesthetic and from opera, so that in, especially, *Taming of the Shrew* (1966) and *Romeo and Juliet* (1968), we are presented with a carefully observed, highly detailed material world in conjunction with a sweeping romantic tone underlined by a strong emphasis on music and spectacle. Zeffirelli, however, exhibits almost as much of the traditions of British Shakespeare as he does a more specifically Italian one; he has, after all, spent a good part of his working life in England, directing Shakespeare

and opera on the London stage, and he has expressed his admiration for
Olivier's Shakespeare films.[18] As a result, Zeffirelli's Shakespearean productions have something of the air of "Euro-pudding" about them: the variety of influences and the emphasis on spectacle do not add up to anything
like a stylistic unity. By the time of *Hamlet* (1990), most traces of neoreal-
ism and opera have disappeared, and in spite of his location filming, he produces a Shakespeare film that has more in common (in its mise-en-scène,
at least, especially costumes and setting) with Victorian and Edwardian
stage productions than with his two earlier films, at the same time that the
casting of Mel Gibson and Glenn Close, together with an orthodox group
of British Shakespeareans, has obvious appeal for a primarily Anglo-American market.

To place Welles's Shakespeare films in their specific cinema-historical
contexts, we can compare the circumstances of their production with the
near simultaneous Shakespeare films of Laurence Olivier, Akira Kurosawa,
and Sergei Yutkevitch. Olivier's *Henry V* (1944), *Hamlet* (1948), and *Richard
III* (1955) were all financed by the two major British producers J. Arthur
Rank and Alexander Korda, with significant governmental encouragement
and institutional support. Each film was conceived of as a prestige production, expected to bring honor and, hopefully, some American dollars, to
Great Britain. Each film (especially *Hamlet*) was provided by its distributor
with a carefully orchestrated publicity campaign. *Hamlet* was released in the
United States under the auspices of the prestigious Theatre Guild, a highly
unusual step by that organization. Handsome illustrated booklets were prepared as press kits, and *Hamlet* generated not one but two hardcover, lavishly illustrated volumes, one of which included both Shakespeare's play
and Olivier's script.[19] *Richard III* had its U.S. premiere on NBC television
in 1956, an event publicized as a significant cultural moment for both
Shakespeare and for television, and one that returned a quick half million
dollars to Olivier's backers.

Kurosawa's *Throne of Blood* (1957), an adaptation of *Macbeth*, and a film
that is often pointed to as an ideal Shakespeare adaptation in spite of the
fact (because?) it does not include on its sound track a single word written
by Shakespeare, was produced, distributed, and exhibited under, once
again, highly favorable conditions. As an "art cinema" artifact, *Throne of
Blood* received extensive cultural support; it was embraced by Shakespeareans in part because its translation to another medium was so complete that comparisons to the original could be made in general rather than
specific terms. Yutkevitch's *Othello* (1955) was produced at a government-

run studio and was the product of a cultural moment when the Soviets, partially freed from the shadow of Stalin, were in the process of redefining their relationship to culture in general and to the West in particular.[20] Significantly, none of these "successful" Shakespearean films reached a large enough popular audience so as to make a lot of money (an accomplishment perhaps more tricky than Bernstein [Everett Sloane], in *Citizen Kane*, quite realized). The undoubted critical success of a number of these films has served to obscure the fact that they were either barely profitable or not profitable at all, their seeming popularity artificially inflated by careful handling and publicity. Though Olivier's *Hamlet* ran in New York for over a year, it played at one theater only and hence could never generate large grosses. And even though an estimated 62.5 million people saw *Richard III* on television, Olivier's film still lost money.[21]

Welles's approach to filming Shakespeare may be more closely related to the circumstances of early modern theatrical practice than are the more orthodox projects of his contemporaries. In a very real sense, as a number of critics have recently emphasized, Shakespeare's plays themselves flourished first in the actual margins of Tudor and Stuart cultures, at the edges of the city of London proper. "The popular theatre in particular . . . was a threateningly liminal space, whose 'mingling of kings and clowns' . . . blurred a whole range of distinctions, evoking the specter of adulterating, crossbreeding, and hybridity."[22] Welles's Shakespeare films, regarded in this light, are part of a countertradition of Shakespeare, what might be thought of as "Shakespeare from the Provinces," a tradition that includes amateur and school productions, abbreviated texts, "foreign" (i.e., non-Anglo-Saxon) stagings—almost any Shakespeare taking place outside the theater capitals of London (including London, Ontario) and New York. These forms of "derivative creativity," to employ Michael Bristol's term,[23] have, in fact, always been around: Shakespeare's own company engaged in provincial performance, employed severely cut texts, performed in makeshift acting spaces, and so forth.

Welles's Shakespeare films could be further marginalized as provincial in the sense that they are products of an American sensibility. Actually, there is very little that can be characterized as specifically American about Welles's approaches to Shakespeare's text; the films combine traces of Hollywood genre elements (this is particularly true of *Macbeth*) with European, art-cinema practices. The marginal status of these films lies precisely in a simultaneous awareness and incorporation of the "great tradition" of British Shakespeare (Gielgud and Richardson in *Chimes*, for example) and a decisive movement away from the center. This is precisely what is meant by marginal: not outside the circle but at the edges of it, reaching simultaneously toward the center and outside the line. Even *Othello*, which might seem most divorced from theater practice, is not innocent of theatrical traditions. Having Roderigo and Iago witness the elopement of Othello and Desdemona is an interpolation that goes back at least to Oscar Ashe's London production in 1907; Welles makes much of having based his visual design on the work of the Renaissance painter Carpaccio, but Beerbohm-Tree did the same in 1912; in the nineteenth century the French actor Charles Fechter, playing in London, made use of a mirror to emphasize Othello's growing consciousness of racial difference, and a mirror figures prominently in Welles's film.[24]

Perhaps because Welles appears to have one foot in each camp, to be both at the center and at the periphery, practitioners of cultural studies and various other modes of poststructuralism have been hesitant to embrace his Shakespeare films. The discourse surrounding *Othello* is particularly telling: in at least four recent studies (Vaughan, Donaldson, Collick, and Hodgdon), Welles's *Othello* has been taken to task for being insufficiently sensitive to issues of race and gender. I will consider the race question in chapter 6; the gender argument, it seems to me, is founded on little more than dubious assumptions concerning Welles's personal life and the difficulties surrounding the production of the film that have scant force as evidence. Vaughan, for example, writes: "Constructed by a male auteur who was known to have difficulty in his own relationships with women, Welles's *Othello* fetishes the female body and demonstrates the tyranny of the male gaze"; Collick claims that "the protracted search for an actress to play Desdemona hints at an indecisiveness on Welles's part and an inability to come to terms with the sexual implications of the Othello-Desdemona relationship in the film"; Donaldson supports a psychoanalytic point in this fashion: "The emphasis on the failure of the beloved's eyes to return an anxious gaze in a reassuring way may draw on Welles's memory of his dying mother's eyes"; and Barbara Hodgdon, apropos of *Filming Othello*, Welles's 1978 documentary, finds that "not only is [the film] organized as a series of male conversations or monologues, with Welles . . . at its center; but none of the three Desdemonas who worked on the film [i.e., *Othello*] appears to tell her story."[25] These comments perhaps reveal, as much as anything else, the limits of contextual criticism.

In spite as well as because of the marginal nature of Welles's Shakespeare films, they undeniably provide a more challenging reading of the plays and, not incidentally, a more useful pedagogic tool than, for example, the vast majority of the BBC/Time-Life Shakespeare plays. Whereas the latter are far more "faithful" to the texts of Shakespeare than are any of Welles's films, with a few notable exceptions they are also, in their bland refusal to explore interpretive possibilities and to challenge theatrical (or even televisual) orthodoxies, dead on arrival. But because the BBC versions have the aura of "official" Shakespeare and because the videos have been aggressively marketed to schools and colleges worldwide, they have filled a significant pedagogic niche. If, however, the goal is to challenge viewers to think about Shakespeare rather than simply absorb the plays passively, Welles's films provide a far more useful model.[26] The gaps, omissions, and quirks of Welles's texts call for some kind of answering intelligence, a challenge to either Welles or Shakespeare. Although John Collick can claim that a film like Welles's *Othello* (or Derek Jarman's *The Tempest*, 1979) is "as institutionalized within the economy of commercial cinema as any other movie," thereby ironing out rather significant differences in production, distribution, and exhibition, he nevertheless recognizes that "it is in these fragmented and contradictory movies that the coherence and apparent consensus over what constitutes culture, Shakespeare, and film, breaks down to reveal an uncertain and grotesque vision of society and social relationships."[27] Welles's films, to put the matter somewhat differently, are unlikely to be perceived as definitive versions of the Shakespearean texts from which they derive.[28]

Welles's Shakespeare films, as we will see, have been more celebrated in Europe than in England and North America, in part because they place less emphasis on language and in part because the theatrical understanding of Shakespeare in Europe—and here I am thinking of such venues as the Deutsches Theater (Berlin), the Piccolo Teatro (Milan), and the Théâtre de Soleil (Vincennes)—is far bolder and experimental, more playful and elastic, than the equivalent venues in Great Britain and North America. As Dennis Kennedy has observed,

> the authoritative and thorough-going rethinkings of the plays we associate with Leopold Jessner or Giorgio Strehler or Ariane Mnouchkine have not occurred to the same degree in the home countries. Even Peter Brook, reinventing the plays in English since 1945, has done his most radical work on Shakespeare in French.[29]

At the same time, of course, it needs to be acknowledged that Shakespeare has a rather different cultural status in Europe, that his plays are often pre-

sented in modern translations, and that French cineastes, in particular, are
less likely to be familiar with Shakespeare's original text than most English-speaking reviewers and critics. No European critic, in short, is likely to
be bothered by the fact that Welles, like many of the producers of Shakespeare in non-English-speaking countries, has virtually translated Shakespeare into another idiom.

Welles's Shakespeare films, in short, circulate more clearly within a range
of European postwar appropriations of Shakespeare than they do within an
Anglo-American tradition of Shakespeare performance. Or, perhaps more
accurately, they exhibit, as do many contemporary Shakespeare productions, "a tension between a decentering aesthetic and the desire to retain
the plays as touchstones of traditional Western culture."[30] Bringing the
witches back at the very end of his film of *Macbeth*, which echoes the similar employment of voodoo drums in the Harlem *Macbeth* in 1936, may not
have been an interpretive invention on Welles's part, but it is a strategy that
has been latterly associated[31] with the theatrical influence of Samuel Beck-
ett and the critical influence of Polish critic Jan Kott; the ending of Polish-
born director Roman Polanski's 1971 film of *Macbeth*, which shows us Malcolm's younger brother, Donalbain, drawn to an encounter with the
witches just as his older brother is being crowned king of Scotland, makes
the point explicit, but it was already implicit in Welles.

European cinephiles, furthermore, who were quick to enshrine Welles
in a pantheon of auteurs, easily incorporated the Shakespeare films into the
Wellesian cinema, recognizing in them themes and dramatic emphases present as well in *Citizen Kane*, *The Magnificent Ambersons*, *The Stranger*, *Lady
from Shanghai*, *Touch of Evil*, and *Mr. Arkadin*: the destructive consequence
of power, even when employed in a just cause; the inevitability of betrayal;
the loss of paradise—all of these films are, in their own way, Shakespearean
texts, if in no other sense than in the way they impose a large, poetic intensity on questions of family and domesticity and thus wed the social with
the personal. So Henri Lemaitre, for example, could write: "Perhaps the
most Shakespearean film in the history of the cinema is not one of those
drawn from his works, but rather a creation of the most Shakespearean of
the masters of the camera, Orson Welles—the film, *The Lady from Shanghai*."[32] In the specific context of a discussion of *Touch of Evil*, Robin Wood
has captured the general affinities between Welles and Shakespeare by
pointing to "the efforts to create a visual-poetic world equivalent to the
'world' of a Shakespearean tragedy; in the constant reaching out for a tragic
weight and grandeur; in the attempts to find a cinematic style that will ful-

fill a creative function analogous to that of Shakespeare's verse." (Wood, however, suggests that *Touch of Evil* may be closer in spirit to Shakespeare's near-contemporary John Webster, "in whose plays the Elizabethan creative energies degenerate into morbidity and decadence.")[33] What Welles's films and Shakespeare's plays perhaps share most directly, apart from their interest in power relations, is a compelling evocation of evil as something at once attractive and horrifying, both in terms of its appeal to characters within the fiction and to audiences outside of it.

Whether produced at the center or from the margins, however, one thing is certain: Shakespeare films, as Welles was no doubt aware, have seldom been big box office. Only such a presumption explains the methods he employed to produce *Macbeth* at Republic: a low budget was all that could justify making a Shakespearean film at all. That Welles returned to Shakespeare twice again, and planned other projects along the way, shows a tenacity quite divorced from sound business acumen. If Warner Brothers and MGM were not able to succeed with Shakespeare, who could? Certainly, the conjunction of Shakespeare and Welles's modernist, avant-garde, and even postmodern cinematic practice was almost guaranteed to produce films of narrow commercial appeal. Welles made few concessions, in these films, to the requirements of popularity. After *Macbeth*, he was working completely outside mainstream Hollywood and had gone over, willingly or not, into the European personal cinema, a cinema that was poised to make an extraordinary cultural, though never truly popular, international impact. This picture is complicated, however, by Welles having positioned himself, or been positioned, as an international maverick during much of the period in question. His limited access to more or less standard modes of production, distribution, and exhibition severely compromised his European films, which were often financed by dubious speculators, processed in not always reliable labs, and released in piecemeal fashion by organizations and people ill-suited to the task.

Welles's Shakespeare films, in other words, were not rationalized productions, even when compared not to Hollywood but, more appropriately, to the international art cinema of the 1950s. It is worth noting, in this context, that the important European and international auteurs who came to prominence in the 1950s—Ingmar Bergman, Federico Fellini, and Akira Kurosawa, notably—made films that were produced, distributed, and exhibited under comparatively ideal conditions, either because of government subsidy (Bergman), major studio backing (Kurosawa), or, with Fellini, a film industry enjoying, by the end of the 1950s, a renaissance both

in terms of prestige and commercial popularity which allowed it to support offbeat projects. These highly individualistic filmmakers did not, for
the most part, have to struggle to find minimum financing, essential facilities, or sympathetic distributors. Welles, on the other hand, in each of the
three instances where he adapted Shakespeare to film, did so within formal
constraints that virtually demanded as well as allowed an expressionist,
highly fragmented solution to the questions posed by the Shakespeare text.

Hollywood's earlier experiences with Shakespeare, in other words,
would have suggested both to Welles and to Republic Studios that, given
the size of the potential market for Shakespeare on film, containing costs
was the crucial issue. Welles knew that filming Shakespeare successfully in
Hollywood would involve creative production techniques. The desire to
see Welles's *Macbeth* as originating from a conflict between the commercial
imperatives of Hollywood, on the one hand, and the aesthetic aspirations
of the artist-genius, on the other, thus needs to be resisted. Welles was just
as sensitive as studio head Herbert J. Yates and producer Charles K. Feldman to commercial values, even if he was often unable or unwilling to turn
that knowledge into practice. Welles's purpose in filming *Macbeth* at a studio known primarily for its low-budget movies was precisely to demonstrate that a financially successful adaptation of Shakespeare could be made
in Hollywood. The conflict, in other words, was not over whether Shakespeare could be transformed into popular art, but over how best to accomplish that goal. Welles and Republic were both, in their own way, attempting to reach a large, popular audience for Shakespeare films.

By the time of *Othello* and *Chimes at Midnight*, the project I ascribed to
Welles at the outset of this study—reconciling Shakespeare (high culture)
with popular culture—was no longer viable. Neither film is "accessible" in
the way the earlier *Macbeth*—at some point in time—was meant to be.
Indeed, the motives behind the 1992 "restoration" of *Othello* (and the plans
to "restore" *Chimes at Midnight*), I will argue, testify to the irreconcilable
differences between these Shakespeare films and the popular audience one
might hope to discover for them. An ironic reversal here takes place. Shakespeare, essentially a popular artist, is rescued by Welles from the late nineteenth-century high classicism which had threatened to imprison and limit
him, had threatened to turn him, in Gary Taylor's words, into "the badge
of cultural elitism and the instrument of pedagogical oppression,"[34] but in
the process the sixteenth-century playwright now becomes a distinctly
modernist figure. As we will see, the deconstruction Welles performs on
Shakespeare's *Othello* and "Henriad" plays (and, to a lesser extent, on *Mac-*

beth) produces a series of irresolutions and complexities that elucidate and sharpen the tensions already present in Shakespeare while at the same time undermining the narrative and structural foundations of Shakespeare's dramaturgy.

In the chapters on *Macbeth*, *Othello*, and *Chimes at Midnight* which follow, I am not primarily concerned with constructing new readings of Welles's Shakespearean films; each has been well served by much recent attention paid both to Welles and to the filming of Shakespeare. Among a number of outstanding discussions, I would select those by James Naremore and Anthony Davies on *Macbeth*, Jack Jorgens, Peter Donaldson, and Lorne Buchman on *Othello*, and Joseph McBride and Samuel Crowl on *Chimes at Midnight*.[35] Bernice Kliman and Barbara Hodgdon, in their volumes in the Shakespeare in Performance series, have provided extremely useful estimates of, respectively, *Macbeth* and *Chimes at Midnight* within the context of performance histories.[36] My goal, which partially overlaps a number of these discussions, is to place each film within a larger contextual field and to suggest the extent to which the meaning and significance of each are intimately tied to the circumstances in which it was produced, distributed, exhibited, and received. Welles's Shakespeare films will be seen to be very much part of the recent cultural debates on Shakespeare's "transcendent" value versus his role in maintaining and justifying what Terence Hawkes has usefully termed "Bardbiz,"[37] a debate that posits Shakespeare either as "an alternative to the culture industry" or as "simply one of its more successful products,"[38] a paradoxical space that Welles himself, partly because of his Shakespeare films, continues to occupy.

FIVE

Shakespeare Rides Again

—

The Republic *Macbeth*

An official U.S. entry in the 1948 Venice film festival, *Macbeth*, directed by and starring Orson Welles, was withdrawn from competition before the judging could begin when it was learned that the grand international prize would be awarded to *Hamlet*, directed by and starring Laurence Olivier. This was only the earliest indication that *Macbeth* would be bedeviled by, among many other things, comparisons to Olivier's film. According to both Welles and columnist Elsa Maxwell, *Macbeth* was shown out of competition to "the largest enthusiastic audience of the entire festival,"[1] although it was "soundly panned by the Italian critics."[2] Welles blamed the Italian attitude on a personal antipathy to himself; he insisted that "MACBETH GOT SUPERLATIVES FROM ENTIRE FOREIGN PRESS REPRESENTATIVES WHO UNANIMOUSLY SAY IT IS SUPERIOR TO HAMLET."[3] From that moment on, nearly everyone involved in the production, distribution, and exhibition of Welles's film, apart from—most of the time—Welles himself, again and again alludes to Olivier's film. From the point of view of Republic Pictures, the poverty-row Hollywood studio which had financed *Macbeth*, the success of *Hamlet* was something both to worry about and to emulate: *Hamlet* had its U.S. premiere in Boston, so *Macbeth* was premiered in Boston. For many critics, however, *Hamlet* became a convenient stick with which to beat *Macbeth*. The success, real and imagined, of Olivier's film, both in terms of prestige and in terms of profits, haunted Welles's film. In part, this was a matter of timing. Not only did they compete at Venice, but Olivier's film opened in the United States on September 29, 1948; Welles's opened on October 7.

To demonstrate most dramatically the relative receptions of Olivier's and Welles's film, we can do no better than look to *Life* magazine. The March 15, 1948, issue of *Life* features an elaborate, eleven-page photographic essay on Olivier's *Hamlet*, and Olivier himself, in costume as the prince, graces the cover. When we turn to the essay, we find that the film, which has yet to open in Great Britain, much less in the United States, is already being treated as a matter of great cultural significance. "In *Hamlet*," *Life* tells us, "the combination of a dramatic masterpiece and a great actor at his peak is certain to be one of this year's artistic events. The film is the most spectacular *Hamlet* ever produced." *Life* then goes on not to discuss or review the film, but to use photographs taken on the set especially for *Life* as a way of illustrating "the story of *Hamlet*." Olivier's film, in other words, is being treated not merely as equal to the play but, almost literally, as if it were the play itself. In one two-page spread, Olivier, on the left-hand page, contemplates suicide; on the right-hand page, *Life* reproduces "The Great Soliloquy" in its entirety: the verbal text and the photograph in effect illustrate each other. And *Life* leaves us in no doubt as to the nature of the "Shakespeare" it here celebrates: "Along with the King James Bible," the anonymous writer tells us, "*Hamlet* has passed into the language so completely that millions of people who have neither seen nor read the play unknowingly repeat fragments of its stirring lines in everyday conversation to describe their own situations and emotions." This is the familiar figure of Shakespeare the Transcendent Genius who provides "proof that, though the condition of man is always changing, men themselves do not change much."[4] Even with only the evidence of still photographs, *Life* could sense that Olivier's film, in the elegance of its decor and richness of its costumes, would clearly support its view of Shakespeare.

Life was, in fact, well prepared to embrace Olivier's film, having reacted with enthusiasm ("a beautiful and uplifting work of art") only a few years earlier to the U.S. release of *Henry V*. Shakespeare's history play itself, according to *Life*, was "a major work by the greatest genius who ever lived, with all his matchless language and deep humanity."[5] Although *Life* appears to have been misinformed on this point (few Shakespeareans, then or now, would rank *Henry V* that highly), the language of praise again suggests the kind of yardstick against which Welles would, fatally, be measured. *Life* actually devoted no less than three stories to Olivier's *Hamlet*—in addition to the March 15, 1948, photo essay, the film makes its initial appearance in *Life*'s pages in the "Speaking of Pictures" feature for November 24, 1947. In this piece, *Life* informs its readers that, among other things, "it has taken Olivier, who plans carefully and works slowly, 32 weeks to film *Hamlet*."

One of the photo-captions adds that the film "will cost about $2 million."[6] The third *Life* piece (October 18, 1948) is a profile of Olivier himself, a "special feature" in that, unlike most *Life* articles of the period, it is given a byline (John Kobler) and it depends much more on a written text than on illustrations. The gist of Kobler's profile is to justify the opening sub-heading claim that Olivier has become the "greatest theatrical figure of his time." The London opening of *Hamlet* is lovingly described:

> The king himself, who had knighted Olivier for his services to the English theater, the queen, their daughters and the Duke of Edinburgh swept into a garlanded royal box while peers and commoners, statesmen and artists, cheered themselves hoarse.[7]

Here as elsewhere throughout the essay, the effect is to associate Olivier himself with royalty.

The contrast with *Life*'s reception of *Macbeth* could not be more stark. *Life*'s review, which was on the stands when the film opened in Boston, was headlined "MURDER!" in large capital letters, and then, in a smaller headline underneath, "Orson Welles doth foully slaughter Shakespeare in a dialect version of his 'Tragedy of Macbeth.'" Welles, *Life*'s anonymous reviewer writes, "has gone back to the senseless violence of all the generations of hams who have hacked and gesticulated their way through *Macbeth* for out-of-town audiences. It is such a jumble of gallopings and sweaty close-ups and fog and bubbling cauldrons that the spectator can only stagger from the theater howling with Macduff, 'Confusion now hath made his masterpiece.'" *Life* also commented on the use of Scottish accents, which would become the most frequently mentioned objection to the film: "Mr. Welles has had the idea that 11th Century Scotsmen appearing in a 17th Century play should express themselves in the accents of Sir Harry Lauder on the vaudeville stage of the 20th."[8]

In contrast to the photos "especially taken for LIFE" that were used to illustrate *Hamlet*, the *Macbeth* piece features particularly poor, static, and unrepresentative Republic stills. One of those stills is reproduced again in the second and final mention of Welles's film in *Life*, in a feature entitled "The Movies of 1948." Under the rubric "Funniest Scene (Unintentional)," Macbeth is shown conspiring with the two murderers of Banquo. The same essay gives space to *Hamlet*, "the best Shakespearean film ever made and a significant event in English dramatic history."[9] Welles himself makes one further appearance in *Life* in the period we are considering. In the September 13, 1948, issue, in an article on the "New International Set,"

Welles is photographed shirtless, lounging with Darryl Zanuck, Elsa Maxwell, and *Macbeth's* producer Charles Feldman. Welles is described as "up from Italy to talk business with Darryl Zanuck." We also read that he "had had a wonderful reunion with Rita Hayworth, his almost ex-wife, but had finally fallen in love with a strong-minded Italian actress."[10]

Life's coverage helps us to identify the major issues that would continue to define the discourse surrounding Welles's film and that in particular would characterize Republic's understanding of what needed to be altered or eliminated before the film could again be released. Generally speaking, objections to the film can be outlined as follows:

1. Most broadly and vaguely, that Welles fails to render the tragic dignity of the original play and that his film is unworthy of Shakespeare

2. That Welles himself occupies too much of the footage, and that his performance is at best uneven and at worst bombastic and incomprehensible

3. That most of the other performers, particularly Jeanette Nolan as Lady Macbeth, are inadequate as well

4. That the Scottish burr Welles employs throughout makes the dialogue and speeches difficult, if not impossible, to understand

5. That the mise en scène—the settings and costumes in particular—is ludicrous and inappropriate and that too much of the film's artifice shows through

Although *Life* set the tone for the 1948 reception of *Macbeth*, it did not by any means determine it. Other reviews appeared, primarily in trade publications, some national magazines, and the Boston newspapers where the film had had its official world premiere (Republic decided to forget Venice). The trade publications were generally quite devastating. *Variety*, for instance, began its review with "William Shakespeare's 'Macbeth' will survive its latest interpretation," and the *Hollywood Reporter* characterized Welles's film as "one of the most disastrous of motion picture enterprises" and found Welles's own performance to be "completely devoid of thoughtfulness or intelligence."[11] The Boston papers, though not quite as harsh overall, echoed these sentiments.[12] *Newsweek* and *Time* were mixed in their responses—surprisingly in the case of *Time*, given its intimate relationship to *Life*. For *Newsweek's* reviewer, Welles's film was "a lusty experiment which again demonstrates [Welles's] penchant for valiantly missing the mark." Calling the film the work of a "master craftsman," the reviewer praised the physical aspect of the film: "The setting—a symphony of gray rock, drizzling rain, darkness, and blasted trees—is terrifyingly appropriate to the play's morbid theme."[13] *Time*'s critic termed *Macbeth* "an interesting, unconventional try" and also liked Welles's mise en scène: "Wonder-Boy Welles has an imaginative way with a camera. His stark and gloomy settings create a fine mood for tragedy."[14] Both newsmagazines deplored aspects of Welles's interpretation of the play ("the story of a dead-end kid on the make"—*Time*) as well as his performance. *Good Housekeeping* ended its review in one summarizing sentence: "It's all pretty bad."[15]

Republic's response to the critics was panic. After allowing the film to run for a few weeks "out of town," the studio decided that, at the very least, *Macbeth* would have to be redubbed before the New York opening. By January 1949 the issue has become one of redubbing and reediting. In the meantime, producer Charles Feldman, together with a number of Republic executives, privately screened the film to a variety of friends and associates in order to collect reactions. According to Richard Wilson, Welles's point man in Hollywood during this period, Feldman "has now memorized the '*Life*' review of the picture and cannot help but quote it to make a point."[16] In one memo to Wilson, Feldman passed on some responses to the studio screening of *Macbeth*. "Some of the boys in the office," he wrote, "couldn't understand the witches." He added that Samuel Goldwyn, the immigrant Hollywood mogul notorious for his creative use of the English language, "said the same thing."[17] One can easily imagine the scene in that Republic screening room as a group of studio executives and their underlings, cigars firmly planted in mouths, scratch their collective heads as "when the hoorly-boorly's doon" is screeched at them in a Scottish brogue.

But the sound track was not the only problem for Republic. In a later memo Feldman suggests that the first scene in which Lady Macbeth appears

> should be cut in my opinion because I think she looks horrible and frightening, and everyone who has seen the picture on the many occasions I have run it, was appalled at the looks of the girl. In her next scene she looks infinitely better—as a matter of fact she looks damned attractive, and I think this next scene is an infinitely better opening for Lady Macbeth. The soliloquy we lose may be of some importance, but I think it is of greater benefit to have the right opening for the girl.[18]

By May the cuts and reloopings could be defined, and Welles reluctantly agreed to a number of changes. Although he refused to eliminate Lady Macbeth's opening soliloquy, deep cuts were made throughout *Macbeth*, including the scene with the murderers that *Life* had found so comic. The remainder of the cutting involved reducing the amount of footage devoted to Welles and eliminating some of his more histrionic moments. Attempts were made as well to lessen the effect of the costume choices, in particular what is referred to as Macbeth's "Statue of Liberty costume," which had moved some audiences to laughter. At the same time, partly on the analogy of Olivier's *Hamlet*, a spoken prologue was added to clarify Welles's interpretation.

Why Herbert J. Yates, president and chief executive officer of Republic Pictures, a studio primarily known for the B westerns it produced with John Wayne, Gene Autry, and Roy Rogers, should have wanted Orson Welles to make a Shakespeare film with his studio's money remains something of a mystery. He would always claim to have liked *Macbeth*, even though, as Richard Wilson reported, his screening room reactions were difficult to gauge: "Mr. Yates does an awful lot of tapping with the foot, and must spit out his chaw of tobacco every four minutes. This is, to say the least, disconcerting."[19] It had been Yates, in any case, who, upon completion of the famous twenty-one-day shooting schedule, wrote Welles to thank him for "the greatest individual job of acting, directing, adapting and producing that to my knowledge Hollywood has ever known."[20] Yates, apparently, had not actually seen *Macbeth* at this point, and his enthusiasm may have been as much for Welles's efficiency and punctuality as for anything else. Nevertheless, Welles, in the following months and years of struggling to complete the film in an acceptable form, must have frequently reflected on the ironic implications of Yates's premature encomium.

Welles was able to convince Yates to finance *Macbeth* in the first place, it may be presumed, because he agreed to stay within the confines of the minimal cost of a "prestige" Republic film—what the studio categorized as a "Premiere" production. This was essentially a new category, developed by Yates as part of an ambitious plan to compete with the major studios on one or two productions each year. The shooting schedules and budgets were still modest compared to the equivalent product from MGM or Paramount, but they were generous by Republic standards. Welles contracted to bring the film in at something under $800,000. The most significant, and unusual, cost-cutting measure Welles took was to prepare the film by presenting it first as a stage production. The Utah Centennial Commission, in collaboration with the American National Theatre Association, gave Welles the opportunity he needed when they invited him to stage a Shakespeare production in Salt Lake City. Drawing on his Harlem experience, Welles adapted the play and designed a setting along the lines of that earlier production, and then took his film cast to Salt Lake City, where *Macbeth* was presented through the end of May and the beginning of June 1947.

The chief advantage to this method of preparation was that it allowed for an abbreviated shooting schedule. To shorten it even further, Welles decided to record all the dialogue in advance, thereby requiring the actors to lip-synch during principal photography. As in the Salt Lake City presentation, the actors adopted a (for the most part) light Scottish brogue. The resultant twenty-one-day shooting schedule, always mentioned by commentators on the film, was, as Richard Wilson pointed out in an article for *Theatre Arts,* "something like a book-keeping trick," and that if all the rehearsal, playing, recording, and preparation days were added, "the number would be something like three times twenty-one days." "We did a project," Wilson writes, "in which preparation, mainly in the form of the stage presentation at Utah, and ten solid months of love, work, and tremendous ingenuity after shooting was used instead of money which we didn't have."[21] Principal photography on *Macbeth* began on June 23 and was completed by July 17 at a cost of around $725,000. Editing, music, and other elements of postproduction brought the total up to nearly $870,000, which was still under the final authorized $885,000 budget.[22]

What Welles gave Republic for its money is a Shakespeare film that, in effect if not in intention, weds the popular with the avant-garde. The opening precredit sequence of *Macbeth* (as constructed by Welles in 1947–48, before the reediting) exemplifies Welles's approach throughout: the viewer is immediately caught up in a series of seemingly unconnected images and sounds, a melding together, as with the opening of *Citizen Kane,* of the rational and the irrational, the concrete and the abstract, the specific and the general. Underlying the images—of clouds, the sea, the witches, rain, flames—is a mélange of sound and musical effects, some of which have only an oblique association with what we see, as when we hear a squealing, machinelike scraping as the witches pull off gobs of mud or clay from a child-shaped effigy. These incongruously juxtaposed images and sounds not only set the tone and create the atmosphere for the events to follow, but provide as well, in microcosm, an exposition of Welles's mode and methods: the film, in its entirety, will be like the mud voodoo figure of

Macbeth the witches pull up from the murky depths of their cauldron—a crude, primitive, roughly molded but at the same time powerful and evocative substitute for Macbeth himself, conjured up from the materials at hand, magically brought to life by the imaginative manipulation of eccentric conjurers.

Welles's very first shot—of soundstage fog—prefigures the film's studio-bound style: Welles does not promise us what he will not deliver. This will be, among other things, a highly "artificial" film, and nothing we see over the next several minutes in any way modifies our expectations. The subsequent collage of images and sounds transports us into a world fundamentally irrational. With the first postcredit image, of Macbeth and Banquo on horseback, galloping over a soundstage moor, Welles both affirms the Republic manner and style—this could be a western—and undermines it: the shots of men on horseback are edited together in a discontinuous fashion, each shot somewhat "off" in relation to the shot that precedes and follows it in terms of speed of movement, scale, and screen direction. As the scene continues, the actual spatiotemporal relationship between Macbeth and his partner Banquo, on the one hand, and the witches they almost immediately encounter, on the other, can only be established with difficulty: when, for example, they greet Macbeth, the witches appear to be facing in the "wrong" direction, away from Macbeth and Banquo.[23] Here, as throughout the film, Welles presents us with B-movie images mediated by avant-garde stylistics.

Macbeth unfolds through a series of relatively long "takes" on what is virtually a single-unit set, a set that suggests a highly stylized, imaginary geography. The effect, in conjunction with the deep cuts Welles has made in the play, is to render the action, particularly in the early scenes, as illogically continuous: space, time, and even character motivation are drastically foreshortened. Shakespeare had already, in the first few scenes of *Macbeth*, created a strong sense of a sequence of events following each other with pell-mell speed and movement.[24] But Welles exacerbates the effect in a manner that might be described as grimly comic. So, for instance, when Macbeth, addressed as "the thane of Cawdor," objects that "the thane of Cawdor lives," the unfortunate thane himself is immediately dragged into view under guard, his badge of office taken from him and passed on hand to hand until it is placed around Macbeth's neck. The sense here is that all one needs to do to conjure up anyone or anything is to give a name to one's desire. Later, within a few mere moments and within a continuous space, King Duncan is killed, Macbeth is pronounced king (in effect) by Banquo,

Malcolm and Macduff are said to have fled to England, and Lady Macbeth
tells her husband that he "lacks the season of all nature, sleep," a line trans-
posed from much later in the play.

Throughout the film, we experience Welles's Scotland as a world of
continuous time and space, a world in which no one is truly alone—the
first colloquy between Macbeth and Lady Macbeth takes place in a courtyard, in the presence of Duncan and his train, and continues while everyone kneels and prays; Macbeth's letter to his wife is dictated in the presence of Banquo—and everyone's actions seem to impinge immediately on
everyone else's. A primary consequence of this compression of both time
and setting is to emphasize the already powerful evocation of a totalitarian
world where everyone is either watching or being watched. That both
Lady Macbeth and Macbeth should be present and personally involved
with the murder of Lady Macduff and her children makes perfect sense in
this context.

The irrational and eccentric organization of space and time in *Macbeth*
would not, perhaps, be noticed on the stage of a theater, where the fluid
and adaptable mise-en-scène Welles here employs is fairly commonplace.
It would not, on a stage set, seem odd or disconcerting that Macbeth's
throne has been located in the courtyard outside the castle proper, for
example. But in the cinema, where the movement of the frame and the
shifts in point of view provide us with the possibility of continuous alter-
nations of time and space, the oddness of the mise-en-scène makes itself
felt. Welles's long takes, particularly the one constructed around the murder of Duncan, not merely reproduces but intensifies the spatial and temporal unities Shakespeare has constructed for his play. Again, the intensification is a consequence of the manner in which cinematic time and space
arouses different expectations than does theatrical time and space. The
longer the take continues, the more we become conscious of its unusual-
ness (unusual, that is, in terms of our cinematic expectations) and the more
intense it becomes. Editing and composition, too, contribute to this sense
of an irrational space, a space where character movement, for example, does
not follow the logic of continuity editing either in terms of how human
figures enter into or exit from the frame or in terms of their relative size
and shape at any given moment (Macbeth himself, notably, seems to grow
in bulk as the film progresses).

We experience a similar tension between the theatrical and the cinematic in some of Welles's technical experiments, many of which have a
"minimalist" effect very much in harmony with the youthful Welles's com-

ment that "one of the very wisest ways to play Shakespeare is the way he wrote it . . . utterly without impediment."[25] That Macbeth, just before his second encounter with the witches, stands in front of what appears to be a blank scrim against which, as lightning flashes overhead, we see his shadow projected, would not be notable on a stage; in a film, of course, it becomes an almost scandalous instance of showing the apparatus, of "baring the device"—Welles, while he was at it, might just as well have shown us the wind machine and the thunder sheets. This scene, referred to as the "mount" scene in the studio correspondence, was clearly an embarrassment to some Republic executives; it is in general highly theatrical, and although the resistance to it may have many sources (the obvious artifice, the unappealing costume, the histrionics of Welles himself—all of which were mentioned in various memos and missives), the objections seem to be nearly as much to the "size" of it, to the grandness of the emotions and the impact of the language—in short, to the untamed "Shakespeareanness" of it. At moments like these, we can experience a central element of what had gone out of fashion in Shakespeare as the nineteenth century knew him: the oratorical style, the grandeur of emotions, the barnstorming manner, the primitive calling forth of pity and terror.

The minimalism of *Macbeth*, the solutions Welles found to compensate for his lack of means, often provide a sense of genuine wonder and magic. A particularly striking instance of this is Macbeth's visit to the weird sisters (Shakespeare's IV.i), which immediately follows the "mount" scene. All we actually see is the face and part of the body of Macbeth himself, seemingly at the bottom of a dark pit, his countenance illuminated by a pinpoint spotlight, the camera descending closer and closer toward him. Flashes of lightning, the offscreen voices of the witches, a few notes of music, the moving camera—which effectively makes Macbeth appear to get bigger and bigger—and the aforementioned wind machine and thunder sheets (not, strictly speaking, visible, but clearly *there* nonetheless), together create a sustained effect of suspense and danger that compels assent at the same time that it calls attention to the simplicity of its own construction. So, too, in the sequence near the end when Macbeth's enemies mass for attack, the Celtic crosses atop the long staves the soldiers carry form a nearly abstract pattern that in a weblike manner crisscrosses the sky, in dramatic and graphic contrast to the figure of Macbeth, alone and substantial against a blank cyclorama in the following sequence.

One way to look at the film's highly stylized and severely stripped-down mise-en-scène, to justify or provide an explanation for the choices

Welles has made, is to assume that Welles has created an essentially psychological landscape. Much of the sympathetic critical literature on Welles's
film has stressed the otherness of setting, costume, props, and so on either
by suggesting the interiority of what would ordinarily be the external
world, or by insisting on the indefiniteness of Macbeth's world, or by
pointing to the timelessness indicated by it. Jean Cocteau thus writes of a
"dream underground,"[26] Claude Beylie discovers an atmosphere "redolent
of both the Paleolithic and atomic eras," imagining the audience as transported "into 'the very bowels of the earth,' or perhaps into some other
planet,"[27] and André Bazin found a "pre-historic universe . . . at the birth
of time and sin, when sky and earth, water and fire, good and evil, still aren't
distinctly separate."[28] All of these are useful perceptions, but they are also
quite fanciful, leaving far behind the material reality of Welles's film. As
much as we may, at some level, assent to Cocteau's wonderfully surreal
vision of Lady Macbeth as "almost a woman in modern dress, . . . reclining
on a fur-covered divan beside the telephone,"[29] it is still, I think, worth
insisting that what we actually see on the screen, a good deal of the time,
are some unusually tacky sets, shapeless and ill-fitting costumes (extremely
eclectic in style, which can suggest "temporal indefiniteness" as well as "let's
see what we can find in this old trunk"), obvious soundstage exteriors,
aberrant lighting schemes, and performers who appear to have wandered
in from some other film altogether. It is necessary to insist, in other words,
that the "look" of this *Macbeth* is a consequence of the material circumstances of production.

Insofar as it resembles anything other than a studio set, the world of
Welles's *Macbeth* suggests postnuclear devastation—objects and clothing
that sometimes seem cobbled together from the remnants of a destroyed
civilization: the castle looks like pulverized rock-face; the chairs, tables, and
other furnishings seem to have been quickly patched up from materials at
hand. Macbeth's throne, in particular, a massive V-shaped monolith seemingly made of poured concrete, appears to have been improvised from the
rubble of some technologically advanced structure—a power station perhaps. Welles's Scotland is not so much prehistoric as outside history; his specific time and place exists as a blur; indeed, we are *beyond* history. Although
it is certainly reasonable to see this world as a mental landscape, a physical
manifestation of interior darkness and evil, it can just as logically be considered an objective reality, a world where the sun never shines, where
nuclear winter has arrived and enveloped everything in mist and shadows.

But however much Welles's mise-en-scène lends itself to metaphoric speculation, it might just as easily be understood as a literal representation of Macbeth's world, a representation that points up the futility and barrenness of the tyrant's ambitious designs. Welles has transformed Shakespeare's essentially—and anachronistically—Elizabethan Scotland into a strange, crude world of rocks and caves and bogs and dens of death, a poor man's hell inhabited by creatures pitiful in their grotesquerie. Not merely visually, but in the whole tone and manner of this production, Scotland is a third-rate kingdom, an almost barbaric horde. The very deficiency of the Republic sets—the cheapness of the film's mise-en-scène—calls into question the worth of Macbeth's ambition. The banquet scene, for a striking illustration of this point, presents us with one of the least appealing social events imaginable—the sense of forced attendance prevails, the food and drink are unappetizing, the atmosphere is grimly minimal, and no one looks as if he or she were having, or expecting to have, a good time. The world of the film is one of uncertainty, a place where, in spite of a seemingly circumscribed space, it is difficult to get one's bearings, to find the "sure and firm-set earth" of which Macbeth speaks. There is even less here than in Shakespeare's play of an established throne and kingship; rather, Duncan appears only nominally in charge, held in check, as it were, by the newly introduced Christianity.

The whole of Welles's *Macbeth* is, in fact, reminiscent of Brecht's description of Macbeth's castle in a production designed by Caspar Neher: "a semi-dilapidated grey keep of striking poverty. The guests's words of praise were merely compliments. He [Neher] saw the Macbeths as petty Scottish nobility, and neurotically ambitious."[30] Here Welles has taken a theme inherent in Shakespeare's play, and one treated in other plays as well (*Richard III* in particular), the theme of the emptiness of achievement, and has rendered it palpable in the very look of the film. This is no great kingdom at stake, but a pitiful world inhabited by small and, for the most part, small-minded creatures. Perhaps in no other production of *Macbeth* have the lines "To be thus is nothing" rung so true; certainly, we are given little sense of what Macbeth has won in achieving the Scottish throne. Whatever financial constraints Welles may have labored under, he turns the film's shabby production values to his advantage. The world he creates for this *Macbeth* has been deliberately and thoroughly deglamorized. This is in many ways a postholocaust vision, a film fully conscious of the darkness at the center of the human soul, a darkness that Shakespeare, of course, had already understood, but a darkness that awaited twentieth-century totalitarianism for its full realization.[31]

If we need a metaphor to explicate and justify Welles's mise-en-scène, we might want to find one in which the tenor and the vehicle are nearly identical. The time and place of this *Macbeth* is here and now (i.e., the soundstages and backlots of Republic Pictures in 1947). Welles, far from attempting to disguise this fact, revels in it. This, he seems to be saying, is how I can put on *Macbeth* in Hollywood today—in fact, this may be the only way they'll let me do anything worthwhile in Hollywood today. Insofar as Republic is Hollywood, Hollywood is itself revealed as a less than prepossessing world, as a dream factory in receivership, well on its way to nightmare. But even if we prefer not to read metaphor or metaphysics into what Welles is doing, the fact remains that we cannot watch *Macbeth* without seeing, undeniably and actually, the mechanism underlying his project: he happily (and unapologetically) bares the device, as it were. The film, in its entirety, projects a constant *Verfremdungseffekt*, a making strange that serves to exhibit the evil of *Macbeth* as both timeless and timely, to bring us from Shakespeare's into our own world, to show us an evil ordinary and terrible, tawdry and frightening at once.

In the end, all attempts to provide an overarching stylistic or thematic core for Welles's film—whether it be "expressionist" or "surreal" or "Freudian" or whatever—must necessarily fall short of the film's effect. What *Macbeth* exhibits is precisely the tension between an interpretive scheme more or less consistently applied, on the one hand, and on the other, the very real constraints a low budget and a consequently compact shooting schedule—combined with the realities of Welles's production methods, which worked at cross purposes to those constraints—imposed on the project. Even in his most fully realized films, Welles appears to be as interested in solving local and contingent problems—how to shoot a particular scene, what effect might be most surprising or intriguing at a particular moment—as he is in providing some version of a "through line," a thematic strand, that will carry the viewer more or less safely from beginning to end.

The eccentric casting of minor characters—for instance, George "Shorty" Cirello, Welles's personal assistant, plays Seyton (a character traditionally conceived of either as merely a plain, loyal retainer, or a dark, sinister figure) in a highly peculiar manner—contributes to what might be described, along with a number of other similar details, as a kind of grotesque scribbling in the margins of the film. In one shot, Seyton, who has nothing to say or do at that moment, is given a large, foreground close-up, while Lady Macbeth is visible but small in the background; it is as if

Seyton were here providing a commentary on the main action. Seyton's appearance and dubious function, along with the thuglike faces of the supernumeraries wandering though the film, or the almost idiotic expression William Alland assumes in his role of the Second Murderer, all reinforce the banality of the depicted world: evil has quite explicitly become a B movie. Macbeth's murderous ambition is not given the dignity or nobility of a traditional production; Welles retains just enough of Shakespeare's words to allow communication among the major characters, but not enough to maintain the verse structure, the texture of poetic language, with which Shakespeare has constructed his play.

Although a contrast can certainly be drawn between the relative largesse of New Deal public works programs which provided Welles with all he might need for his "voodoo" *Macbeth* in 1936 and the penury of Republic Pictures, which forced on Welles an economy that all but banishes pomp and circumstance in 1947, Welles's Republic *Macbeth* owes a good deal more to the voodoo production than Welles was ever willing to acknowledge.[32] The design for the central castle set, for example, is virtually identical in both; the way the witches become a pervasive presence and voice also stems from that production, as does their final appearance at the end, chiming in on Macduff's "untimely ripp'd" and speaking the final line, "peace, the charm's wound up." Many other details could be adduced to demonstrate that, once again, Welles recycled and refurbished already existing material, like the careful, thrifty craftsman he in so many ways was. Nevertheless, the context in which the two productions appeared were quite different. In 1936 America, World War II (including the Holocaust) was still only an impending catastrophe, a matter of (mostly) distant social turmoil, localized warfare, and slightly ludicrous European dictatorships. It was still possible, in this context, to see evil as a cosmic force that held mere humans in its thrall. By 1947, however, evil had a very different face, and that difference is reflected in Welles's view of Shakespeare's *Macbeth*.

If the supernatural still plays a key role in this version of *Macbeth*, Macbeth himself is no longer a mere victim of external forces. Evil has been internalized and made an aspect of his psyche. The structure of the film enacts a shift from the 1936 view of evil to a postwar view of evil. Or, perhaps more accurately, one might say that the whole film is built on a tension between the external and the internal. On the one hand, Macbeth can be seen as a victim among other victims in a world enthralled by the forces of darkness. On the other hand, Macbeth's world—including the supernatural forces—appears to be an emanation of his mind and will. In the initial moments of the film, the first interpretation seems to predominate. Welles begins with an emphasis on the supernatural: the early part of the film suggests that Scotland is in the grips of a contest between the forces of darkness, embodied in the witches, and the forces of light, embodied in the invented character, the Holy Father. But we gradually come to see that this dichotomy, too, is internal rather than external; even the presence of a voodoo doll manipulated by the witches, though technically "un-Shakespearean" and reminiscent of the Harlem production, serves primarily to underline the tension between a view of the witches as possessing supernatural powers and a view of them as old women with a simple faith in their own magic. And when, late in the film, Welles dissolves from the tree Macbeth contemplates as he speaks the lines about the "crow making wings to the rooky wood" to the image of Banquo's murderers, perched like vultures on the branches of another tree, we are encouraged to believe that his will has summoned up these harbingers of death.

In going back to his voodoo *Macbeth* for inspiration, Welles has at the same time significantly inverted some of the implications of that earlier production: whereas on the Harlem stage the elegant costumes and other elaborate production details were, to some extent, a cover for elemental passions and irrational evil, in the film the forces of evil work at taking the characters back from a civilized state—Western customs and habits are revealed, through the shabbiness of the external world, as the pretensions of civilization itself. In the "voodoo" version, the external trappings of Western society—specifically, the costumes and objects associated with the French governing class during the Napoleanic era—provided a mere cover, newly acquired, for elemental emotions and desires only barely suppressed; in the film, the elemental is, in a sense, externalized, as if those same trappings, long worn but gradually fallen into disuse, revealed a fragile and poor attempt, no longer effective, to disguise the rising savagery beneath. Welles's mise-en-scène suggests not so much a primitive world as a world attempting, with meager resources and without quite knowing how to go about it, to keep a tenuous hold on form and structure, to raise itself back to some kind of higher realm from which it has descended.

In this light, much of the discussion of Welles's un-Shakespearean invention of a Christian priest, the "Holy Father" (an amalgam of several of the play's minor characters), and in general of his view of the play as a struggle between Christianity and the Old Religion, misses the thrust of his design. That Alan Napier's Holy Father, the object of much ridicule, seems ineffective and even sinister, is precisely the point. Christianity is not offered by the film as a positive alternative to the old religion, but rather as an equally oppressive system, itself collaborative with savagery. Thus, the elaborate and impressive prayer scene early in the film is juxtaposed with the decapitation of the thane of Cawdor. Macbeth, from the very beginning, resists the blandishments of the new religion. He eagerly follows the witches ("Stay, you imperfect speakers, tell me more") even after the priest has chased them away. As a direct result of the way Welles rearranges dialogue, asides, and soliloquies, Macbeth, shown by Shakespeare in these early scenes to be struggling with his own conscience, now appears rather to be placed in opposition to external interlocutors. "Goodness" has been almost completely externalized in codes and rules of behavior embodied in such figures as the Holy Father. Macbeth, it appears, has no internal checks against ambition and desire. Welles's reassignment of verse is thus not arbitrary. The Holy Father, who often voices some moral and theological point, sometimes speaks lines Shakespeare had given not only to Ross and Banquo but to Macbeth himself. In the end, it is the Holy Father—who appears more as a military man than a priest—whom Macbeth singles out for death as Malcolm's forces besiege his castle; one senses a certain glee on the part of Welles the director as Macbeth's spear neatly impales its finally ineffective victim.

Welles is incapable of sentimentalizing Macbeth, whom he transforms into little more than a drunken thug. The "nobility" of Macbeth (an aspect of Shakespeare's character that has, in any case, been greatly exaggerated in the critical literature) has been thoroughly suppressed until the very end, when he is allowed to rise, if only for a moment, to the occasion of his own destruction. Again, the postholocaust context, however far it may take us from what we presume to have been Shakespeare's intention, serves to integrate the character into the experience of the modern world. Although Jan Kott never refers to Welles's film, his interpretation of Shakespeare's *Macbeth* in many ways runs parallel to Welles's own: "Not only can a man kill; a man is he who kills and only he. . . . This for Macbeth is one end of his experience. It can be called the 'Auschwitz experience.'" "In Macbeth's world," Kott claims, "—the most obsessive of all worlds created by Shakespeare—murder, thoughts of murder and fear of murder pervade everything. In this tragedy there are only two great parts, but the third *dramatis personae* is the world."[33] However adequate or inadequate this may be as a description of Shakespeare's play, it nicely summarizes the effect of Welles's film.

In the end, Welles could claim that he had rendered Shakespeare in

forms familiar to an audience of the popular cinema: the traces of melodrama, horror film, and even the western, that virtually all critics have dis-
cerned, not to mention the overall B picture aura that envelops the film,
would seem to be the logical conduit for appealing to a broad con-
stituency. Shakespeare, of course, is always already "popular" in these terms:
melodrama, Grand Guignol effects, narratives of adventure and incident,
unearthly presences, are all part and parcel of "Shakespeare." But insofar as
Welles maintains and indeed accentuates the Shakespearean artifice and
larger-than-life theatricality, he perhaps works against easy popular accep-
tance. His stylistic trademarks—relatively long takes, mid-distance staging,
respect, in general, for the integrity of time and space—guarantee that the
formal shape of Shakespeare's most highly charged moments will be
retained, but they are aspects of style harder for viewers accustomed to classical Hollywood decoupage to accept.[34]

From Republic's point of view, Welles had produced an uncommercial
product, and something had to be done to make *Macbeth* acceptable to as
wide an audience as possible. A close comparison of the 1948 film and the
version eventually released in 1950 demonstrates that the alterations, particularly those made to the sound track, were more complex and thor-
oughgoing than is usually thought.[35] Simply detailing the cut footage or
making reference to the elimination of the Scottish accents does not sufficiently indicate the extent to which the two films are fundamentally different. For one thing, the burr was *not* eliminated, and only parts of the dialogue track were rerecorded. The 1950 release version, as a result, includes
both Scottish and non-Scottish accents. At the same time, in those portions
that were rerecorded, and even in some that were not, the sound mix has
often been altered. In the 1948 version, Welles created, at certain moments,
a three-dimensional sound space, with lines spoken in the "background"
in distinction to those spoken in the "foreground." So, for example, in the
scene where the murder of Duncan is discovered, the Holy Father's line
"God's benison go with you, and with those / That would make good of
bad, and friends of foes" (II.iv.40–41) is spoken from deep in the shot,
"overheard" by Macbeth. The effect is lost in the 1950 version, where the
dialogue has been recorded pretty much at one level, presumably in order
to effect greater comprehension.

The issue of "comprehension," of the difficulties audiences had in
understanding the dialogue, was in fact unrelated to the Scottish accents,
although Republic was never able to see that. The real problem, as Richard
Wilson, among others, was quite aware, is that it is primarily Shakespeare's

vocabulary, syntax, and imagery that is difficult for a twentieth-century audience to understand.[36] Furthermore, in Welles's *Macbeth*, as in his *Othello* and *Chimes at Midnight*, the normal problem of understanding Shakespeare is considerably exacerbated by the extreme editing and rearranging of the original text, which results in something quite similar to a Charles Marowitz theatrical "collage": Shakespeare's play has been taken apart, the pieces of text shuffled around, in the process of which some have been lost, some broken, some thrown away, and what is left is then put back together according to a plan or pattern that treats these bits and pieces as so many shards of colored glass, to be placed into the design wherever they will appear most useful and aesthetically pleasing, given the entirely new purpose and structure governing its deployment. Such a process, of course, though perhaps not confusing to an audience familiar with the original, can be extremely perplexing to audiences with no prior knowledge of Shakespeare, an audience for whom, presumably, context and continuity would be of some aid.

Furthermore, Welles's use of a prerecorded sound track contributes to an effect he frequently strives for in his films—a perceptible disjunction between sound and image.[37] What we often hear in *Macbeth* is what film theorists refer to as "displaced diegetic sound." The sound is *diegetic* in the sense that it emanates from within the film world, but it is *displaced* in the sense that it is not synchronized with the ostensible source from which it can be presumed to emanate. Even the decision to employ voice-over for soliloquies, which today appears relatively unadventurous, has specific and complex consequences. By separating voice from image, Welles intensified the splitting of Macbeth's personality and, simultaneously, the disassembling of his own performance. The words Macbeth speaks at such moments turn into a commentary on the image of Macbeth we watch; Welles's performance thus becomes, like Macbeth's character, schizophrenic, split, dissolved. Welles's sound design, in short, often constitutes in itself an instance of *Verfremdungseffekt*.

Although much of Welles's sound design remains in the 1950 version, specific details have been significantly altered. Welles himself, notably, completely rerecorded—at long distance (he was in Europe at the time)—some of his own speeches and soliloquies, and in nearly every case, the new readings are less intense, less expressive, more polished, more conventional, than the old. Particularly notable in this regard is the "blood will have blood" rumination (Shakespeare's III.iv.123f.). In the 1948 version, Welles's reading suggests a powerfully disturbed, overcharged imagination; the rhythm of

the lines is erratic and highly modulated; some words are grunted or
groaned, some strangled. One line illustrates the point. When Welles says
"And push us from our stools" in the 1948 version, the word "push" is
given great emphasis, and "stools" is both emphasized and drawn out:
STOOOLS. The release version smooths out the line, modifies the
emphasis, and eliminates the drawing out at the end. (Since the line is spoken "off," Welles did not have the image of his lips and face to guide him
when he "looped" the line, so that the actual timing differs as well.) The
overall effect of the rerecording is to tame the emotions at this point, to
normalize what Welles had originally conceived as a moment of near nau-
sea. The 1950 reading suggests rational thought, as if Macbeth were working through a difficult point in logic, whereas the 1948 version gives us a
Macbeth viscerally responding to a world gone mad. A similar decline in
intensity can be detected in the "dagger" speech: the 1948 version is much
more "tightly" spoken, more disturbed in tone, than the 1950 version.
Again, one example can suffice. Welles, in the original, speaks the phrase
"and on thy blade and dungeon, gouts of blood" as if he were choking on
the words—and on the blood: the word "gouts" emerges from deep in his
throat; the 1950 reading exhibits far less tonal variety and completely eliminates the sense of overwhelming panic.

Welles, of course, was quite aware of these and other consequences that
would result from altering the sound track, especially via cables, memo-
randa, and air-mailed recordings. A new voice track, for one thing, would
inevitably mean that lines lip-synched to one sound track—in which a
Scottish burr was used—would now be relooped with a different accent as
well as a different rhythm and a different emphasis. The slowed-down effect
Welles claimed to have wanted to achieve by using a Scottish dialect would
remain in the actors' visual performances, the movement of their mouths
and facial muscles, of their hands, arms, and, in general, their whole bodies. Though Welles was willing to accept a certain amount of disjunction
by prerecording the dialogue in the first place, it was at least a planned, considered effect.

In a memo from London presumably sent to Republic executives,
Welles, having just seen parts of the redubbed version, identifies changes
"not only in speech, but also in *character*" (Welles's emphasis). He notes, for
example, that

> when [Jeanette] Nolan moves from the Scottish speech (*in which she had
> been rehearsed*) to what she considers normal speech for Shakespeare, her

vocal tone moves at least an octave upwards, and the entire personality of Lady Macbeth vanishes. We are given instead an intense and some-times intelligent reading of the lines by an American farm girl. It would be impossible to state strongly enough the gravity of the mistake. Nolan is not a large woman; her personality is not commanding. She lacks what the French call "presence." Her success in the role of Lady Mac-beth was entirely based on her intelligence and on the vocal authority which informed and underlined the playing of all her big scenes. The unfortunate Montana whine, wheeze, and scrape completely nullify this authority.[38]

Welles, in other words, was quite conscious of the fact that redubbing, even by the same actor, is not merely a matter of lip synchronization, but that it affects, in terms of rhythm, pace, emphasis, tone, and so forth, the entire shape of an actor's performance. In other moods and at other times, of course, Welles was happy, or at least willing, to substitute his own voice for the voices of other actors, particularly when only a few lines or small parts were involved, but, once again, it must be stressed that he did so with full and sophisticated awareness of the problems and principles involved. The issue, thus, is one of "authority," of responsibility for the final product. That Welles was, once again, attempting to maintain that authority long distance is only one part of this complicated drama.

The tampering with the sound track, though highly significant, is not as dramatically obvious as the deep cuts Republic persuaded Welles to make, cuts that reduced the film's running time from approximately 112 minutes to 86 minutes. Although small deletions of words and lines, as well as some transpositions, were made throughout the film (several of which destroy the effect of Welles's long takes—both the murder of Duncan scene and the England scene, each close to a full reel in the original, have been cut), several sequences were eliminated altogether. The most extensive single cut is the scene of Macbeth instructing the murderers of Banquo. The elimination of this scene, as Richard Wilson rightly saw, was a complete capitulation to *Life* magazine. Certainly this scene, as Welles had staged it, departs about as far as possible from what *Life* and other middlebrow pub-lications conceived of as "Shakespearean." Macbeth is clearly drunk; the murderers, embodied by Bernard Duffield and William Alland, are a couple of animalistic lumpen-proletariat of unprepossessing appearance. The scene as a whole takes us a good distance from the genteel Shakespeare: this is, rather, Hannah Arendt's banality of evil with a vengeance.

Rereleased in the final days of 1950, *Macbeth* was reviewed once again, with the new set of reviews offering a somewhat different picture from the earlier one: they could best be described as mixed, not so much among themselves as within each review. Nearly every reviewer found something to praise and something to blame. Taken together, the praise and the blame suggest an ironic point of view toward Welles and his work. Even when a reviewer, on balance, liked the film, the temptation to have some fun at its expense was evidently irresistible. Robert Hatch, in the *New Republic*, informs his readers that the film, at first glance, looks like it had been made "in the Carlsbad Caverns by a company of Mongolian yak herders."[39] John McCarten's entire *New Yorker* review is so caught up in a tone of light bemusement that one would be hard put to demonstrate by quotation what is clear at least to me—that the review is more positive than not. The bemusement is aimed not so much at the film as at what McCarten perceives to be the likely response of the average filmgoer. "I'm afraid," he writes, "that communication between Mr. Welles and his public is going to be hellishly confused in the course of this 'Macbeth.' "[40] The move is a familiar one: the reviewer implies that he, certainly, can find much of interest in this odd piece of work—but what will the hoi polloi make of it?

Several points emerge from an examination of the reception of Welles's *Macbeth*. First, there is a certain discomfort, not unique to this film or this period, with coming to terms with filmed Shakespeare. The reception of Welles's film was—at least to some extent—conditioned by the expectations conjured up by the name "Shakespeare": reviewers were unable, in the nature of things, to accept *Macbeth* as simply another Republic film (and, one hastens to add, rightly so—for *Macbeth* was *not* just another Republic film, if for no other reason than that the name Orson Welles was associated with it). Although Welles—in retrospect, at least—would have liked *Macbeth* to have been seen as an experiment, a "violently sketched charcoal drawing of a great play,"[41] he could not have expected, or wanted, the film to be treated as other than an Orson Welles production. It should also be kept in mind that if *Macbeth* was a modest production by the standards of the major Hollywood studios, it was fairly expensive by Republic standards—though certainly not as costly as Ford's *Rio Grande* or Frank Borzage's *Moonrise*, both made at the studio at around the same time. In any case, everyone involved in the production, including Welles himself, created a climate of expectation that virtually guaranteed, if it did not welcome, controversy.

Newspaper and mass circulation magazine reviewers, in any event, at times found themselves caught between a desire to applaud Welles for his daring disregard for the niceties of Shakespearean production and a fear that Welles has gone too far and that, in applauding Welles, the reviewer may reveal his or her own cultural insecurities. There is, in any case, a real difficulty in separating out Welles's film as a text in its own right and judging it as an adaptation. Arthur Knight, in his dismissive one-paragraph review, simply notes that "there is precious little Shakespeare here."[42] Somewhat overlapping with this approach is one whereby the reviewer wants to differentiate his or her response from the probable response of the larger audience. Hatch has already been quoted in this regard, and a similar mixed message is evident in the final paragraph of the *Scholastic* review (one aimed, presumably, at a college-educated group of secondary school teachers): "Although we personally did not like the film, we will give Welles two checks for effort—and our readers the warning that they may wish they had saved their money on this round." "For really good Shakespeare," the reviewer adds, "we'd advise seeing Olivier's *Hamlet* twice."[43]

Complicating the Shakespeare question was, as the preceding quotation indicates, the Olivier factor. Here again, the issue is a complex one: not all reviewers liked *Hamlet* and not all reviewers compared Welles's Shakespeare to Olivier's (though of course many did). Upper middlebrow publications (to adopt the discourse of the time), such as *Atlantic Monthly*, in fact disliked Olivier's film[44] (and, as far as I can tell, made no reference at all to *Macbeth*), as did Parker Tyler in the highbrow *Kenyon Review*.[45] Overall, however, *Hamlet* was well received by the popular press, and it was perhaps inevitable that it would be used as a means of measuring Welles's perceived shortcomings.

And then there is the matter of Orson Welles himself. In 1948 Welles's reputation was, to a degree, in limbo. *Citizen Kane* (1941), and all that preceded it, was still relatively fresh in the public mind. At the same time, "Welles the Failed Genius" had not quite been formed in his full dimension. Welles's problems with his 1942 "docudrama" *It's All True*, the failure of *The Magnificent Ambersons* (1942), the limited success of *The Stranger* (1946), the problems surrounding the filming and release of *Lady from Shanghai* (though filmed long before *Macbeth*, it was not released until April 1948): all of this contributed to an apprehension of declining powers, though this is a theme played in a minor key. *Life*, again, makes the point most forcefully, noting that Welles "a few sad years ago was the Boy Wonder of Hollywood."[46] The criticism, taken so much to heart by Republic executives, that stressed the amount of time and the number of close-ups devoted to Welles ("too much footage being given to Orson"),[47] now seems incredibly petty and obtuse, underlining the irrational dislike Welles seemed to draw upon himself. Within the context of the film, where mega-lomania is so clearly projected as central to Macbeth's degeneration, this criticism must be thought less than irrelevant. The shots in which Welles's figure, back, or head fill the entire screen makes sense primarily as a response to the image of the dictator in so many newsreels and films of the thirties and forties; one might simply point to *Triumph of the Will* (1934), whose images of massed crowds are constantly juxtaposed to close shots of Hitler, his head at times silhouetted against a blank sky. Although Welles deliberately eschews the grandeur of Riefenstahl, and certainly did not have the resources to reproduce her crowd scenes even if he had wanted to, he nevertheless hints at a similar effect.

Overall, the critical reception of Welles's *Macbeth* was not as devastating as legend would have it, although any clear estimate needs to distinguish between who was doing the reviewing, and when. Insofar as the American (and British) reviews were negative, they tended to see the film as failed Shakespeare. The European critics, on the other hand, appear totally unconcerned over Welles's treatment of the Shakespeare text; they sensed that Welles had captured the spirit of *Macbeth*, even if he had not been true to the letter. The American reviewers, even the sympathetic ones, saw papier-mâché sets and road company costumes and inappropriate phys-iognomies; the European critics saw absurdist poetry or surrealism or expressionism or alienation effect or the unconscious. Some of the Amer-ican critics, along with a number of Republic executives, saw an egocen-tric ham hogging the screen; the European critics saw *un grand cineaste* exploring the contours of an individual consciousness. The Anglophone critics failed, for the most part, to allegorize Welles's mise-en-scène; the European critics, probably, overallegorized it.

In spite of its reputation as perhaps the ultimate *film maudit*, then, *Mac-beth* was neither a massive critical nor commercial failure. The reviews, as we have seen, were at times at least respectable. They were not, for the most part, reviews that would have been likely to pull a general audience into the movie theaters, but then, Shakespeare wasn't likely to, either. And although figuring the profit and loss situation for any film is always a tricky matter, what evidence there is suggests that *Macbeth* probably recouped Republic's investment in the long run; the studio, in any case, could not have lost very much. Indeed, the film probably would have done better at the box office if Republic had not gotten cold feet and put additional money into extensive redubbing and recutting—not to mention the negative publicity the revision process generated. Furthermore, neither *Henry V* nor *Hamlet*, whatever their final profits, were so successful as to make the financing of future Shakespeare films easy; Olivier had to look for television money for *Richard III*, and he never was able to find the backing for his own *Macbeth* project.

At once an experimental film and, stylistically, at least, a B movie, *Macbeth* fell between several stools, being neither sufficiently "tasteful" to compete with Olivier's style nor sufficiently experimental to qualify as, at least, a succés d'estime. Welles seems to have produced, from some points of view, the worst of all worlds—an inaccessible B movie, a Shakespearean western. If he succeeded in meeting the terms of his contract with Republic, which is certainly the implication of Yates's glowing memo, his solution to the problems of filming Shakespeare at a reasonable cost was not, as it turned out, one that either studio executives or much of the film's first audiences were prepared to accept with any real enthusiasm. He adapted Shakespeare's play in a fashion that paid little respect to the "High Art" tradition in which Shakespeare was seen to find his significance and value. What the studio seems to have wanted from Welles was something both commercially viable and prestigious, both "accessible" and "artistic"—in other words, something very much like Laurence Olivier's *Henry V* and *Hamlet*. (One thing Republic seems not to have sufficiently considered was that both of Olivier's films were far more expensive than Welles's; *Hamlet* cost more than twice as much as *Macbeth*.) What Welles provided instead was something raw, gutsy, modern, and eccentric, commercially viable (at least in theory) because of its relatively low cost, but otherwise unlikely to please anyone expecting a tasteful, "entertaining," straightforwardly traditional adaptation of Shakespeare's tragedy.[48]

SIX

The Texts of *Othello*

Orson Welles's *Othello*, even more than his *Macbeth*, presents us with a complicated and confused textual history which is itself related to the complexity of the production process. We can identify a number of different Welles *Othellos*: the one shown at the Cannes film festival in 1952 (generally regarded as the film's "official" date), the one distributed in Europe soon thereafter (which may or may not be the same as the Cannes version), the version Welles prepared for U.S. and British distribution in 1955, and the "restoration" (actually, as we will see, "restorations") of 1992—to which we could add several newly edited sequences from the original film Welles constructed as illustrative material when he made *Filming Othello* in the late 1970s. Anthony Davies found "no fewer than six versions" of *Othello* catalogued in the British National Film Archives, though some of these, one suspects, are what bibliographers refer to as "ghosts," works alluded to and sometimes even described, which nevertheless do not, and probably never did, exist. Davies also notes that the *Othello* screened by the BBC in 1982 "varies significantly" from the version available from the British Film Institute Library; the BBC version differs from the 1955 U.S. and Great Britain release in having "no printed credits at all (all credits being spoken as 'voice over' by Orson Welles)," in omitting the narrative introduction, in curtailing the closing sequence, and in placing the "montage of ship-rigging and water-reflection shots among the opening sequences of the film."[1]

For the moment, however, the text of Welles's *Othello* we are all most likely to be familiar with is the 1992 rerelease, referred to in the publicity as "Welles's Lost Masterpiece." Welles's film, of course, was never "lost," though it is fair to say that, throughout much of its history, it has been something of an invisible text, a film more frequently remarked upon and alluded to than seen, available to scholars and aficionados, primarily. You might catch some version at a retrospective, as I did for the first time at the Orson Welles Theatre in Cambridge, Massachusetts, in 1977 (with Welles himself present), and by the eighties you could see it both in a 16mm version at the Folger Shakespeare Library and, a few blocks away, in a 35mm version at the Library of Congress. The 1992 Castle Hill version (now available on videocassette) has brought *Othello* back into circulation, but only as yet another text: though the restorers have aimed to be definitive and final, they have instead foregrounded the complexities involved in any attempt to reconstruct Welles's film.

Examining the textual puzzle that surrounds *Othello* serves in part to reaffirm what others have noted before: the provisional, unfinished, never-to-be-fixed state of so much of Welles's work. The fascinated interest Welles continues to inspire can be related quite directly to textual indeterminacy and to the related difficulties in accessing what texts there are. Much like the "lost" Hitchcocks, especially *Rope* (1948), *Rear Window* (1954), and *Vertigo* (1958), the very inaccessibility of *Othello* has lent to it an aura, a cult value (in Walter Benjamin's terms)[2] not associated with your run-of-the-mill classic. With *Othello*, one could argue that the film itself is not, cannot be, the text; the film—or, more precisely, the various traces of the film we have—is merely part of a larger text, one that includes, for example, Michael MacLiammoir's tour-de-force account of the filming (*Put Money in Thy Purse*) and Welles's own comments, both in interviews and in his "documentary" *Filming Othello* (1978). These texts, together with a great variety of other materials (I will just mention Beatrice Welles-Smith's introductory comments inserted at the beginning of the video version of the rerelease and therefore now part of that text), have helped to construct an anecdotal frame, an accumulation of more or less reliable commentary which at times complements and at other times becomes a replacement for or alternative to the film text itself.

Michael MacLiammoir's *Put Money in Thy Purse*, a highly entertaining account of the making of *Othello*, details the sporadic, peripatetic, drawn-out nature of the production. In its essential outlines the story has been told many times and has become well worn in the telling: how Welles, forced to finance the film himself when the original backers went bust, would frequently interrupt production so that he could take on one acting job or another in other people's films, thus raising much-needed cash. Then he and his company were off to a new location—Mogador (Essaouira),Venice, Viterbo, Safi, Rome, and so on. The story, in fact, is retold one more time by Welles himself in one of his most intriguing projects, *Filming Othello*, a "documentary essay," to employ Jonathan Rosenbaum's term,[3] made for West German television. Without tackling the unanswerable question of truth value, both Welles's documentary and MacLiammoir's account provide yet more source material with which to construct the textuality of *Othello*. Both are texts generated, as it were, by Welles's original film, and they now constitute a portion of that text that cannot entirely be separated from the original.

Put Money in Thy Purse is itself something of a postmodern text, fairly evenly divided between descriptions of personal discomforts and illnesses and the enthusiastic embrace of work, however sporadic and incoherently undertaken. MacLiammoir's account, in its journal form, at times duplicates the structure and effect of the film—a continual attempt to make sense from chaos, a series of sketches and incidents seemingly loosely connected but ultimately revealed as having been carefully arranged to produce the desired end. MacLiammoir throughout evokes the nature of the international film world in the postwar era, a period of runaway production, of inexpensive location work and low-paid extras, of actors transported all over the globe in search of blocked dollars and cheap but luxurious accommodations. The general tone of all this is nicely rendered at one point when Welles announces, in the course of a lunch at the famous (and notoriously expensive) Paris restaurant, the Tour D'Argent, that the company will have to shut down owing to lack of money. At times, *Put Money* reads like a novel by Paul Bowles in its uneasy mix of attraction toward and repulsion from the Orient, which perhaps is another way of saying that it reflects Iago's view of Othello.

Filming Othello complements and overlaps with *Put Money in Thy Purse*, in part because MacLiammoir figures prominently in both and also because the two texts tell approximately the same story, albeit from quite different perspectives. Welles's documentary essay almost creates, or at least evokes, another film *Othello* in place of the one Welles actually made. Welles gives us a bit of production history, snatches of autobiography, and some adroit commentary on Shakespeare's play. Like his earlier *F for Fake* (1973), *Filming Othello* exhibits a variety of self-reflexive moments, mixing fact and fiction,[4] combining disparate materials, employing editing strategies that work at cross-purposes to documentary "truth." And, again like *F for Fake, Filming Othello* projects a sense of fragmentation, incompleteness, and nonlinearity.

At the same time, Welles's strategies in *Filming Othello* have their origins in the pedagogic role I have ascribed to Welles more than once in this study: as he had on television in the 1950s, he combines a discussion of Shakespeare with a performance of Shakespeare, reciting several of Othello's and Iago's speeches and soliloquies. At a number of points in the film, he even cites what others have written about his *Othello*. In particular, he paraphrases, with acknowledgment, Jack Jorgens's excellent analysis of *Othello* in his book *Shakespeare on Film*, and then treats Jorgens's comments as if they were the expression of his intentions for *Othello*: "The attempt of our camera," he remarks at one point, "was to create that sense of vertigo, a feeling of tottering instability." The words, however, are from the Jorgens essay.[5] By the end of *Filming Othello* we can no longer tell when Welles is citing Jorgens and when he is commenting in his own person.

Both *Put Money in Thy Purse* and *Filming Othello*, in their emphasis on production history and in their own fragmented and provisional self-constructions, imitate and reinforce the stylistic and thematic strategies of Welles's *Othello*. If the manner of filming *Macbeth* resulted in a closed, claustrophobic world inhabited by a monomaniacal personality, as I earlier argued, the manner of filming *Othello*, in contrast, can be seen to have resulted in a fragmented, mosaic world of shards and shattered bits,[6] all brilliantly exposed to sun and sea, a world of jigsaw-like confusion and uncertainty, where the innocence and clarity of nature becomes in itself suspect and frightful to the protagonist's imagination.[7] *Othello* is, in a sense, *Macbeth* turned inside out, the internal becoming external, the implosion becoming explosion, the act of pulling all toward a central point becoming a moving out and away from the center. While dispensing with so much of Shakespeare's verbal poetry, Welles creates a visual poetry of his own, a poetry inspired rather than dictated by Shakespeare. If this new visual poetry cannot, in the nature of things, replace the verbal while maintaining Shakespeare's meaning, it can and does create its own meaning, sometimes reinforcing, sometimes ignoring, the thematic and emotional resonances of the play.

A brief look at how Welles has transformed the opening movement of Shakespeare's play can illustrate his methods of adaptation. Welles begins with a wordless (apart from crowd noises and Latin chants) prologue followed by a spoken narration, neither of which, of course, has any textual authority. (These will be further considered below.) The first Shakespearean line we hear, spoken by Iago, is "I have told thee often and I retell thee again and again, I hate the Moor," which is from act I, scene iii, lines

360–62. Iago's next words, "I'll poison his delight," are from act I, scene i, line 65. After a non-Shakespearean interpolation from Roderigo ("How, how, Iago"), Iago continues with lines 66–68. After another interpolation from Roderigo, we are transported forward to I.iii for three lines (298–300). Soon we are back to I.i.76–82 for "Awake! What ho, Brabantio," minus a few lines and with one change in speech heading. We skip to lines 118 to 123 (with cuts), back to line 116, forward to line 134, forward to I.iii.358 for part of one line, back to I.i.157, then to 168 for Brabantio's line "Is there not charms, etc.," which, however, Welles assigns to Iago. After line 172, we are in act I, scene ii, line 58 for Othello's first line, "Put up your bright swords." An interpolation by Brabantio ("There is the Moor") follows, and we once more hear Welles's voice-over narration. We then go to I.iii.60 (for the scene with the senators). The remainder of act I can be summarized as follows: I.ii.62–70; I.iii.74–75; I.iii.111–12; I.iii.76–94 and 127–87; I.iii.19–20 and 27–30; I.iii.287–89; act II, scene i, 219–22; I.i.10; I.i.24; I.i.14–21 and 29–30; I.iii.289–90; I.iii.390–93; I.i.40–62; and I.iii.293–95.[8]

Welles, clearly, is here not so much adapting Shakespeare as creating a collage (made up, in the example just described, of some forty distinct bits and pieces) based on Shakespeare, a free variation on the original. *Othello* can be described as a film of shreds and patches at the same time that an overarching coherence works against the local incoherence of specific moments and scenes, subsuming any straightforward concept of unity and wholeness. In effect, Welles's style destabilizes the seemingly straightforward dichotomies—white/black; Venice/Cyprus; male/female; human/monstrous—that govern Shakespeare's text. His radical deconstruction of Shakespeare's *Othello*, which, while maintaining the general dramatic contours and much of the imagistic and linguistic texture of the original, reorders its constituent elements at will, is neither more nor less extreme than what other adapters and redactors of Shakespeare's plays have done from his time to our own. It is true, however, that in the process of reordering and reshaping the elements of the original play, Welles eliminates much of the text (e.g., the 673 lines of act 1 have been boiled down to some two hundred lines), and hence much of the context for the actions and motivations of the characters, a context an audience necessarily has to reconstruct as best it can.[9]

The initial expository foundations of the play (Shakespeare's I.i and I.ii) are rendered, after the credits and the voice-over, as an almost dizzying sequence of events. Welles has robbed Iago of much of his expository func-

tion and in the process plunges the viewer far more directly and immediately than Shakespeare does into the narrative action. This may account, in
part at least, for the perceived difficulties many commentators have had in
following the sound track. The verbal patchwork Welles has constructed
lacks continuity and coherence—we are forced to pay close attention to
the primarily visual clues for the meaning of this verbal structure.

Welles's precredit prologue to *Othello*, frequently analyzed as a bravura
piece of filmmaking, partly functions to orient the viewer; it also keys us
to Welles's visually metaphoric approach to Shakespeare's text and at the
same time announces his independence from it. The sequence is, without
question, a tour de force, though it is also much more than that. After the
momentary darkness that begins the film, a vertical slit of light appears in
the center of the screen and then expands outward left and right, revealing
the upside-down black face of the dead Othello. The shot clearly begins
inside a church, and the expanding light is created by the church doors
opening to allow the funeral procession to exit. In a series of shots, we see
Othello's body borne and accompanied by black-robed priests; the line of
this procession is then seen to be walking parallel to another procession of
white-robed priests bearing a blonde, dead Desdemona. Soon, another line
of people, this time soldiers dragging a stumbling prisoner by a chain,
passes by in the opposite direction (from right to left), and we then see the
prisoner placed in a cage which is raised high above the city square. From
his vantage point, the caged man watches as the funeral processions continue on their way. Finally, as the choral and instrumental music that has
accompanied this sequence from the beginning stops to be replaced by
Latin chants, we see, from a low camera position, the file of mourners
accompanying the man, and as they turn away from us into the background, Welles's camera tilts down to take in a black wall which soon fills
the entire frame, returning us to total darkness.

This opening, for one thing, announces at the outset the European, classical art-cinema status of the film—the influence of, most particularly, the
Danish Carl-Theodore Dreyer and the late Eisenstein of *Alexander Nevsky*
(1938) and *Ivan the Terrible* (1944–1946); *Othello* thus places itself in immediate contradiction to Hollywood practice. More significantly, perhaps,
Welles's prologue radically alters the narrative structure of Shakespeare's
play. We are, as true in several of Welles's films (*Citizen Kane*, *Mr. Arkadin*,
Chimes at Midnight), beginning at or near the end of the story: Othello and
Desdemona dead, Iago about to begin his period of torture. So *Othello* is
going to be, again like so many of Welles's films, a mystery story: what hap-

pened to these three people; how did they end up as they did; indeed, to the uninitiated, the main question may simply be, who are they? One effect of using a flashback is to emphasize the pattern of inevitability inherent in the story; the events have already been played out, and we wait to see them replayed before our eyes.

It may be argued, of course, that even for a half-way literate viewer, any production of *Othello* will have this effect. After all, can there be anyone, above a certain age, who goes to a performance of *Othello* unaware of its outcome? Though this is true enough, it is also true that Shakespeare's skills as a dramatist have a way of making us forget that we know the outcome, and a successful performance of the play will always have the power of making us hope, against our knowledge, that Desdemona, at least *this* time, will not die. Welles, in any case, does not allow for the suspension of our knowledge. He may have begun *Othello* this way because, as he has said, he needed a "grabber"[10] at the outset, but just as plausibly, he was drawn by the sense of inevitability that Shakespeare's play projects.

The story Welles is telling us will become an act of reconstitution, retelling, retrospection. The opening of the film allows us to adopt several points of view—in a sense, we are encouraged to see a double narrative movement—Iago's "inside view" and the outside view of the relatively minor characters, Lodovico and Cassio, the only survivors (together with Montano) shown in the prologue that we can subsequently recognize in the narrative proper. The combination of Lodovico's minimal, Cassio's partial, and Iago's larger—but never total—understanding provides us with and justifies the mosaiclike retelling that follows this prologue. A related effect of Welles's opening is the creation of a closed narrative form, one that ends where it began. Welles emphasizes this not only by returning to the initial funeral processions at the end of *Othello* but by going further and using, over again, the same shot that had immediately preceded the credits. The story proper, in effect, does not merely fill an imaginary time warp between two nearly contiguous events or moments; rather, the narrative occupies negative time, as it were, slipped in during the brief moment it takes to reverse the film for several dozen frames.[11]

The opening of *Othello* prefigures (and partly includes) the manner in which Welles uses imagery throughout the film. One aspect of this centers on the manipulation of black and white, darkness and light. It should not be surprising that a story primarily concerned with the relationship between a black man and a white woman should call forth the metaphoric use of these light and color values, but Welles goes beyond the obvious in making light/dark imagery a pervading and in no way simplistic concept in his film. It might be objected that the juxtaposition of black and white is inevitable in any film shot in black and white, but this is only superficially true. As we watch most black-and-white films, we tend to forget this limitation of the color spectrum, to "fill in" colors ourselves. In *Othello*, Welles does not really allow for this—he emphasizes, time and again, the sharp contrast between areas of light and areas of darkness; the film is filled with shadows, with darkness engulfing light, and with illumination emerging, or thrusting itself, out of the void.

The whole opening sequence begins and ends in blackness, and even the light comes into being to reveal Othello's black face. (The fact that Welles begins with Othello's face lets us know that for him, as for many if not most others, the tragedy is decidedly Othello's tragedy, not Desdemona's and certainly not Iago's.) And, again to repeat, the monks accompanying Othello's body are robed in black, those with Desdemona in white. Other contrasts are more abstractly rendered. We, as viewers, begin our apprehension in total darkness (the interior of a church) and then are thrust, along with Othello and the camera that follows him, into a square literally bathed in bright sunlight. The funeral processions, as they march from left to right, are silhouetted against the bright, white sky; beneath the feet of the mourners, taking up nearly half the frame, is the blackness of shaded streets and palisades. In short, black and white are constantly juxtaposed in the first few minutes of the film, as they will be at the end.

In Welles's design, the symbolic tonalities of black and white suggest complementary realities, the necessary contrast that renders all human experience rich, complex, and variegated. At the simplest level, black/white merely represent or symbolize Othello/Desdemona. Welles's Desdemona is not only white (Caucasian) racially, but she is nearly always dressed in white, and the paleness of her skin is emphasized by her blonde (equals white in a black-and-white film) hair. When we first see her, a corpse, the transparent black veil which covers her face and head not only calls attention to the whiteness beneath; it also prefigures (retrospectively) her manner of dying and the instrument of her death: (black) Othello strangles Desdemona with a portion of her (white) silk nightgown and his own suffocating kiss. Black and white have no preordained or absolute meanings. The priests in the funeral procession are dressed in either black or white, though their function is identical. Just as Othello himself can be more or less "black" in the course of the narrative, depending on how Welles has lit himself, what tonal values surround him, and how heavily his

—

makeup is applied, so a white-robed figure can momentarily become a black silhouette against a brilliant white sky, and a black-robed figure can reflect light in such a way as to appear white.

As his prologue might lead a viewer to expect, Welles throughout the film freely transforms much of Shakespeare's verse and a good deal of his dramatic form into objects, symbols, and motifs, most notably the Cage, the Bed, the Mirror, the Pit, and the Maze. These objects and symbols are as much part of Welles's mythology as they are suggested by Shakespeare's text: one might say that Welles has adapted Shakespeare's imagistic universe and reconstituted it in his own terms. None of these images is stable or isolated; they blend and merge at will, consume, subsume, and echo each other. They provide to Welles's *Othello* the coherence and stability that are locally absent from virtually every individual scene or shot of the film. The Cage, the Bed, the Mirror, the Pit, and the Maze. These are, in some instances, literal, concrete things: this cage—Iago's cage; this bed—Othello and Desdemona's bed. But, just as much and just as well, the Cage becomes, on a larger, physical scale, Cyprus itself—a place, a world. Or, in a metaphoric move, the cage of doubt, suspicion, and fear in which Othello entraps himself. On the other hand, the Pit may never be a true or actual pit, not a hole in the ground in which anyone might be thrown or imprisoned. The Pit is a depth, a level below another level, a darkness that shuts out all light.

The Cage, the Bed, the Mirror, the Pit, and the Maze. They are at once local and pervasive, things and moods, substance and style. Welles's *Othello* is, as Jack Jorgens and others have noted, from beginning to end a labyrinth.[12] Individual mazes there are: passageways, vaults, tunnels, cellars, stairs. But these all become, on a grand scale, pieces of a greater maze, a labyrinthine geography in which signposts are absent and directions are unclear: top and bottom, front and rear, light and shade, inside and out, contribute to the world of *Othello* an Escher-like ambiguity and confusion. We cannot find our bearings, cannot establish space or even time. The labyrinth is, of course, the well(e)spring image par excellence: from the very form of *Citizen Kane*—a search for something that, within the film's diegetic universe, at least, is never found—to the Chinese box conundrums of *F for Fake*, the Wellesian cinema posits a world in which goals are never reached, or are reached too late, or turn out not to be the goal one had hoped for, or are reached at too great a price. *Othello*, like *The Trial*, constructs a world where the protagonist can never know, for certain, what is going on around him.

In sharp contrast to *Macbeth*, there are few long takes in *Othello*. The most memorable of these is the extended tracking shot Welles employs for the dialogue between Iago and Othello in the course of which Iago plants the seeds of jealousy (Shakespeare's III.iii); the film's longest take, it provides intensity and tension for a scene always difficult to make convincing in stage productions: in a very short period of time (some five hundred lines of virtually uninterrupted dialogue in the original), Iago turns Othello from a loving husband to a raving maniac. The tracking camera, which parallels the movement of Othello and Iago as they walk along the battlements, binds the two men together, reinforcing and locking into place what the dialogue tentatively but inexorably works for. Welles, who does not have the luxury of five hundred lines, gives us an Othello who is both impatient and puzzled: he seems a bit worried from the outset. Iago, grim and straightforward throughout, makes no effort to be subtle in his probings; he seems genuinely concerned, bothered by the direction of his own thoughts.[13] While it serves the purpose of intensifying a crucial movement in Shakespeare's play, the long take simultaneously makes us aware of the fragmentary nature of the film as a whole.

If the formalist rigor of *Citizen Kane* contributes to our impulse to see it as quintessentially "modern," the ragged edges, the absences, dispersals, and disjunctions of *Othello* are what constitute that film as postmodern.[14] Design gives way to chance, hierarchy to anarchy. *Citizen Kane* was, in a sense, Welles's farewell to modernism: the one Wellesian film that stands as a textually stable, finished work, as opposed to the provisional, improvisational nature of virtually all his other films. With *Othello*, the (modernist) labyrinth merges into "a cistern for foul toads to knot and gender in": a labyrinth is a rational construct for those not lost in it; a cistern incorporates in itself a loss of rationality. A labyrinth has an outside as well as an inside and has been made according to a plan; hence, the formal perfection of a *Citizen Kane* (or, for that matter, *Last Year at Marienbad*) compensates for the unsolved mystery at its center. With *Othello*, outside and inside are one, the formal imperfections reinforcing the emotional chaos. Whereas *Citizen Kane* ends with a movement that reverses and thereby completes the movement with which it began, *Othello* ends with a movement that duplicates and repeats its beginning.

The above discussion of *Othello* as a black-and-white film foregrounds what for some viewers appears to be a crucial absence in Welles's film: race. "When Orson Welles filmed his cinematic adaptation of *Othello* in the late 1940s," Virginia Mason Vaughan writes, "he minimized race as an issue."

Peter Donaldson makes a similar point: Welles, he writes, "plays a light-complexioned Moor and consistently underplays racial difference."[15] As theatrical history shows us, however, the impulse to make Othello, a man who murders his wife in a fit of sexual jealousy, as black as possible, especially when played by a white actor, is a two-edged sword. Which, in the end, is more "racist": to underplay Othello's blackness or to overplay it? The eighteenth-century actor-manager David Garrick believed that Othello was black in order to make his jealousy more believable and awful.[16] Julie Hankey, in her discussion of the scurrilous and racist, but highly popular, production of the burlesque opera *Othello* (1836), notes that its success "serves to mark the arrival of a peculiarly unwanted distant relation to Othello. A Shakespearean actor would have had to keep that distance."[17] The recent (1996) film of *Othello* directed by Oliver Parker poses the issue in a different way. With an African-American actor in the title role, the drama ironically loses much of the racial tension we expect to find in it; Laurence Fishburne gives a quiet, dignified, but nearly bloodless performance, almost as if he were afraid of exhibiting the passion, violence, anger, and rage that the part clearly demands. Everyone involved seems to be anxious to eliminate all stereotypical signs of "blackness," anything that might suggest that Othello acts as he does because he is black.

In this context, it is worth remarking that Welles goes against theatrical tradition by restoring two nearly contiguous scenes that have frequently been eliminated in the theater (although he alters their order): the epileptic fit and the eavesdropping scene. Both disappeared from virtually every British production of *Othello* from the beginning of the eighteenth to the end of the nineteenth centuries; one or the other or both have been cut from many twentieth-century productions as well. Godfrey Tearle, whose Othello was contemporary to Welles's film, did away with the fit. In 1954 in New York, Earle Hyman, an African-American Othello, omitted the eavesdropping. The discomfort with these moments are understandable—they detract from the dignity of Othello as a character as well as, one suspects, from the dignity of the actor who has to play Othello. But that, of course, is precisely their purpose.

Although scholars have demonstrated beyond any doubt that Othello was conceived by Shakespeare, and so perceived by Elizabethan audiences, as black, he was, at the same time, of course, undeniably played by a white actor—this, too, is part of the play's meaning. We have, unfortunately, no way of knowing how that white actor (Richard Burbage, by all evidence) performed the role. The only eyewitness account we have of a seventeenth-century performance of *Othello* makes no mention of race or color.[18] The question of what role race plays in Shakespeare's *Othello* is not itself clear-cut.[19] It is not even demonstrable that, as Vaughan claims, "the Venetian outlook in Shakespeare's play is predominately racist."[20] Although we would assume that the marriage of a dark-skinned foreigner to a high-born white woman would have been a matter for scandal (if not for revulsion and hatred) in Venetian society, most of the characters in the play in fact find nothing remarkable about Desdemona's choice of a husband. Only her father Brabantio, Roderigo, a rival for her hand, and Iago, the play's arch-villain, ever give voice to racial slurs. Brabantio, for his part, acts very much like any father in Shakespeare whose daughter elopes or refuses to marry the man he chooses for her: Egeus in *A Midsummer Night's Dream* or Old Capulet in *Romeo and Juliet*, for example.

It is in any case ahistorical to suggest that the issue of race somehow disappears from Welles's film. By photographing on location in Venice, Mogador, Perugia, Safi, and elsewhere, Welles makes vivid and tangible the implicit orientalizing tendencies of Shakespeare's text. At moments filling the screen with "local" color, employing local extras, and in general re-creating the texture of a non-Western culture, Welles replicates the tension that takes place in Othello himself, a tension between "primitivism" and "sophistication," between being true to one's origin and adopting the customs of the host culture. From this point of view, the fact that Welles's performance of Othello presents him as neither wholly black nor wholly white can be seen as strategic rather than evasive. That Othello is a Negro would not have been lost on a contemporary (1950s) audience, however much Welles underplays the blackness—indeed, I would suggest that he underplays Othello's race precisely because it is so evident.[21]

If *Macbeth* was released during a period of postwar cultural anxieties, a time when a predominantly middlebrow culture was having difficulty coming to terms with either "high" or "low" cultural projects, *Othello*, only a few years later, found its context in a Cold War atmosphere of paranoia and xenophobia, on the one hand, and, on the other (among a variety of other issues one could isolate), a powerful drive for Americans of African descent to achieve legal, social, and cultural parity in a deeply racist society. In this context, Shakespeare's tale of a black man's love for a white woman, combined with Welles's Europeanized—even "Russianized"—film aesthetic, presented another puzzling cultural object for American viewers to negotiate. Nor was U.S. culture prepared for a story of a black man in love with a white woman. The 1943 Margaret Webster production of *Othello* with Paul Robeson in the title role marks the very first time a black actor played the role with a predominantly white cast on the New York stage. Photographs of Robeson embracing Uta Hagen (Desdemona) that had earlier been published in *Life* magazine provoked a strong racist response from some readers. When news of Welles's *Othello* plans was made known, the Breen office (the self-censorship arm of the motion picture industry) informed one possible backer that it would not pass on the film were Othello to be played as a black man, even if that black man was a white actor in blackface.[22]

The issue of race is not unconnected to an understanding of Welles's own performance as Othello. Welles sometimes seems uncomfortable with the role, with the pretense, with (perhaps) the blacking up. As James Naremore observes, "Welles has been a bit too wary of his own romantic inclinations, and never generates an acting intensity equal to the drama itself."[23] He is physically right for the part, and his voice would seem to have been perfectly suited to express what Laurence Olivier has called Othello's "purple tones" (although, as Jack Jorgens notes, "Welles speaks in muted tones, and holds himself to a narrow emotional range"),[24] and individual scenes and moments are powerfully and movingly presented. But Welles's rendition of the part asks as many questions as it answers: what is his Othello about, what makes him tick? In all fairness, this is a problem many actors have had with the role, and there are ways—other than through performance—that Welles gives us some hints as to Othello's nature and identity. But, overall, we are given more a recital of the part than an embodiment of it, more a series of attitudes and set pieces than the presentation of a whole man.

Like his Macbeth, Welles's Othello is very much a bear tied to the stake, continuously worried and snapped at by the hound that is Iago; he is a distant, somewhat unapproachable figure whose love for Desdemona is very much a compound of lust and respect, of desire and something resembling fear. Physically, he barely moves (hence, perhaps, Eric Bentley's judgment that Welles does not act, he is photographed);[25] other characters, especially Iago, move around or to him, like flies worrying an elephant. Welles seems to have conceived of Othello as self-contained and self-sufficient, above the normal needs of average humanity, wrapped up in his own sense of self, until his fateful meeting with Desdemona. All at once, he finds himself desiring, needing, but this is an emotion he does not know how deal with. Even more than is usually the case, we have a sense that Welles's performance here is projected outward, as a commentary on Shakespeare's Othello more than as a presentation or even a representation of the character.

Welles's performance has a static grandeur and studied rhetorical manner that suggest the romantic/exotic approach of nineteenth-century
British and American "gentleman" actors from John Philip Kemble at the
beginning of the century to Edwin Booth and Henry Irving at the close.
Welles gives us very little of the other tradition, the one best represented
by the Italian actor Tomaso Salvini, whose performance as Othello is often
characterized in terms of his animal-like passion and his "fierce tender-
ness"; Salvini has been described as rushing into Desdemona's arms in the
first Cyprus scene speaking his lines with "such intense joy that the audience at once seemed to enter the feeling."[26] Welles, in contrast, does not
even touch Desdemona in this scene: he delivers the line "O, my fair warrior" standing awkwardly by, avoiding eye contact with her. The overall
effect of Welles's performance is to make Othello appear uncomfortable
with himself, uncertain of his "role," of his thoughts and actions, especially
when these involve Desdemona, whom he treats somewhat like a creature
from another planet.

Many of the objections to Welles's performance and to the film itself, I
would argue, originate with misreadings of Shakespeare's play. Othello, we
are told, is not black enough; Iago must be more subtle; Desdemona should
be more sympathetic. These are not objections that naturally arise from a
careful study of Shakespeare's text, but rather from unwarranted assumptions and preconceptions the critic has made about Shakespeare: they are,
in fact, criticisms that could be equally applied to Shakespeare's text. Othello not black enough? The question of Othello's color and appearance has
in fact been vigorously debated from at least the late eighteenth century
on.[27] Iago not subtle enough? This has been a criticism leveled at actors
from Colley Cibber in the eighteenth century to Christopher Plummer
and Bob Hoskins in very recent times. Desdemona not sympathetic
enough? Any actress playing the role finds herself navigating between
Scylla and Charybdis: those who have been most sympathetic have been
condemned for being too sweet, too obedient, or too passive, while
actresses who have played Desdemona as self-assertive, argumentative, and
physically active against Othello in the final scene have been faulted for
bringing an insufficient pathos to their performances. A normalization and
idealization of Shakespeare too often becomes the yardstick for measuring
the success of an adaptation of Shakespeare.

A similar impulse to normalization and idealization lies behind the 1992
restoration and rerelease of *Othello*. But if, as I have suggested, *Othello* was

never actually lost, neither has it been, in any meaningful sense, "restored." Indeed, to term the project authorized by Beatrice Welles-Smith as a "restoration" is to make nonsense of the word. One cannot restore something by altering it in such a way that its final state is something new. To restore means, if it means anything, to bring back to some originary point—itself, of course, an extremely dubious concept. What the various people involved with the *Othello* rerelease have done is to "improve" (by their lights) Welles's film, not restore it. If you find a Greek statue with a left arm missing, you might be able to restore it if, *(a)* you can demonstrate, through internal and external evidence, that it once had a left arm and, *(b)* you can discover some evidence of what that left arm looked like when it was still attached. If, however, the statue was meant to have no left arm (a statue, perhaps, of a one-armed man), or if the statue was never completed by the sculptor, or if, assuming the arm did once exist and had broken off, you have no evidence of what the missing arm had originally looked like, then adding an arm of your own design is not an act of restoration. You are, instead, making something new.

In practice, even under the best of circumstances—when scrupulous care has been taken to establish what the original state of the work might have been like and what the intentions of the artist were—acts of restoration are always compromises and are inevitably controversial (consider the arguments around the cleaning of Michelangelo's Sistine ceiling). Nevertheless, one can confidently differentiate between the restoration of, say, David Lean's *Lawrence of Arabia*, undertaken with the full cooperation of not only Lean himself but of a number of artists and technicians involved in the production of the film, along with a wealth of external evidence testifying to the film's original state, and the case of *Othello*, with Welles dead, with none of the original artists consulted, with Welles's own intentions uncertain, and with only a theoretical, not a material, original to go back to.

But, one may reasonably ask, why "restore" *Othello* at all? The restorers, if pressed, could undoubtedly cite evidence, both from the film's original reception and from the critical commentary that had accumulated around it over the years, to encourage their work. Much has been written about what was wrong with Welles's "original" *Othello*. The 1955 U.S. reviews would be one place to start, though, as was true of *Macbeth*, these were not as uniformly negative as legend would lead one to expect. Both *Time* and *Newsweek*, for example, were favorable, *Newsweek* unreservedly so: "a powerful, darkly beautiful movie . . . the Bard treated right."[28] The most nega-

Suzanne Cloutier as Desdemona (top), Orson Welles as Othello, and Fay Compton as Emilia in the labyrinthine world of *Othello* (1952). (Author's collection)

Orson Welles as a "light-skinned" Othello. (Photo courtesy of Christopher P. Jacobs)

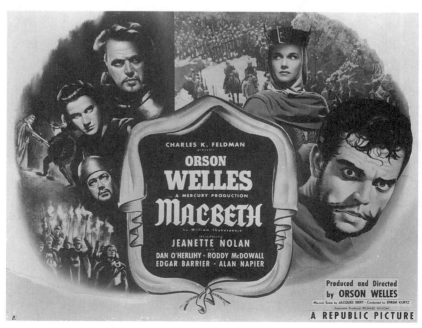

Poster design for *Macbeth* (1948). (Courtesy of Jerry Ohlinger's Movie Material Store)

Orson Welles as "Guest Star": Cesare Borgia in *Prince of Foxes* (dir. Henry King, 1949) (Courtesy of Jerry Ohlinger's Movie Material Store)

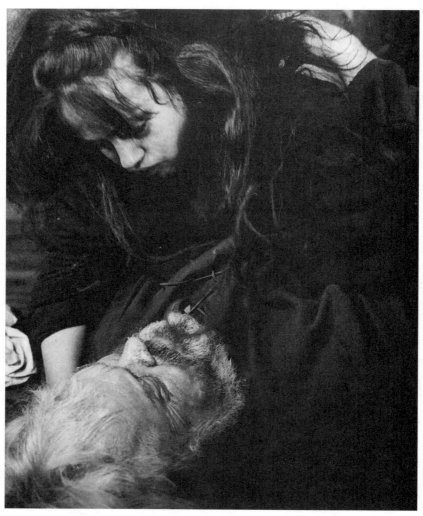

"A tun of flesh": Jeanne Moreau as Doll Tearsheet tries to embrace Orson Welles's Falstaff in *Chimes at Midnight* (1967). (Photo courtesy of Film Favorites)

A comic view of chivalry: Norman Rodway as Hotspur and Marina Vlady as Lady Hotspur in *Chimes at Midnight*. (Photo courtesy of Film Favorites)

Keith Baxter as Hal, caught between the call of duty (represented by his father's castle) and the temptations of irresponsibility (represented by Welles's Falstaff) in *Chimes at Midnight*. (Photo courtesy of Film Favorites)

The "Mr. Wu" factor: turning a small role into a memorable one. Orson Welles as
Harry Lime in *The Third Man* (1949). (Photo courtesy of Jerry Ohlinger's Movie
Material Store)

The Oratorical Style: Orson Welles as Charles Foster Kane (*Citizen Kane*, 1941). (Photo courtesy of Jerry Ohlinger's Movie Material Store)

Yet another false nose: Orson Welles as Sigsbee Manderson in *Trent's Last Case* (dir. Herbert Wilcox, 1952). (Author's collection)

A historical figure with a Shakespearean aura: Orson Welles as Cardinal Wolsey in
A Man for All Seasons (dir. Fred Zinnemann, 1966). (Photo courtesy of Jerry
Ohlinger's Movie Material Store)

tive reviews were those by Philip Hamburger in the *New Yorker*, Eric Bentley in the *New Republic*, and, most crucially perhaps, Bosley Crowther in
the *New York Times*.[29] Bentley's review is essentially an attack—more in sorrow than in anger, one senses—on Welles himself. Crowther's review, however, together with a follow-up article, insured *Othello*'s fate. As an "art
house" film playing in a single theater in each of a few selected cities, *Othello*'s success or failure in New York meant everything, and the *Times*
review was essential to that reception. United Artists clearly thought it
important to have the *Times*'s blessing: its ads feature a paragraph of carefully chosen and artfully arranged excerpts from Crowther's review which
almost sounds positive.

The main points in the negative reception of *Othello* can be summarized, as follows: (1) Welles fails to capture the essence of Shakespeare's play;
(2) the dialogue is difficult to understand; (3) the film is "technically
gauche" (Bentley); (4) the performances are inadequate, especially Welles's;
(5) content is too often sacrificed to form (Welles indulges in "half a hundred cinematic tricks," per Hamburger); (6) humanity has been sacrificed
to "art" ("We wish that Mr. Welles . . . could recognize that people, not
walking shadows, populate Shakespeare's plays," Crowther wrote).
Although the assumptions behind both the leaning-toward-positive and
the leaning-toward-negative reviews are essentially the same (i.e., that a
film adaptation of a literary work—especially Shakespeare—should be in
some specific but never defined ways "faithful" to the original; that films
are about real human beings; that acting should be psychologically credi-
ble, naturalistic, and invisible; that a sound track exists primarily to support
and clarify the images and the narrative; that the conventions of classical
cinema—transparency, coherence, clarity, motivated action—must be
adhered to), the most surprising aspect of the reception of *Othello* is how,
given these premises, critics should be so lacking in unanimity in their
responses to what they see on the screen. Even the question of the sound
track, for example, receives a mixed response. Bentley notes that the dialogue "is all too obviously dubbed," and Robert Hatch (*The Nation*) complains of not being able to "hear [understand?] half of what [Welles] said."[30]
But reviewers who liked the film made no reference to the sound track,
while one of the most destructive reviews (Hamburger's) claims that Welles
delivers his lines with "understanding and nobility."[31]

The major area of complaint, of course, has always focused on the
sound. Although there are brilliant aural moments, particularly musical
moments—the entire opening sequence, for example—much of the sound

track, the argument goes, is a mess. The dubbing, perhaps a necessary procedure given various financial exigencies and production difficulties, is poorly carried out at least half the time and barely adequate for most of the rest. Some of the actors, clearly, were no longer available when the sound was recorded in postproduction: Robert Coote, for a glaring instance, seems to speak mostly with Welles's voice, and quite apart from any synchronization difficulties, the very fact that we recognize Welles's barely disguised tones is, for some viewers, disconcerting and distracting. But the aural problems in *Othello*, it has been argued, go beyond dubbing. Sound levels are erratic, and some of the dialogue is lost entirely. Considering how much of Shakespeare Welles has cut, most viewers would like what remains to at least make sense and be reasonably clear.

To add to the aural confusion, the editing of the visual track sometimes works at cross-purposes to the sound: Othello's famous line, "Put up your bright swords, or the dew will rust them" (I.ii) is virtually thrown away, since (1) we don't know who is speaking, (2) or to whom, and (3) because of the way Welles has framed and edited his shots at this point, we can only barely catch the words anyway. In Shakespeare's play, this line is highly significant: it establishes Othello's calm command over a confusing situation, his natural mastery over his fellow men, and his desire to prevent bloodshed. It is a line that *characterizes* in a typically Shakespearean manner. So dissatisfaction with Welles's craftsmanship here goes beyond technical matters to a point of interpretation. Welles, we may feel, has missed an opportunity to say something important about Othello (and about *Othello* as well). In short, purely technical or primarily stylistic issues intersect with, and inevitably affect, larger concerns of purpose and meaning.

Although the restorers played with the contrasts of the photographic image and occasionally fiddled with the editing, they primarily concerned themselves with the sound track. It is therefore with the sound track that I am most concerned, and here some precision—in place of the impressions I have been summarizing—would be useful. The assumed "problems" can be characterized as follows:

1. The frequent absence of precise synchronization of the dialogue track with the visual track

2. Occasional difficulty in identifying the source of spoken words

3. Frequent use of offscreen diegetic sound

4. Unmotivated shifts in sound levels

5. Absence of ambient sound (music, effects) in scenes where such sounds would ordinarily be expected

6. Difficulties in understanding speech

7. The "thinness" of the music

8. Missing or dropped or half-finished words and phrases

9. The effect of voice-over speech when synchronized speech is expected (Othello's line "Come, Desdemona, I have but an hour of love to spend with thee" [I.iii.293f.] is spoken "over" an image of Welles's face, his lips clearly visible and not moving)

10. Substitution of one actor's voice for another

As a glance at this list soon makes clear, some of these items represent, at first sight, clear-cut, observable, and testable phenomena while other items are subjective and disputable. It is not possible, in some instances, to separate out "flaws" and "errors" from deliberate choice. Many of these supposed problems (items 2, 3, 5, 6, 8, 9, and 10) can all be attributed to intentionality or to issues that are unrelated to errors or flaws. It is certainly true enough, for example, that there are moments when even someone thoroughly familiar with Shakespeare's text will have some difficulty in hearing precisely what has been said. Here, however, we are, to some extent, dealing with subjectivity and degree. Nearly all Shakespeare adaptations present difficulties in comprehension. Perceived shifts in sound levels and the supposed thinness of the music are similarly subjective: a shift in sound level is a measurable phenomenon, certainly, but evaluating its purpose and significance is another matter. Even the issue of synchronization is relative, not absolute: if there is sufficient motion within the frame, lip movement may be indistinct, and we may therefore "read" unsynchronized sound as if it were synchronized if the context so encourages us.[32]

The issue of one actor dubbing another, too, has complex ramifications. That Othello and Roderigo both speak with Welles's voice—a fact not noticeable, perhaps, to first-time viewers of the film—may save one actor's salary at the dubbing stage, but it also has the effect, however subliminal, of equating Othello and Roderigo, linking them as common dupes, in very different ways, of Iago. Roderigo is a burlesque version of Othello, an echo, a caricature of Othello's propensity to be twisted and turned as Iago so wills. That Welles chose to loop Roderigo's dialogue himself suggests that he was aware of the value of equating the two, at some affective level, in the minds of the audience (late in the film, Roderigo glances in a mirror and is photographed from the same angle Othello had been when he had looked at his image in a mirror at an earlier moment). The high-pitched, nasal whine Welles uses for Roderigo is a parodic inversion of Othello's (and his) normally low-pitched and orotund delivery.

In short—and this is my major point—none of the issues listed, nor all of them taken together, justify a "restoration" of Welles's *Othello*. Although we may wish that Welles had had better facilities, more sophisticated equipment, less haphazard financing, and so forth, we can only deal with what is, not with what might have been. Furthermore, many, if not all, of the supposed flaws of *Othello* are, as in so many of Welles's films, symbiotically linked, at least to a degree, to the virtues. Rather than lament the sound track, we might better attend to how Welles employs it. In some sequences, for example, the sound is not simply mismatched; rather, the visual track and the sound track are deliberately conceived of as *separate* entities. When, for example, Othello requires of Iago "ocular proof" of his wife's betrayal, Welles appears not to be speaking at all. Othello's lines are delivered when his back is to the camera. The editing scheme together with the absence of any lip movement when we do see Othello's face contributes to the illusion that Othello does not speak, that his language is divorced from his essential self. Only in moments of comparative calm and stasis do we have perfect synchronization between word and image. Synchronization, in effect, comes to stand for calm and stasis. Just as the images present a fragmented, chaotic, disintegrating world, so, too, words are fragmentary and unclear, and the relationship between word and image constantly falls apart.

The circumstances of filming, therefore, though they can explain some of the eccentricities with the sound track, cannot be evoked at every point as an explanation for what a particular viewer finds inadequate with Welles's film. Clearly, for one example, Welles meant to have speeches and soliloquies—notably, "the Pontic Sea"—delivered with the actor's back to the camera. It may have been convenient, circumstantially, to film a particular speech or soliloquy in that manner, but it was also, we must assume, what Welles wanted to do. Again and again, Welles's methods—the economies he adopted, the difficulties in achieving continuity (in one scene, the sacking of Cassio, Othello appears, seemingly, in two different costumes, and Iago's beard, to choose a somewhat frivolous but nevertheless easily observed example, throughout the film moves over different parts of his face almost at will), the drawn-out production schedule, the frequent changes in location—all can be shown to have interpretive significance. If we ignore, at least momentarily, questions of intention—or, rather, if we more reasonably assume that intention is always an issue, that there are no accidents—then the anomalies, the "mistakes," the "flaws" that have been identified in *Othello* take on a rather different character.

Consider, for example, the following "fault": the last shot (outside the framing narrative) of the murdered Desdemona. We see her on the floor of the bedchamber photographed in an oddly frozen, surprisingly grainy, medium close shot. We can "explain" this image in at least two ways. On the one hand, we can account for the shot's provenance with reference to Welles's improvisational necessities. In the course of editing the film, Welles evidently decided that he needed a reasonably close shot, some four hundred frames in length, of Desdemona lying dead. Desdemona—Suzanne Cloutier—herself was long gone by this time. Welles therefore took a medium shot of the dead Desdemona some thirty frames in length, step-printed it to lengthen it and blew it up to create a tighter close-up. We can guess that this is what Welles did because, moments earlier, we see the thirty-frame medium shot in question. The result is a slightly enlarged freeze-frame of Desdemona. If, however, we ignore the circumstances, the effect of this shot is both startling and extremely moving: what we seem to be looking at, in the context of this otherwise richly photographed film, is a blurry tabloid photo, seemingly taken surreptitiously, of a dead woman lying on the floor, tangled in a wrinkled bedsheet, the pitiful, coldly observed, degraded victim of a tawdry domestic melodrama. (Here, one could cite G. B. Shaw's critical view of Shakespeare's *Othello* as exhibiting a "police-court morality.")[33] This moment offers a stark contrast to the almost ethereal image of Desdemona lying on her bier in the opening moments of the film.

What I am suggesting, in short, is that what the restorers of *Othello* have succeeded in doing, in their light, is to smooth the rough spots in the film and in the process to conventionalize the unconventional.[34] They have also, admittedly, "corrected" some mistakes. I am far from arguing that Welles's film is free of technical inadequacies or that Welles was able, at all times, to fulfill his own intentions: clearly, he was not. *Othello*—as, of course, is true of virtually all films—is the product of *compromise*: what Welles wanted to do and what he was able to do are two different matters. We know, for one striking example, that Welles, when he came to edit the film, very much wanted a close-up of Roderigo (Robert Coote) emerging from the well in which he had hidden himself in the course of the nighttime brawl in Cyprus. Welles sent instructions to his associate in Hollywood, Richard Wilson, directing him to find Coote, "take him to a swimming pool and make a big head close-up of him sticking his head out of the water, ducking, sticking his head out and ducking again."[35] Wilson was not able to find Coote, and the film therefore lacks the close-up Welles wanted. Does this knowledge justify creating a close-up and "restoring" it to the film? Few would think so, even though, in this (perhaps unique) instance, we have documentary evidence—including a small sketch in Welles's own hand—of what that close-up might have looked like.[36]

Ironically, the "restoration" of *Othello* is itself fraught with textual uncertainties: there are, we now know, two (and perhaps three) "states" of the restored version, as David Impastato and Jonathan Rosenbaum have pointed out.[37] Evidently, the thorough overhaul of the sound track undertaken by the original restorers—which included a complete rerecording of the music—was unacceptable to Welles's daughter, so that a second, less restored version was prepared and put into general release and, later, on video.[38] The video version, furthermore, differs in at least one detail from the general release: the Latin chants which conclude the prologue of Welles's American release version (and, one presumes, the others as well), were unaccountably eliminated from the restored film. They were rerestored on video.

A careful viewing (and hearing) of the restored version, moreover, reveals that the restorers have violated their own stated principles.[39] In some instances, dialogue has been relooped with new actors. Roderigo, for example (who, ironically, was dubbed by Welles himself), has a completely new voice at several points. His early line, "I would not follow him, then," spoken in a muffled manner but clearly in Welles's voice in the original, is now spoken by someone else and with a different emphasis. At the conclusion of the Cyprus brawl scene, we have both new voices and rewritten dialogue. Welles's version includes the following exchange (between two unidentified characters): "Please you come [with?]." "At whose command?" "Our generals." This becomes, in the restored version: "You are ordered above." "At whose command?" "Why, Sir, the generals." At a few points, words have simply been eliminated so that a lip-synch could be achieved. Iago no longer says that he would not drown himself for love of a guinea hen, but simply for love. The restorers have even reedited at least one sequence entirely: the exchange between Iago, Cassio, and Bianca which centers on Bianca's questions concerning Desdemona's handkerchief has been altered so that both the order of shots and the arrangement of dialogue is new. (One of Welles's shots, in fact, is actually edited to constitute two shots.) At other points, dialogue and music are displaced. In the scene where Desdemona appears on the ramparts (immediately following the cashiering of Cassio sequence), Welles's muffled timpani have been replaced by what sounds like kettle drums.

What, then, is Orson Welles's *Othello*? The question continues to be asked, restoration or no restoration. Victor Paul Squitieri, in his 1993 dissertation "The Twofold Corpus of Orson Welles's 'Othello',"[40] claims that the "real" *Othello*, what he terms Welles's "final cut," is represented by a unique copy in the Cinémateque française, a copy of the version shown at Cannes. In essence, Squitieri's argument is that this version differs significantly from, and is superior to, the 1955 release (and, necessarily, to the Castle Hill "restoration" based upon the 1955 version); a corollary to this argument is that Welles's reediting and relooping of his "final cut" was made unwillingly and under the watchful eye of United Artists executives. Serious problems, however, arise both with Squitieri's claims and with the arguments supporting them: simply stated, we have no way of knowing that the version of *Othello* shown at the Cannes film festival in 1952 was regarded by Welles in any way as a final cut. As Jonathan Rosenbaum has pointed out, "Definitive versions of many of [Welles's] films are impossible to establish." Rosenbaum believes "that Welles preferred the version [of *Othello*] featuring his spoken credits,"[41] but even if we presume that Rosenbaum is referring to the same version Squitieri refers to as the "final cut," the phrase "final cut" is much too definitive. In at least one instance, Welles loaned his personal copy of *Othello* for a retrospective of his work: this print was, without doubt, the 1955 version. Furthermore, Davies's description of the BBC version shown in 1982[42] makes it sound a lot like the "unseen" version in the Cinémathèque.

But our story does not end there. We now have the Criterion laser disk of *Othello*, and it provides us with more mysteries. Voyager's 1994 guide to the Criterion Collection announces the availability of the "fully restored version, along with a documentary on this major restoration effort and its relationship to the film's original production challenges."[43] But if you mail in your $49.95, what you will receive is a beautifully produced transfer of what appears to be the 1955 U.S. release version, or something very close to it. The production information is not entirely clear on this matter: the source is simply identified as the 35mm composite fine-grain master made from the original camera negative, but the exact provenance is not given. This is a treasure, certainly, Welles's film in a form otherwise unavailable, but it is also quite definitely not what Voyager had originally planned to release. Supplementary materials include the short film *Return to Glen-nascaul*, an excerpt from *Filming Othello*, and portions of an Italian documentary, *Rosabella*, featuring interviews with Suzanne Cloutier and others involved in the production. All very commendable, but what, one wonders, happened to the restored *Othello*?

Rather than attempting to resolve all these puzzles, we might better regard Orson Welles's *Othello* as yet another variation of a text which has always been unstable and unfixed. The textual history of Welles's film uncannily recapitulates the textual history of Shakespeare's play, which exists in two distinct early versions, together with variants thereof. The First Quarto (Q1, 1622) and First Folio (F1, 1623) texts of *Othello* differ from each other in a number of ways. Without going into great detail, suffice it to say that the folio has some 160 lines not in the quarto, while the quarto has some fifty-three lines not in the folio. A comparison of the two texts, furthermore, reveals at least a thousand variations in vocabulary, phrasing, and stage directions. Until very recently, editors of *Othello* have been happy simply to "conflate" the quarto and folio versions, thereby creating a new, composite text made up of readings from both and favoring, when choices had to be made between evenly balanced alternatives, whichever version the editor believed to be the most authoritative. Needless to say, in our poststructural, postmodern age, this procedure no longer seems acceptable. Textual scholars now believe that neither text necessarily represents that elusive single text, Shakespeare's original: instead, we may very well have two "original" versions, both to some extent authoritative, albeit in different ways.

To further complicate this picture, it is interesting to note that in 1630, some fourteen years after Shakespeare's death, we have what could easily have been called, with about as much authority as the restorers of Welles's film could claim, a "restoration" of Shakespeare's play, what is now known as the Second Quarto, or Quarto Two (Q2). In the absence of any independent authority, the anonymous editor of this version of *Othello* reproduced the First Quarto, adding to it those passages unique to the First Folio, and choosing, in a seemingly haphazard fashion, whatever variant readings from the two texts he found most acceptable. This version was frequently reprinted and served as the basis for a number of acting editions well into the eighteenth century, becoming further embellished and altered over time, so that Shakespeare's play can be said to incorporate many textual and theatrical variations and alterations, among which Welles's film itself has a place. Although it is convenient to speak of Shakespeare's *Othello* as if it were a fixed, singular work, the implications of the textual history I have just sketched out would suggest otherwise.

In a letter to Hilton Edwards and Micheal MacLiammoir ("Dearest Gents"), his Brabantio and Iago, respectively, Welles outlined some of the ways his production of *Othello* both resembled and failed to resemble a typical Hollywood production, and at the same time justified his past and, evidently, continuing failure to pay his actors regularly and promptly for their services. We read of cutthroat deals in blocked lira, of field maneuvers directed by mail, of a French lawsuit, and of a disappearing partner. The letter itself as material object, with its penciled-in corrections, second thoughts, crossings-out, and so on, nicely suggests the chaotic state of the *Othello* production and of Welles's life in this period of exile; it also bears the material evidence of its own production: in the upper left-hand corner of the first page, a dark smudge has been identified by Welles as partly sand, partly suntan oil.[44]

In the end, Welles's film, too, bears the marks of its own production, but, flaws and all, it is the film (or, perhaps, the films) we have. The very fluidity implied by the existence of multiple versions and multiple texts makes the act of restoration both presumptuous and unnecessary. No fixed text of *Othello* exists. I would go further and suggest that any appreciation of Welles's film requires a recognition of its fragmentary essence—that it is a film, in a sense, *about* fragmentation. The textual histories of Shakespeare's play and Welles's film might even be said to recapitulate a problem endemic to Othello's predicament as a character acting in the worlds of Venice and Cyprus: what is the truth about Desdemona, about Iago, about Cassio? What do the words *black* and *white* really mean in a world in which identities are not fixed? How do we tell the real from the unreal, the true from the false, the faithful from the unfaithful? How do we negotiate the maze that is the world in which we find ourselves? "What is the text?" thus becomes a subset of the larger question, "Who tells the truth?"

If it is true that *Othello*, like a number of Welles's films, truly resists the tendency of film to present us with a fixed, unchanging text, we may use that observation to formulate another explanation for Welles's lifelong interest in Shakespeare. Shakespeare, a professional playwright, created texts that were by their nature unfinished and imperfect, that were open to change, that could be and undoubtedly were abridged, expanded, and generally rewritten according to need or convenience, either by the author or by anyone else who had a stake or an interest in their fortunes. Like Shake-

—

speare's plays, Welles's films will always be works in progress, open to change, to alteration, even to desecration. Rather than lament the multiple versions, the textual uncertainties, of Welles's *Othello*, we might instead celebrate them, as we are beginning to celebrate the textual uncertainties of Shakespeare's plays.

John Heminge and Henry Condell, the editors of the Shakespeare First Folio, justified their project with the claim to be replacing "stolen and surreptitious, . . . maimed and deformed" copies of Shakespeare's plays with the genuine articles, "cured and perfect of their limbs." But their texts were frequently just as maimed and deformed as the ones they were replacing. They were, after all, trying to make a few shillings: "Whatever you do," they several times exhort their potential readers, "Buy." So, too, the restoration of *Othello* was a commercial enterprise, and extremely questionable claims were made on its behalf. "This is a film," Beatrice Welles-Smith tells us in the video release, "that no one has seen." Michael Dawson, one of the restorers, is quoted elsewhere as saying that Welles's original dubbing job made the film look like "Japanese sci-fi."[45] We also read that *Othello* was "never given a real theatrical release" and that Welles's voice was "lost and has now been restored—to us and to Orson Welles."[46] But however misguided a project in its intentions and however well- or ill-executed, the restoration of *Othello* has helped to insure the film's continuing life, very much as Welles, in making the film, contributes to the continuing life of Shakespeare's play. The technology that allowed for the "restored" *Othello* has simultaneously served both to preserve and to destroy the very concept of an authorized text. Perhaps ironically, given Welles's exalted auteur status, the only textual authority *Othello* can finally claim must be found in the interplay between all the texts we have at our disposal.

SEVEN

Chimes at Midnight

—

Rhetoric and History

Of the many cinematic allusions to Orson Welles that have prolifer-
ated since his death in 1985, one of the more surprising comes
about a third of the way through Gus Van Sant's exploration of street
hustling in the urban underworlds of the Pacific Northwest, *My Own
Private Idaho* (1991): an extended borrowing from Shakespeare's Fal-
staff/Hal plays, which is at the same time stylistically indebted to Welles's
Chimes at Midnight (1967). The debt to Welles is most evident in the photography (wide-angle lenses) and mise-en-scène (low-key lighting, costuming, etc.) Van Sant employs to present his Shakespeare-inspired
sequences. Although the resemblance between the underworld of late
medieval London and the milieu inhabited by Van Sant's characters may
not strike one as immediately obvious, the analogy presents intriguing,
albeit largely unexplored, possibilities having primarily to do with the
homoerotic and Oedipal subtexts present both in Shakespeare's history
plays and in a number of Welles's films.[1] The homage to Welles nevertheless seems, at first thought, somewhat gratuitous, and Van Sant's
mélange of Shakespearean thought and modern-day idiom ("It will
impress them more, when such a fuckup like me turns good") is a dis-
traction that nearly brings his film to a halt on several occasions. What is
appropriate, perhaps, is that Welles serves here in a typically postmodern
manner—part homage, part pastiche, part nostalgia. Appropriately
because *Chimes at Midnight* itself, as I will suggest, presents Welles in his
most postmodern guise: a Shakespeare adaptation that seemingly negates
language and radically deconstructs the thematic polarities of its originary texts.

Campanadas a la Medianoche/Falstaff/Chimes at Midnight: the three titles by
which Welles's third Shakespeare adaptation is variously known suggest
something of the film's complexity and variety. *Campanadas a la Medianoche*
points to the circumstances of production: a Spanish-Swiss sponsorship,
filmed and copyrighted in Spain. As a Spanish film, it could be thought to
stand in for the never-completed *Don Quixote* which so fascinated Welles
throughout much of his life. The opening, precredit images of *Chimes/
Campanadas* can then be seen as an allusion to that other film project and
to the Spanish masterpiece on which it was based. Two figures in a landscape, one very thin, almost emaciated, the other enormously round: Don
Quixote and Sancho Panza in old age, perhaps? Certainly, Shakespeare was
as much concerned with chivalry and honor, and with the potential for
parodic reversal inherent in the codes that define these values, as was his
near-contemporary Cervantes. Hotspur and Pistol, for instance, provide us
with differently caricatured versions of knighthood, as, in a more subtle
way, Falstaff might be said to be a tragicomic melding of Don Quixote and
Sancho Panza, at once knight and squire, idealist and realist, gentleman and
buffoon.

The titles *Falstaff* and *Chimes at Midnight* point in other directions. The
former, apart from the emphasis it places on the titular character, highlights
the congruence between Welles's Shakespeare projects and Guiseppe
Verdi's: *Macbeth*, *Otello*, and *Falstaff*, in that order, were Verdi's three Shakespearean operas, just as *Macbeth*, *Othello*, and *Falstaff* were, again in that
order, Welles's three completed Shakespeare films. Verdi's operas, like
Welles's films, are bold, highly individual reworkings and reinterpretations
of their source plays. *Falstaff*, its libretto based primarily on *The Merry Wives
of Windsor*, incorporates a good deal of material from *Henry IV*, parts 1 and
2,[2] while Welles, for his part, in adapting the Henriad (the title often given
to the three plays concerned with Prince Hal/Henry V), borrows both a
few lines and, more generally, a spirit from *Merry Wives*, especially the manner in which that play makes Falstaff central; it is, throughout Welles's film,
Falstaff/Welles who occupies the most screen time and the most screen
space.

Chimes at Midnight, as a direct citation from Shakespeare's text, takes us
in yet another direction, toward Welles's intentions, his reading of the
Henry IV plays from a nostalgic, somewhat sentimental mode as a lament
for "the death of Merrie England . . . the age of chivalry, of simplicity, of
Maytime and all that" and as expressing the theme of the "lost paradise,"
which Welles saw as "the central theme in Western culture,"[3] a theme evi-

dent elsewhere in Welles's work, especially *The Magnificent Ambersons* (1942). This view, it must be emphasized, functions in the domain of Welles's intentions primarily: although a number of critics and scholars have taken Welles at his word, there is, in fact, very little evidence of "Merrie England" in the film, present or past. As Bridget Gellert Lyons writes, the phrase "chimes at midnight," "which is given further resonance by the repeated intoning of bells throughout the film, is associated for the audience with sadness and mortality more than with youthful carousal."[4] The several references to the youthful activities of Falstaff and Shallow cannot be taken at face value, and they do not, in any case, add up to anything that might be described as a medieval paradise.

The title *Chimes as Midnight* also alludes, indirectly, to the origins of Welles's film. As was true of *Macbeth*, *Chimes* had had several earlier manifestations. While still at the Todd School, Welles had created and starred in a streamlined conflation of eight of Shakespeare's history plays (the three parts of *Henry VI*, *Richard III*, *Richard II*, the two parts of *Henry IV*, and *Henry V*), which provided him the first opportunity to play, among other characters, Falstaff. In 1939, at the height of his New York theatrical career, he directed and played Falstaff in *Five Kings*, an elaborate, technically complex, and ultimately unmanageable staging of the Henriad (*Henry IV*, parts 1 and 2, and *Henry V*); after brief runs in Boston, Philadelphia, and Washington, D.C., the production closed down, never reaching New York.[5] In 1960, in collaboration with his old Dublin Gate employer and colleague Hilton Edwards, Welles restaged part of his *Five Kings* project in Belfast and Dublin under the title *Chimes at Midnight*. Again, Welles played Falstaff and hired a young actor named Keith Baxter to play Hal. It was this production, essentially, that served as a primary inspiration for the film.[6]

Although *Chimes at Midnight* has gradually come to be recognized both as one of the most intelligent and imaginative of films adapted from Shakespeare and as one of Orson Welles's finest achievements, a film at least equal in energy and brilliance to *Citizen Kane* (1941) and *The Magnificent Ambersons*,[7] the chorus of praise occasionally includes a few sour notes; as so often with Welles's post-*Citizen Kane* films, various qualifications temper even highly enthusiastic assessments.[8] The criticism of *Chimes* echoes that of *Othello* in centering on the sound track and on the uncertain relationship between sound and image: the recording is technically faulty, Shakespeare's words are frequently unintelligible (Welles's Falstaff, in particular, is difficult to understand much of the time), several sequences are poorly synchronized, and, disconcertingly, a number of the minor actors have been

dubbed by Welles himself—all signs that inadequate financing forced artistic compromise. Additionally, critics find fault with Welles for the film's
haphazard continuity and for a general inattention to detail, especially in
the casting and playing of the secondary roles. In short, *Chimes at Midnight*
is often discussed in terms that remind us of Shakespeare's Sir John Falstaff
himself: attractive, vibrant, large, and complex, but, withal, so deeply flawed
as to negate many of its virtues.[9]

Chimes at Midnight is a difficult film to come to terms with, in part
because it seems at once premodern, modern, and postmodern: if Shakespeare's play provides a classic text of the early modern era, Welles's cinematic style transforms it into a modernist work while his interpretive
strategies push it into the postmodern, deconstructive mode. In particular,
Welles prefigures the New Historicist turn, whereby the Renaissance
becomes the Early Modern era, and C. S. Lewis's "Merrie England"
becomes a steely terrain of realpolitik.[10] Although Welles's way of discussing the film in interviews ("Merry England and all that") may seem
unhistorical and slightly naive, his practice is quite otherwise. *Chimes at
Midnight* can be regarded as a work that both deconstructs its source material at the same time that it invites a deconstructive reading.[11] In this light,
both the unquestioned successes and the supposed defects of the film need
to be placed within the context of what I take to be the film's governing
strategy: the rewriting of Shakespeare's text, a rewriting that includes an
attempted erasure of writing, a critique of rhetoric, indeed an undermining of language itself. Taking up what is undeniably present in Shakespeare—no writer shows more awareness of the dangerous seductiveness
of words—Welles carries the questioning of language much further than
Shakespeare, whose primary resource was language, ever could. *Chimes at
Midnight* centers squarely on a conflict between rhetoric and history, on the
one hand, and the immediacy of a prelinguistic, prelapsarian, timeless physical world, on the other. This conflict comes to us primarily through the
actions and character of Falstaff, as we might expect, but it informs as well
the texture and style of each moment of Welles's film. Welles has made a
Shakespearean film in which both rhetoric and poetry seem to undergo
rigorous devaluations.

Welles, of course, given the institutional and economic constraints governing the production of a Shakespeare film in the early 1960s, would have
found it imperative to rewrite, and in rewriting, condense, Shakespeare's
texts as part of the process of adaptation: no Shakespearean film—with the
notable exception of Kenneth Branagh's recent *Hamlet* (1996)—repro-

duces even one Shakespeare play in its entirety (nor, for that matter, do most stage productions). In fact, in incorporating and reordering material from both *Henry IV* plays, *Henry V*, *Richard II*, and adding a few lines from *The Merry Wives of Windsor*, Welles, once again, joins a long and hallowed tradition. The two parts of *Henry IV* were conflated for performance as early as 1623, when Sir Edward Dering prepared a playscript for amateur theatricals. The actor Thomas Betterton performed in a highly abridged adaptation in the early 1700s, and from his time on the Falstaff/Hal plays were combined and individual scenes and speeches rearranged in order to fit preconceptions of one kind or another.[12] In addition to the more or less faithful adaptations and redactions, various pastiches and offshoots have appeared over the centuries, from *Falstaff's Wedding* (1760) to *The Life and Death of Sir John Falstaff* (1923) and beyond.

Welles's editorial decisions, as was true of many of his predecessors, aim at a particular end and have a specific focus. He compresses and reshapes his source material at will, reducing it to a bare minimum of words. He also gives Shakespeare's story of a prince's coming of age a single plot line and a new emphasis. In *Henry IV, Part I*, Hal, the heir apparent to the English throne, attempts to evade his responsibilities by staying away from the court of his usurper father, for whom he substitutes Falstaff and his low-life world until the need to defend his father's crown against internal enemies compels him to reject his unworthy companions and embrace his destiny. At the beginning of *Henry IV, Part II*, it is as if much of Part I had never happened: Hal once again is found in the tavern world and once again must work his way into his father's good graces and to a final rejection of Falstaff and all that he stands for. In short, *Henry IV, Part II*, as readers and playgoers have often noted, in many ways recapitulates, albeit in a different key, the structure and theme of Part I: Shakespeare presents two scenes of reconciliation between Hal and his father, two military engagements (Shrewsbury and Galtree Forest), two moments when Hal realizes his destiny, and so forth. Welles does away with much of this repetition and shifts scenes and parts of scenes around at his convenience, placing Falstaff's recruitment of soldiers in Part II, for example, before Part I's battle of Shrewsbury.[13] Although his refashioning of Shakespeare's text(s) has a number of consequences, the primary effect is to shift the thematic emphasis away from Hal toward Falstaff, thereby blunting the chiasmatic movement of Shakespeare's Henriad whereby the rise of Hal roughly parallels Falstaff's decline. Welles, in short, moves away from history and toward satire.[14]

The critique of history in *Chimes at Midnight* completes a process already begun by Shakespeare, whose *Henry IV, Part II* functions, at some moments, to call into question what we have learned in Part I. The character Northumberland (Hotspur's father), for example, is too ill to fight in Part I. In Part II, however, we are told that he was "crafty-sick." History, in other words, cannot be distinguished from report and rumor ("Rumour," as a character, speaks the Prologue to Part II), and Shakespeare is willing to revise his own historical materials to justify the different tone he wishes to employ in his new play. The contradictions are not resolved by anything like the yardsticks of "truth" or "history." Welles's attack on history, however, is harsher, his conclusion far less optimistic. "History," for the purposes of my argument, includes the whole world of kings and politics, of war and chivalry, as well as the language, the rhetoric, which inevitably is that world's chief expressive medium. As critics since at least Cleanth Brooks and Robert B. Heilman, in their influential New Critical textbook *Understanding Drama* (1945), have argued, Shakespeare's Henriad holds in continuous tension the values of the court world and the values of the tavern world. Brooks and Heilman, however, as Hugh Grady has suggested, could not entirely accept a relativistic interpretation of Shakespeare, and so the formula of balance which they developed in their commentary to *Henry IV, Part I* ended up valorizing, if only very slightly, the social over the personal, politics over friendship.[15] As Grady demonstrates, however, throughout much of their discussion Brooks and Heilman come very close to a deconstructive solution to the relativistic dilemma facing them by hesitating again and again to choose one interpretation over another.[16]

Welles, I would suggest, does deconstruct this antinomy, along with many others. Shakespeare's Henriad can be shown to comprehend a large cluster of binary oppositions that are posed as potential choices for Hal—court/tavern, honor/dishonor, Hotspur/Falstaff, Henry IV/Falstaff, time/timelessness, word/being, serious/nonserious—where either the first term is the privileged one or where both terms have been suspended in an uneasy equilibrium, leaving to Hal the task of determining which to choose, or indeed if a choice has to be made at all. In Welles's film, these paired alternatives are unbalanced, diminished, reversed, or exploded. Shakespeare's Hal has always already made the choice, though he appears to be choosing all the time. For Welles's Hal, the choice possesses genuine and insoluble problems.[17] The various embodiments of "positive" values, what I have simply termed "History," have little exemplary force in *Chimes at Midnight*, tending at times to degenerate, at the level of language, into the incoherent babbling of poseurs, cynics, and fools. At the same time, any attempt to bypass language, to ignore the power of words, leads inevitably to destruction. Here, Falstaff stands as the cautionary figure, and his desire to abolish language and put sheer physicality in its place becomes the tragic fulcrum upon which Welles's film turns.

Although Welles has said that, for him, Falstaff is "the greatest conception of a good man, the most completely good man, in all drama,"[18] *Chimes at Midnight*, as James Naremore has argued,[19] presents a far more ambivalent portrait of Falstaff than these words suggest. Welles's view of Falstaff had, of course, been formed in the 1930s, but again and again in his career he demonstrated his tenacity at sticking to a conception once he had formed it. Nonetheless, by the time of *Chimes at Midnight*, he could not have been unaware of the 1951–52 Stratford Festival productions of the *Richard II* to *Henry V* cycle whereby Falstaff (as interpreted by Anthony Quayle) was, to a considerable extent, desentimentalized. Here, one needs to emphasize the distance between what Welles tells us and what we see in the film. We cannot doubt that Welles sympathizes, both as director and as actor, with Falsfaff's desire to bypass language and thereby gain access to an unmediated reality. At the same time, we know, and Welles knows, that in a fallen world such a desire is folly. And we know as well that, like many Wellesian heroes, Falstaff longs for an Edenic world only because he has long since forfeited it.

Welles's Falstaff, in any case, is far from the jolly knight seen in various theatrical interpretations of the role. Rather, he seems more the corrupt, gross "misleader of youth" that Hal and others claim he is. Some readers have seen two Falstaffs emerging from the two parts of *Henry IV*, the second considerably less pleasant than the first. But whether the Falstaff of Part II is really a different character from the Falstaff of Part I, or whether he evolves naturally in the course of the two plays, Welles chose to combine both Falstaffs in his performance. To Peter Bogdanovich, Welles claimed that "the closer I thought I was getting to Falstaff, the less funny he seemed to me. . . . I found him only occasionally, and then only *deliberately*, a clown."[20] One critic, commenting on Shakespeare's Henriad, claims that "Jolly Falstaff has too much dominated our thinking. He is not a comic character in the second part nor finally in the first. He *plays* a clown in the first part, just as he *plays* in the second a pathetic old man closer to his real self."[21] As Welles interprets the role, even Falstaff's bonhomie and sentimentality are, to some extent, fraudulent.

It may be simply an effect of Welles's performance style but, whatever the cause, his Falstaff appears always to be acting, to be manufacturing the appropriate, expected response, fitting each emotional note to what will most please or placate Hal. In a film whose imagery centers significantly on faces and bodies, Welles's own face becomes an especially sensitive indicator of many moods and feelings only suggested by the words he speaks: Falstaff's geniality, his cowardice, his weariness at Justice Shallow's ramblings, his suspicions of Hal's intentions, and his final humiliation and defeat, all find expression in Welles's plastic features. Welles's Falstaff is, in Beverle Houston's felicitous phrase, a "Power Baby," both in temperament and in appearance, an "eating, sucking, foetus-like creature"[22] whose benignity is an illusion. Prelinguistic, he is forever locked in the imaginary world of infancy. Like Kane, like Arkadin, like Quinlan (*Touch of Evil*, 1958), like Clay (*Immortal Story*, 1968), Falstaff is fundamentally, irredeemably corrupt. A larger-than-life figure flawed by hubris, he tragically collaborates in his own destruction.

Welles's interpretation of Falstaff, both as director and as actor, and his reshaping of Shakespeare's texts are two of the primary ways he undermines the historical and rhetorical foundations of the Henriad. He additionally employs stylistic, expressive devices that have a similar effect. History and (verbal) rhetoric are constantly displaced, replaced by Welles's nervous, erratic, decentered, unstable visual and aural style, a flow of images and sounds that thoroughly dismantle Shakespeare's text, peeling away layers of strategically placed and carefully joined verbal and thematic checks against confusion. In this context, the inadequacies of the sound track become at least as much a matter of Welles's intentions and methods as a matter of technical flaws—though flaws there certainly are, as Welles has publicly lamented.[23] In some shots, for example, the actors deliver their lines as they, or the camera, or both, are in rapid motion.[24] Or a character will make an important speech from the depths of an extreme long shot, depriving us of lip movement and facial expression, both important cues for the understanding of unfamiliar language and syntax. Furthermore, Welles constructs jarring editing patterns that easily distract from the spoken word. At several points, even what Welles has structured to resemble continuity editing turns into something unexpected. A simple reverse shot, for example, may involve illogical changes in time and/or space. These and other stylistic idiosyncrasies help to explain why we can follow the sound track of *Chimes at Midnight* more easily if we keep our eyes closed. In effect, Welles generates a constant tension between what we see and what we hear,[25] a tension that points to the ambiguous status of language in its relation to action.[26]

Welles further exhibits his ambivalence toward rhetoric in his handling of soliloquies. In his previous Shakespearean films, as we have seen, Welles had already suggested some discomfort with filmed soliloquies, resorting to a variety of voice-over techniques in *Macbeth* and in *Othello* having some of his actors deliver soliloquies and speeches with their backs to the camera. In *Chimes* Welles virtually does away with soliloquies as such by not allowing anyone to speak directly to the camera or to be truly alone: Hal's revelation (in Shakespeare, to the audience only) that his madcap humor is primarily for show ("I know you all") is spoken in Falstaff's presence; Falstaff delivers both his catechism on honor and his later dissertation on the virtues of sherris-sack directly to Hal. Even King Henry is not allowed a true soliloquy. His famous meditation on sleep, to choose a notable instance, though filmed in a single, uninterrupted take and in close-up, becomes an address to his courtiers; he is not, as he is in the play, alone. All soliloquies have thus become, at least implicitly, attempts at conversation, at communication within the diegetic universe, and not, as soliloquies can be, privileged moments where language provides a more or less unmediated access to thought.[27]

We can see Welles's strategy ideally realized at that moment when Hotspur—whose bath has been interrupted by the pressing demands of history—cries "That roan shall be my throne" and simultaneously drops the towel in which he has draped himself and turns away from the camera, revealing his bare behind. Hotspur's towel falls in the midst of a highly rhetorical gesture, a wide sweep of the arm that, having forgotten its anchoring function, serves as punctuation for his words. Welles comically undermines Hotspur's rhetoric, lays bare his linguistic bravado, and—with some affection—ridicules his historical pretensions, his (partly unconscious) desire for the English throne. Hotspur's words have already been mocked throughout this scene by the trumpeters who echo his belligerent posings with elaborate, comic fanfares. The trumpets say as much as he does, and are equally meaningful as rational statements. Hotspur's dropped towel suggests an additional meaning as well, one contiguous with that just described: for a moment, Hotspur reveals the physical he tries to deny or push aside in the semiplayful, semiserious exchange with his wife, Kate, that follows this scene. The dropped towel signifies the return of the repressed, canceling Hotspur's attempt to replace sensuality with rhetoric (war, history, etc.), to deny the body by asserting the word.[28]

In what is perhaps the most remarkable sequence in *Chimes at Midnight*, the battle of Shrewsbury, Welles presents us with another kind of history—

a history stripped of all rhetoric, denuded of language, and at the same time supremely eloquent. Here the rhetorical dismemberment of the body politic, the scenes of accusation and counteraccusation between the royal party and the highborn conspirators, become displaced and mocked by the literal dismemberment of the body physical. In this sequence, Welles both imitates and ironizes Laurence Olivier's battle of Agincourt in *Henry V* (1944; both Olivier and Welles, in different ways, owe much to Sergei Eisenstein's "battle on the ice" sequence in *Alexander Nevsky*, 1938). When Kenneth Branagh made his Prince Hal film (*Henry V*, 1989), he showed his debt to Olivier throughout, but it was to Welles he turned for the battle of Agincourt. Though Welles thoroughly demystifies warfare throughout the film, nowhere does he do so as dramatically and compellingly as at this moment. "The social consciousness of the movie is as alert as Shakespeare's," Daniel Seltzer wrote in an early, astute reading of the film, "and thematically pertinent in Shakespearean terms too: . . .the footage of the Battle of Shrewsbury itself must be some of the finest, truest, ugliest scenes of warfare ever shot and edited for a movie."[29] *Chimes at Midnight* emerges here as very much a sixties film, a film that, like *Dr. Strangelove* (1964) or *Culloden* (Peter Watkins, 1964), takes a bitterly sardonic view of politics and warfare.[30]

In the Shrewsbury sequence, Welles forcefully underlines the brutal, unheroic character of hand-to-hand combat in a nervously edited mosaic of varied shots, some photographed with a handheld camera, some filmed with wide-angle lenses, some in slow motion, some speeded up, some shots static and others that employ swish pans or other kinds of rapid movement, together with a complex, many-layered sound track of shouts and screams, of the clash of sword against sword, armor against armor, of grunts and cries and cracking bones. In the words of James Naremore, in this sequence "the underlying eroticism of the chivalric code . . . is exposed in all its cruel perversity."[31] Welles conjures up Armegeddon, a nightmare vision of destruction which points up the futility of this or any other war. By the end, both armies have become one huge, awkward, disintegrating war machine, a grotesque robot whose power source slowly begins to fail and finally comes to a frozen halt. Verbal rhetoric—language itself—seems, for the moment, both irrelevant and obscene.

In this context, the highly verbal King Henry IV, the only character in the film whose words and speeches are allowed their full Shakespearean weight and style, stands in ironic counterpoint to the carnage of Shrewsbury. As John Gielgud plays him, and as Welles directs his scenes, King

Henry is reduced to a nearly disembodied voice. The most "poetic" and rhetorical figure in Welles's film, he is also the most ethereal. Cold, pinched, ascetic, photographed sitting on or standing near his throne set on a high stone platform, his face illuminated by a harsh, white light, he is an isolated, distant figure of overbearing but brittle authority. As Falstaff seems to be all flesh, Henry seems all words. But even the king's voice fails him: he can neither govern his son with it nor tame the rebels, who refuse to credit his verbal promises. Henry's highly rhetorical manner, meant to gloss over his insecurities and fears, finally serves to reveal them. His voice becomes an object of parody: at various points in the film, Hotspur, Hal, and Falstaff all imitate Gielgud's immediately recognizable vocal characteristics. The "beauty" of Henry's speech only serves to place in an even harsher light his asceticism, coldness, and largely self-imposed isolation; a supreme poseur, he cannot see beyond his role. Although never really alone, Henry seems to speak only to himself.

King Henry's dependence on words becomes ideally focused in a scene Welles has totally refashioned from Shakespeare. After the battle of Shrewsbury, Falstaff takes credit for killing Hotspur, spinning another one of his outrageous lies for Hal's benefit. Welles gives the scene a special emphasis by having King Henry present as Falstaff tells his tale. The king, for once, says nothing, and Hal, too, is silent, but their faces tell a clear enough story. Earlier, Hal had told his father that he would redeem himself for his bad behavior "on Percy's head / And in the closing of some glorious day, / Be bold to tell you that I am your son." Now is the moment when this prophecy should come true, when the moving rhetoric should be realized in action. But Hal fails to make good on his promise. Unwilling to expose Falstaff, he refuses to say the words his father so much wants to hear, and the moment slips by. The silence, emphasized by a series of static close-ups, takes on precise thematic significance. We can tell, from Henry's expression, that he knows very well who killed Hotspur, but the knowledge, without the words, is not enough. We see, too, the conflict within Hal. And, finally, we can read in Falstaff's face his understanding of what the other two are thinking. For all three as well as for us, silence acquires a rhetorical force ordinarily reserved to speech.[32]

If the world of kings overvalues words, the tavern world fatally undervalues them. In the tavern world (which for my purposes includes the Justice Shallow scenes), words are acknowledged to mean very little. Falstaff's notorious lies, and the ease with which everyone sees through them, are symptomatic, but many of his cohorts share his linguistic deviance. Shal-

low constantly reminisces about the old days, but "every third word" he
speaks, according to Falstaff, is "a lie." Falstaff's hanger-on, Ancient Pistol,
is perhaps the most unintelligible character in the film. In Shakespeare, he
is already rhetorically tedious: his primary function is to cast in ironic light,
through highflown speeches and outrageous behavior, the chivalric code.
But in a world where rhetoric and history are so constantly and thoroughly
brought into question, Welles takes the extreme course of reducing Pistol
to little more than noise. Against Pistol's meaningless bombast, we have
Silence's inability to say anything at all. Welles afflicts him with a stutter so
severe that he cannot complete his sentences. Shallow must speak for him,
must become in effect his voice (a nice joke in a film where so many characters are clearly dubbed, a number of them, including Westmoreland and
the Sheriff, by Welles himself). Words are interchangeable, attach themselves to no one in particular, have no individual meaning. Speech, in short,
appears to be as debased through undervaluing in the tavern world as it is
debased through overvaluing in the court world.

The difficulty of penetrating language, of determining the truth and
weight of words, of reading history, comes to be, in especial, Falstaff's
dilemma. Falstaff distrusts words; in a sense, he himself has nothing to say,
certainly nothing with which to answer King Henry, who is all speech, all
words, the very incarnation of logos. Falstaff's own words are frequently
unintelligible, or nearly so, because he wants to deny the efficacy of language. Welles the actor here exaggerates his post-*Citizen Kane* tendency to
downplay the orotund and avuncular qualities of his vocal delivery by
deliberately "throwing away" words and lines and even entire speeches. He
even adopts a peculiar accent in which, for example, "my" is pronounced
"me" ("Who picked me pocket"), a kind of parodic devaluation of proper
Shakespearean diction somewhat reminiscent of John Barrymore's Shakespearean speech, an "Americanization" through vernacular emphases: we
might be reminded here of how W. C. Fields played Mr. Micawber. But
though words may be questioned, subverted, and parodied, they cannot be
abolished. Falstaff's refusal to credit words at all leads to his undoing. Even
Hal's words—especially Hal's words—mean little to Falstaff, though Hal is
at great pains throughout to make his motives clear.

Welles's presentation of Hal, an attractive, appealing prince as played by
Keith Baxter, runs counter to some modern, especially theatrical, views of
the Henriad which condemn him as a cold, hypocritical careerist who
cynically uses Falstaff for his own ends. Welles's Hal is a poignant figure, in
part because the film puts significant weight on a theme barely present in

Shakespeare: the suggestion that Hal will have to face loneliness in power as his father did before him. This is especially evident in the tense scene (Shakespeare's *Henry IV, Part II*, act II, scene ii) between Hal and Poins, the tavern acquaintance who seems closest to Hal in age and general demeanor, a scene which, in part because Welles allows it its full verbal weight and films it with a generally still camera, receives a particular emphasis that it does not carry within the context of the Henriad as a whole. Both Hal and Poins recognize that something has come to an end, and Hal recognizes as well that the "friendship" between them has been based on a hope of gain on Poins's part ("But is this true, Ned, must I marry your sister?") and has involved a great deal of deception, especially self-deception.[33] Poins, a sour, rather nasty fellow, is clearly using Hal, just as Hal and Falstaff use each other. Genuine affection there may be in all of this, but it is virtually impossible to separate it out from a good deal of cynicism. Hal's ultimate allegiance to historical necessity finally makes friendship impossible.

Although it may be true that, as Bridget Gellert Lyons claims, "in his alliance with Falstaff he [Hal] has reservations that are more visible to the film's viewer than to the inhabitants of either the tavern or the court,"[34] it is also evident that Welles softens Hal's character by deliberately distorting Shakespeare's text at several points in order to stress Hal's straightforwardness. I've already noted that Hal's revealing "I know you all" meditation is no longer a soliloquy in the film; it is delivered in Falstaff's hearing, the second half of it spoken directly to him. Falstaff may or may not be able to hear each word of Hal's speech, but he can certainly gather its import. Similarly, when Hal, pretending to be his own father at the end of the famous play scene, tells Falstaff that he will indeed banish him ("I do; I will"), he gives the words a moving, near-elegiac tone that renders their meaning unmistakable to anyone not as bent on self-deception as Falstaff is.

Against language, Falstaff posits being, presence, physicality. We are made aware, throughout Welles's film, of Falstaff as sheer physical mass. His huge figure—sometimes just his face alone—often dominates the frame. Although he enters the film from the far distance of an extreme long shot, a small, round object on the horizon, he gradually moves toward the camera until his head alone fills over three-fourths of the image, leaving what remains to his companion, Shallow. In the play scene, two men and a boy must help Falstaff onto his makeshift "throne." Before the battle of Shrewsbury, his followers valiantly attempt to raise him to his saddle with block and tackle, only to drop his armor-encased body to the ground. The stairways and corridors of the Boar's Head tavern seem too narrow for his passage. The point is made most strikingly in the Gadshill episode, where Falstaff's monk's robe transforms him into a huge white tent which sharply contrasts with the thin, black trees that surround him. Falstaff's girth is, of course, a running joke in Shakespeare, but Welles goes out of his way to elaborate on the theme; he seems intent on suggesting the extent to which Falstaff's world is physical, corporeal, of the flesh. Falstaff's relationships are expressed in predominantly tactile ways, his rotund figure giving others, especially Hal and Doll Tearsheet, something to grasp, to hold on to, or— in Doll's case—to climb on.

But Falstaff's corporeal substance cannot prevail over the demands of history, and his final defeat, appropriately, has a specifically linguistic dimension: Hal's rejection of him is a rhetorical act, the new king of England's maiden speech, the son's entrance into the symbolic world of his father. (By staging this scene in the midst of the coronation ceremony, Welles puts the emphasis as much on Hal's humiliation as on Falstaff's.) Falstaff's response to Hal's elaborate, majestic, and witty rebuke is nonverbal: we must read it in Welles's expression. What we see are emotions in conflict: awe, perhaps pride (this is *his* king, after all), and a wistfulness not unmixed with cunning (is he already thinking of a "starting hole," a way out?). The dominant emotion, however, is disbelief: Hal's words cannot be meaningful, they are rhetoric only; Falstaff sees through and beyond them. Shakespeare's Falstaff, we feel, indulges himself in sheer bravado when he tells Shallow, "This that you heard was but a color . . I shall be sent for soon at night."[35] For Welles's Falstaff, these words suggest not bravado so much as a deeply felt hope, a nearly desperate attempt to render words meaningless. But Hal not only means what he says, he now has the power to turn words into deeds, and his words and deeds kill Falstaff.

In keeping with his method throughout the film, Welles strips even Falstaff's death of easy sentiment. Mistress Quickly's description of Falstaff's last moments functions as a piece of information for a clearly unmoved Poins; spoken with Falstaff already in his coffin, her words lack the immediacy they have in Shakespeare's *Henry V.* Welles barely prepares us for this crucial finale: one moment Falstaff is alive, if crushed; the next moment he is dead. No illness, no tears, no bedside scene as in both Laurence Olivier's and Kenneth Branagh's films of *Henry V.* Only a final irony: words continue to fail Falstaff, even after death. In a complete departure from Shakespeare's text, Welles concludes his film with the image of Falstaff's coffin passing away in the distance while on the sound track Ralph Richardson recites a passage from Holinshed's *Chronicles of England, Scotland, and Ireland*, a passage in praise of King Henry V, who, we are told, "was so humane withal that he left no offense unpunished or friendship unrewarded."[36] Whatever we may think of the truth or justice of Holinshed's words, one irony, at least, is certain: in *Chimes at Midnight*, a film that thoroughly reveals the hollowness of kings and their fine words, language and history stubbornly abide when all else is gone.[37]

There is in the end no unity, however, no final point of stasis to which *Chimes at Midnight* arrives. The death of Falstaff is not the death of Merrie England, since, as I have argued, Welles's film bears no trace of this sentimental concept. Welles himself, it should be noted, became somewhat uncomfortable with the Edenic vision: "Even if the good old days never existed," he told Bogdanovich, "the fact that we can conceive of such a world is, in fact, an affirmation of the human spirit."[38] Nothing has been finally resolved, or could be resolved, by any ending Welles could have fashioned. My discussion of rhetoric and history points to something I recognize in the text of Welles's film, but my discussion, like nearly all discussions of *Chimes*, pretends to find a far more coherent text than in fact can be found. When, for example, Anthony Davies, a sensitive reader of Welles's film, claims that "the function of the landscape [in *Chimes at Midnight*] is specific,"[39] he is treating the film as if it were more neat and precise than it really is. At a certain level, *Chimes*, like Welles's late films in general, approaches something resembling pure cinema, images and sounds that have an emotional and intellectual resonance apart from rational discourse. Welles's film, in this regard, is both more and less than interpretation allows us to discover.

The critical reception of *Chimes at Midnight* took place in a somewhat different context than had obtained for Welles's previous Shakespeare films. The release of *Chimes* marks a moment when Welles, pretty much written off by Hollywood, a prophet with very little honor in his own country, had achieved, in Europe, the status of international auteur, an artist at the top of the pantheon. Interviews and commentaries began to appear regularly in the pages of *Cahiers du Cinéma* and elsewhere in the 1960s, the decade that, of course, saw auteurism become the dominant theory in film studies. We thus know what Welles had to say about *Chimes at Midnight*, what his intentions were in making the film, and how he regarded the final product, to a greater extent than for almost any of his other films. One interview, which deals largely with *Chimes*, was first published in Spanish in the journal *Griffith*, then translated into French (from the Spanish? from the original English?) for *Cahiers*. Portions of the original English text were then published in the British journal *Sight and Sound*, while an English translation of the French translation appeared in the American publication, *Cahiers du Cinéma in English*, edited by the premier American auteurist, Andrew Sarris. Since each version arranges the questions and answers in a slightly different fashion, it is not possible to reconstruct with absolute confidence what Welles might originally have told his Spanish interlocutors. My point, in any case, is that what Welles had to say about a film he was working on was considered by European cinephiles and their American disciples to be of considerable significance.

In spite of all of that, Welles was unfortunate, once again, in the release and distribution of his film in the United States, though the reviews were, all in all, more favorable than he might have expected. Bosley Crowther, predictably, was mean-spiritedly dismissive ("Mr. Welles has always wanted to play Falstaff. Now he's had his chance. Those who are interested may see him at the Little Carnegie"),[40] but Crowther was no longer the prime voice of American film criticism; in fact, he was becoming something of an embarrassment. New, younger voices were now making themselves heard, though they were not yet as influential as Crowther and the *New York Times*. Pauline Kael, then writing in the small-circulation *New Republic*, and Judith Christ, in the *World Journal Tribune*, were far more sensitive to what Welles had accomplished. Kael called the film "a near-masterpiece,"[41] and Christ was almost unreservedly enthusiastic. Once again, however, it is highly unlikely that even positive reviews would have made a commercial success of a black-and-white Shakespeare film, especially one as idiosyncratic as this one. Whatever his intentions, Welles had produced a film essentially alien from the Hollywood norm: he had, in Jonathan Rosenbaum's apt formulation, "entered the treacherous domain of the avant-garde"[42] and had ceased, for all intents and purposes, to be a popular artist and had instead become a cineaste in the European mold.

Chimes at Midnight has in fact been described on a number of occasions as Welles's most personal film; biographers, in particular, have been quick to provide a more or less psychoanalytic explanation for Welles's impulse to play Falstaff and to restage and reconfigure this particular Shakespearean scenario, one rife with the psychodynamics of fathers and sons, of betrayal, abandonment, and regret, not to mention the literary and mythic echoes of the Prodigal Son story. Jack Jorgens makes the parallels with Welles's personal experience explicit: "To a man who directed and starred in a masterpiece and has since staggered through three decades of underfinanced, hurried, flawed films, scores of bit parts, narrations, and interviews which debased his talent, dozens of projects which died for want of persistence and financing, the story of a fat, aging jester exiled from his audience and no longer able to triumph over impossible obstacles with wit and torrential imagination might well seem tragic."[43] Apart from the dubious biography here, and conceding that a biographical reading has its uses, the point needs to be made that Welles performed Falstaff at the age of sixteen, at the age of twenty-three, at the age of forty-five, and at the age of fifty. Presumably, the psychodynamics would be rather different each time.[44]

This is not to deny, however, that Welles was remarkably consistent in the way he approached aspects of the play. Robert Hapgood has noted that Welles made "essentially the same selection of materials from *Henry IV* [for the film script] as for the two stage versions."[45] In both early scripts, a narrator spoke passages from Holinshed. Even in 1939, reviewers commented on Welles's downplaying of Falstaff's humor. Photographs of *Five Kings* suggest that Welles, in 1939, staged the Shallow/Silence/Falstaff "chimes at midnight" scene in a manner very similar to the mise-en-scène he employed in the film, and, again on the basis of photographs, his design for the Boar's Head Tavern in the film echoes the 1939 designs.[46] Even the battle sequence, so "cinematic" in all of its elements, was already remarkable in *Five Kings*; Welles's Mercury associate, the actor and director Martin Gabel, described the effect:

> He [Welles] must have imagined the medieval battlefields as a sort of no-man's land, like in World War I, with everybody fighting over it and uprooting it and so forth. So, he had a single leafless tree for the scene, and a lot of mounds on the stage covered with tarpaulin painted to look like Belgium after Ypres, or Mons, or what-have-you.[47]

Even Welles's use of a large revolving turntable, which proved mechanically disastrous, reminded viewers, when it worked, of a cinematic effect. In a way, Welles was already making a movie.

Without rejecting the biographical influence on *Chimes*, one needs, nonetheless, to see Welles's film as part of a theatrical tradition, a tradition from which he drew and to which he continued to contribute. Welles was clearly aware, over the years, of theatrical interpretations of the Henriad. He had seen Ralph Richardson (as Falstaff) and Laurence Olivier (as Hotspur and Shallow) in the famous Old Vic production of the two parts of *Henry IV* in 1946,[48] and he very likely knew of the Anthony Quayle staging of the the entire second tetralogy (*Richard II* plus the two *Henry IV* plays and *Henry V*) at Stratford-upon-Avon in 1951, a production notable for the way Hal's final rejection of Falstaff was prefigured repeatedly by earlier mini-rejections and for the darker-than-usual presentation of Falstaff himself.[49] The downgrading of Hotspur from a charming, if doomed, hero—which is the way Welles thought of him in 1960[50]—to a slightly ridiculous posturer, too, may have been influenced by reports of Roy Dotrice's performance in Peter Hall's RSC production which had opened at Stratford some six months before Welles began filming in Spain.

And Welles, in various ways, can be said to have influenced subsequent productions of the Falstaff plays. One rather unexpected influence was reported by Joss Ackland, who played Falstaff in 1982. Ackland claims not to have been inspired by Welles's performance of Falstaff, but by

> the real Orson Welles. . . . As a man Welles exploded brilliantly, and then didn't know where to go. Like Falstaff, I believe he could have achieved so much, but it was frittered away. He gives everyone a lot to laugh about and he can laugh at it too. But inside he is crying. He can see the waste, because he is not a stupid man.[51]

(This, presumably, is the psychoanalytic explanation, but backwards.) Barbara Hodgdon saw the influence of *Chimes* in Terry Hands's "predominantly elegiac" 1976 production,[52] and Michael Bogdanov in 1986 incorporated Welles's idea of having Falstaff appear before King Henry with Hotspur's body. Kenneth Branagh, as I have noted, was influenced by Welles in the direction of his battle sequence in *Henry V*, and his interpolation of the rejection of Falstaff (as flashback) very much recalls the regretful, pained tone of Keith Baxter's Prince Hal. *Chimes at Midnight*, in short, has become a text that can be claimed equally by those whose interest in Welles is primarily an interest in cinema and by those who study the ways Shakespeare's plays have been reconfigured and revivified via various cultural venues. To put it somewhat differently, the symbiosis of Shakespeare and Welles fulfills itself in a text that does more than justice to a complex of Shakespearean themes while it effectively summarizes and distills much of what we know as the Wellesian cinema.

EIGHT

Welles as Performer

—

From Shakespeare to Brecht

Virtually anyone who has seen *The Third Man* (Carol Reed, 1949) remembers Orson Welles as Harry Lime, especially his first appearance—his "entrance," as it were—more than halfway through the film. When Harry's friend Holly Martins (played by Welles's friend Joseph Cotten) first senses his presence, Harry is standing in a doorway, all but his shoes hidden by the darkness. A light goes on in an upstairs room, illuminating his face. After several cuts—to Holly's reaction, back to Harry, to the woman in the window—the camera moves in for a close-up. Harry Lime's expression is pure Welles: head slanted down, eyes glancing up, eyebrows slightly raised, the skin on the outside of his eyes crinkled, the lips formed into the hint of a smile. Welles's performance here, witty and highly self-conscious, points back beyond Harry Lime to the actor-personality who plays him. Here's what you've been waiting for, Welles seems to be saying, the most interesting character in this film, portrayed, not surprisingly, by the most interesting actor. Welles enters the film much like a rabbit pulled from a magician's hat; we know the rabbit is going to come out (that's what we have come to see), but we are still pleased and impressed when it does. Indeed, Welles's whole performance in *The Third Man* takes on the aspects of a magic trick. Because Lime figures so centrally in the story (he is, after all, *the* third man of the title), and because other characters mention, discuss, describe, and allude to him so frequently, we experience the role, and hence Welles's presence in the role, as far more extensive than it really is. Welles transforms what is essentially a guest appearance into a star turn.

His performance as Harry Lime can serve to remind us that for all of Welles's accomplishments as producer/writer/director in radio, theater, film, and television, his fame derives perhaps as much from the projection of a specific and readily identifiable public persona. As even a cursory glance at the currently available biographies reveals, Welles was, from earliest infancy to the end of his life, quintessentially a public performer, sometimes as a real-life personality—boy wonder, magician, storyteller, bon vivant, pitchman—and sometimes as a professional actor; often, as both at once. Even if we limit our definition of performance strictly to professional acting, we find ourselves immediately at the center of the Wellesian universe. Orson Welles as writer, director, and producer invariably focused his energies, one way or another, on Orson Welles the actor. He appears in or narrates all his completed films, most often in a leading or major role. But even in a relatively minor role—Hastler in *The Trial* (1962), for example—Welles makes an impression out of proportion to his time on screen. His acting career, indeed, proves the old theatrical dictum that there are no small parts, only small actors. Welles was always a large actor, in more than the obvious way.

It seems all the more surprising, therefore, that Welles the actor has seldom inspired the sustained attention Welles the director receives as a matter of course.[1] The oversight can in part be explained by the sheer difficulty involved in attempting to analyze the art of acting in the absence, until quite recently, of adequate theoretical paradigms.[2] Equally to blame, perhaps, has been Welles's own tendency to dismiss his acting as merely something he did in order to raise money for more important activities. Even when they occur in his own films, however, Welles's performances tend, in the critical discourse, to be overshadowed by and in a sense absorbed into considerations of his authorship. More generally, his distinctive qualities as a professional actor have been collapsed into a view of him as a personality, a real-life "performer" on the lecture platform, the talk-show circuit, the various radio and television commercials that seemed to occupy him in his last several decades. Welles, furthermore, appeared in so many "bad" films over the years, a number of which remain virtually unseen, that the critical community eventually ceased to regard him at all seriously as an actor.

Although Welles was able to shape his acting persona into a key element of his creative personality, he has been perceived, almost from the beginning of his career, as representing excess, as someone whose acting lay outside the boundaries of what was acceptable or at least desirable in the twentieth century.[3] Among the variety of barbed practical jokes played on him when he arrived in Hollywood, buoyed up by a uniquely generous contractual arrangement with RKO studios, one in particular reflected an attitude that dogged him throughout his career: he was sent a large, smoked ham, decorated, as Welles himself was at the time, with a beard. This view of Welles, which he would live up to in a number of ways, had perhaps as much to do with the context in which his performances took place as it did with the specifics of his performance style. Welles was a ham in part because of his association with stylized roles—in particular with Shakespeare and with what may broadly be designated as "Shakespearean" characters. By the age of twenty-five, Welles had played, professionally, a rather remarkable variety of parts. In Shakespeare alone, on stage, radio, and recordings, he had played Macbeth; he had played Hamlet, Claudius, Fortinbras, and the Ghost of Hamlet's father; Brutus, Cassius, and Marc Antony in *Julius Caesar*; Mercutio, Tybalt, and Chorus in *Romeo and Juliet*; Malvolio and Orsino in *Twelfth Night*, and Shylock and the Prince of Morocco in *Merchant of Venice*.

That he may or may not have "overacted" by one standard or another is almost beside the point. He was associated with Shakespeare, with larger-than-life characters like Marlowe's Faustus, Buchner's Danton, and Mac-Gaffey in Archibald MacLeish's *Panic*. On the radio, he not only played the necessarily flamboyant Lamont Cranston ("the Shadow"), but Count Dracula, Long John Silver, Edward Rochester in *Jane Eyre*, Conrad's Kurtz, Sherlock Holmes, Edmond Dantes in *The Count of Monte Christo*, and Sidney Carton in *A Tale of Two Cities*. Some of these roles were staples of the nineteenth-century popular theater, the kinds of roles that actors in the Romantic tradition excelled in. Henry Miller, James O'Neill, and William Gillette spent good parts of their careers playing, respectively, Sidney Carton, Edmond Dantes, and Sherlock Holmes. In other words, Welles drew from a repertoire of characters associated with a nineteenth-century acting tradition, a tradition that, from the perspective of the 1930s and 1940s, was thought of as old-fashioned, excessively histrionic, unrealistic, and actor-centered—vehicles for outsized egos.[4] In the 1940s, Eugene O'Neill would depict, in barely disguised form (*Long Day's Journey into Night*), his father's long career playing in *The Count of Monte Christo* as a tragic waste of talent.

As an actor in the movies, furthermore, Welles has necessarily been judged according to a fairly narrow standard. Richard Dyer has summarized the general view of what constitutes "good acting" in film as "the elaboration of character within a loose narrative structure and upon naturalistic devices such as interrupted speech, hesitation, mumbling, tics and other techniques that give an air of improvisation to the performance."[5] By these standards, of course, Welles's performance style in film could seldom be mistaken for "good acting." Though actors are sometimes rewarded for what might otherwise be thought of as excessive performances—John Wayne, an otherwise low-key performer, was given his Oscar when, late in his career, he gave a highly mannered, self-parodying, *excessive* performance of an eccentric character in *True Grit* (1969)—such performances generally take place within a context where excess is part of the film's essential visual and thematic strategies. The highly flamboyant performance Lee J. Cobb gives in *On the Waterfront* (1954) can be accepted in part because of the contextual support both of the Method actors who surround him and of Elia Kazan's expressive mise-en-scène and dramaturgy.

Welles's particular excess stems in part from the theatrical mode he nearly always brought to his films, by which I mean that his approach to a role, his method of attack, was closely tied to specific theatrical devices. As Virginia Wright Wexman notes, "On stage actors are prone to use wigs, makeup, and costume to project a variety of images. On screen they are more likely to employ less obvious strategies such as hair coloring, plastic surgery, and weight control to project a single image that operates intertextually."[6] Welles, notoriously, nearly always depended on wigs, makeup (he seldom wore the same nose twice), and costume to construct something like a Brechtian alienation effect, to *look* as well as *be* theatrical. His acting repertoire was more or less consciously drawn from a wide range of performance styles, from the "histrionic" at one end to the "verisimilar" at the other, to adopt terminology employed by Roberta Pearson in her discussion of acting in Griffith's Biograph films,[7] just as his roles ranged widely over a historical spectrum.

Even considered in the context of a hit-and-miss acting career—he appears at times not so much to have chosen his roles as to have been chosen by them—Welles managed to act in films that draw on a variety of theatrical modes, including Greek tragedy (Tiresias in *Oedipus the King*, 1967), Renaissance plays (various Shakespearean roles), American thirties' style social realism (as reborn in *Compulsion*, 1959), fifties' style family melodrama (*The Long Hot Summer*, 1958), Theatre of the Absurd (his own *The Trial*), and free-form improvisation (the films he made with Henry Jaglom, especially *Someone to Love*, 1987). In *Citizen Kane* (1941), and perhaps uniquely in that film, the distinct acting styles Welles adopts in his portrayal of Charles Foster Kane contribute richly to the meaning of the film by serving to characterize each stage in Kane's physical and moral development. Never again in Welles's career, however, will actor, role, and mise-en-scène mesh so definitively: his control over his performance has only infrequently been as absolute, even in his own films.

Along with adopting numerous performance modes, Welles has functioned within a wide variety of performance contexts. In his own films, Welles the actor complements Welles the director. Both as actor and as director, he expresses a desire to control, to amaze, to shock, to perform magic; his impulse is toward the flamboyant, toward what may not improperly be called mannerism. In other people's films, Welles's acting presence frequently turns into an authorial presence. The question here becomes not the tired one of whether Welles literally directed parts of, say, *Jane Eyre* (1943) or *The Third Man*, but whether his style of acting, his presentation of self, does not in fact become a form of direction, a way of imposing himself on the film. In a similar vein, one can see Welles's acting as sheer survival. Throughout his career, Welles acted in films not only for money, I would argue, but also to keep the phenomenon of "Orson Welles" alive as phenomenon. His performances, at times condemned as "hammy," excessively theatrical turns, "Shakespearean" in a negative sense, function as something like bold-faced quotations or bracketed areas within the body of the film-texts (a number of them otherwise uninteresting) in which they appear: for example, *Moby Dick* (1956), *The Long Hot Summer, Compulsion*, and *A Man for All Seasons* (1966).

In many of these films, Welles manages to carve out an area in the discourse which he uniquely dominates, sometimes throwing the governing tonality of the film off-kilter with what appears to be a minimum of time and effort. Frequently, both the official and unofficial publicity surrounding a particular film takes special note of Welles's contribution, making space for yet another commentary on the phenomenon of Orson Welles. Richard Fleischer's *Compulsion* provides a good example. Welles's time on screen is relatively brief and confined to the last third of the film. In compensation, he delivers a ten-minute monologue near the very end that gives him complete control of the film-text not only while on screen but, so compelling is he both in terms of context and mise-en-scène, retrospectively for the entire film. Playing against the grain of the film's somewhat overheated intensity, Welles delivers a powerful condemnation of capital punishment in a resolutely antirhetorical style, one pitched more to the intimacy of the camera than to the diegetic courtroom audience. In the publicity for *Compulsion*, what became important is that Orson Welles played Clarence Darrow (he is called Jonathan Wilk in the film); *Life* magazine, blithely ignoring the filmmakers' fictional pretenses and at the same time deliberately confusing actors with characters, headlines its story on the film "Orson Welles, as Darrow, Defends Leopold, Loeb," and goes on to praise "one of the longest and certainly one of the most gripping soliloquies ever filmed."[8]

Life's use of the term "soliloquy" points, I believe, to the essentially Shakespearean manner Welles brings to so many of his roles, whatever the context. By Shakespearean, I am alluding to the tradition of performance Welles inherits—the outsized, grandiloquent, egotistic, "royal" approach to performance that I briefly discuss in chapter 1. The Shakespearean aspects of Welles's acting personality, however, are balanced by a quality that can be found in Bertolt Brecht's discussion of the "epic" actor. The epic actor, as Brecht conceived him, is first and foremost an instructor, one who speaks his part "not as if he were improvising it himself but like a quotation." Emotions, Brecht believed, had to be externalized; an actor must not "allow himself to become completely transformed on the stage into the character he is portraying." Instead, he should be constantly engaged in a "direct changeover from representation to commentary."[9] "Even if he plays a man possessed he must not seem to be possessed himself," Brecht wrote, "for how is the spectator to discover what possessed him if he does?" (193). Ideal acting, for Brecht, needed to be "Witty. Ceremonious. Ritual" (26). Although the epic actor does not aim for empathy in the usual sense of the word, he nevertheless must "put some artistry into the act of showing" (194). As Walter Benjamin remarked, "The art of the epic theater consists in producing astonishment rather than empathy."[10] The epic actor always appears in a double role: as the character he plays and as the actor who plays him. This is how he produces the *Verfremdungseffekt*, the making strange, that Brecht considered essential to any genuine theatrical experience.

In certain roles and at certain moments in all his roles, Welles approaches the Brechtian ideal of performance. What Welles most obviously shares with Brecht, apart from a lifelong interest in Shakespeare, can best be described as an irresistible pedagogic impulse. From *Citizen Kane* on (and before *Kane* on stage and in radio), Welles combined performance with a desire to explain the meaning of his performance. Welles interprets his roles for us, projects both the emotion required by and the explanation of each dramatic moment. His performance style hearkens back to the rhapsodes of ancient Greece. "A sort of combination actor and teacher of literature," the rhapsode "gave public recitations from the *Iliad* and the *Odyssey*, especially of the more exciting passages; and he undertook to deliver critical and moral lectures."[11] Here one recalls, in particular, the appearances Welles made on television in the mid-1950s when he was rhapsode and Shake-spearean at once. His makeup box in front of him, he would discuss some aspects of *Othello* or *Macbeth* while applying the greasepaint and wig and false whiskers required for a portrayal of the eponymous heroes of those plays. He would then recite one of the famous speeches or soliloquies. To a certain extent, of course, all acting combines emotion and interpretation, but Welles makes the combination particularly visible, foregrounds the interpretation, demystifies performance.

Welles adopted a decidedly pedagogic manner in his radio work, func-tioning simultaneously as presenter and presentee, as master of cere-monies/narrator and as star. As presenter, Welles would be urbane, engag-ing, informative, and, nearly always, slightly pompous in terms both of the content of the narration and the style of presentation. One might describe this as a self-conscious pomposity, as if he were quite aware of the pre-sumption of a man in his early twenties functioning simultaneously as pro-ducer/director/narrator/actor/writer—a veritable "Johannes-factotum," to employ a description applied to the young Shakespeare by a contem-porary. This rather arch self-consciousness remained in his personal appear-ances—those moments when he played "himself"—throughout his life, but it informs his other performances as well, providing a clue that points to the pedagogic aspect of Welles's performance style. The knowing gaze and its aural equivalent, what might be termed the knowing voice, with their promise of secrets revealed, of something rich and strange, or at least bizarre, become salient characteristics of Welles's histrionic gestures.

Welles, furthermore, delights in playing characters who have occasion to recite pointed moral tales—exempla, minisermons, parables, or anec-dotes of one kind or another.[12] Consider Gregory Arkadin's tale of the scorpion and the frog in *Mr. Arkadin* (aka *Confidential Report*, 1955), Harry Lime's brief comparative history of Italy and Switzerland in *The Third Man*, Michael O'Hara's shark frenzy story in *Lady from Shanghai* (1948), or Charles Rankin's dissertation on the German character in *The Stranger* (1946). In *The Trial*, in his roles as narrator and as K's advocate, Welles twice recounts Kafka's allegory of the law. He appears as Father Mapple in John Huston's *Moby Dick* only long enough to deliver a sermon on the theme of Jonah and the whale. *F for Fake* (1973) indulges in this mode from begin-ning to end; the entire film might be considered an extended anecdote. Much the same could be said of *The Immortal Story* (1968). At other times, the effect is more subtle, more a matter of Welles adopting the exemplary style than recounting an actual exemplum. As Quinlan in *Touch of Evil* (1958), to cite a minor example, Welles gives an especially pointed, anecdotal emphasis to his remarks to the murder suspect, Sanchez: "There was an old lady on Main Street last night picked up a shoe . . . and the shoe had a foot in it. We're going to make you pay for that, Sanchez."

Welles's oft-reviled, self-directed performance in *The Stranger* can be best understood in terms of this pedagogic tendency wedded to a Shakespearean approach to performance. As Franz Kindler, a Nazi war criminal who has eluded his postwar pursuers and is hiding under the assumed name and identity of Charles Rankin in a small, picture-postcard New England town, Welles acts in a highly presentational manner, never letting us forget for a moment the overwhelming evil Kindler represents. Joseph McBride, otherwise highly sympathetic to Welles, describes his performance as Kindler/Rankin as "impossibly hammy" and adds that it "just about single-handedly destroys the story's tenuous credibility."[13] If, however, we approach the film with some Brechtian principles in mind, Welles's work here in fact makes a good deal of sense and contributes a rich and complex dimension to an unjustly neglected film. The key to understanding what Welles achieves in *The Stranger* lies in seeing that the actor and the character are locked in an irresoluble conflict: Welles's desire to expose Franz Kindler as a mad Nazi is in direct opposition to Kindler's desire to keep that fact well hidden. Welles wants to play Kindler, while Kindler wants to play Rankin. In this contest, Welles wins throughout.

Welles's Kindler is, like Shakespeare's Richard Crookback, so transparent a villain, so clearly not what the all-American inhabitants of Harper, Connecticut, think him to be, that America's complacency and naïveté become dominant issues in the film, just as, in *Richard III*, the imperceptiveness and doggedly willed innocence of Richard's victims create a continuous ironic tone to the drama. Welles performs in such a way that no member of the film audience could possibly make the error his fiancée, and nearly everyone else with whom he comes into contact, make. Almost as if afraid of allowing the evil of Nazism to appear even momentarily attractive, Welles refuses to act out the charm and plausibility that other characters presumably see in Franz Kindler. Much like Iago in *Othello*, Welles here adopts an extreme form of what James Naremore, following Erving Goffman, discusses as "disclosive compensation," a convention that allows actors "to reveal information to the audience without much regard to the other characters,"[14] itself, of course, a very Shakespearean mode. Welles performs for the audience *of* the film, not for the audience *in* the film. He could be responding directly to Brecht's dictum that "everything to do with the emotions has to be externalized; that is to say, it must be developed into a gesture."[15] Throughout *The Stranger*, Welles delivers even the most inno-cent-sounding lines with the guilty subtext clearly indicated, continually providing commentary in tandem with representation.

No film performance, of course, can be separated from its context: the mise-en-scène of Welles the director has as much to do with his con-struction of Kindler as do the gestures, movements, expressions, and vocal modulations of Welles the actor. Our first close-up view of Welles in *The Stranger* illustrates the point and establishes the tenor of his performance throughout. He is initially seen in profile, his hair somewhat disheveled, his face heavily shadowed, the whites of his eyes, in contrast, brightly illumi-nated. As he glances furtively around, he seems almost savage and slightly mad, an effect intensified by antirealistic makeup. Welles looks, in fact, much as he does in the Republic *Macbeth* after the killing of Duncan. On one level, his manner and appearance throughout are perfectly under-standable: according to the conventions and rhetoric of such fictions—conventions and rhetoric the film is in fact establishing—he behaves pre-cisely as a Nazi war criminal should. The problem, from the viewpoint of Hollywood naturalism, is that almost no one in the film notices any of this, at least on the conscious level. On the contrary, Kindler/Rankin is referred to at one point as "above suspicion." His pursuer, speaking of Nazis in gen-eral and of Kindler in particular, claims that "they look like other people and act like other people—when it's to their benefit." Given the whole tenor of Welles's performance, these words are very nearly ludicrous: he never looks or acts like "other people" at all. Here again, the Brecht effect can be qualified by the Shakespeare effect: just as, in *Othello*, we are appalled and irritated with the gullibility of Iago's victims, so, in *The Stranger*, we become impatient with the self-delusion, the willed innocence of the "good" characters.

As Franz Kindler, Welles may reach an extreme in "alienated" acting even for him, but his performance in *The Stranger* nevertheless underlines a characteristic effect of his acting persona, especially as that persona oper-ates in his own films. Time and again, Welles the actor, like Welles the direc-tor, subverts classical cinema's tendency to construct coherent subjects and seamless narratives. Even when Welles plays a more or less "straight" lead-ing man, as he does in *Lady from Shanghai*, he does so in such a way as to deconstruct the whole concept of the Hollywood hero. Michael O'Hara, admittedly, is a film noir protagonist and hence a highly compromised hero to begin with, but Welles, in his triple function as actor, writer, and director, intensifies the compromise. Welles's Michael O'Hara presents a handsome enough appearance, in a baby-faced sort of way, and if we charitably ignore his lumbering walk and the poor figure he cuts in sports coat and trousers, we might be tempted to accept him as a film noir hero. But Welles conspires against Michael O'Hara at every turn. About three minutes into the film, O'Hara participates, with near-comic ineptness, in a clumsily staged fist fight, in the course of which he defeats several opponents in violation of all known laws of pugilism. O'Hara's voice-over narration makes the matter explicit: "I start out in this story a little bit like a hero, which I most certainly am not," he tells us. "When I start out to make a fool of myself, there's very little can stop me," he had remarked moments earlier. One begins to suspect that Welles has written these lines as an apology for playing a role more suited to, say, Robert Mitchum or Burt Lancaster or Glenn Ford.

At the same time, other moments in *Lady from Shanghai* seem to counter Michael's self-deprecating tone and manner. "Mike's got a lot of blarney in him," his pal Goldie comments, "but he knows how to hurt a man when he gets mad." Later in the film, a radio news story identifies Michael as "Black Irish O'Hara, notorious waterfront agitator." We have, however, seen absolutely nothing of these notorious activities. All the allusions to how much of a tough guy O'Hara is seem, in fact, calculated precisely to call his toughness into doubt. Although quite capable of playing dangerous men, Welles deliberately avoids doing so here. Throughout *Lady from Shanghai*, in short, a tension exists between the way the genre wishes to construct Michael O'Hara and the way Welles, primarily though not exclusively as performer, chooses to construct him. If, as Barbara Leaming claims, Welles was actually reading Brecht at this time,[16] he must have found there ample justification for much of what he does in *Lady from Shanghai*. But, as I have been suggesting, a reading of Brecht would only have reinforced a tendency already well developed in Welles's practice. Brecht, who responded with unwonted enthusiasm to Welles's stage production of *Around the World* (1946), calling it "the greatest thing I have seen in American theater.... This is what theater should be,"[17] had already recognized in Welles a fellow spirit.[18]

Nearly all of what characterizes Welles as a performer can be identified in *Citizen Kane*, where he gives a dazzling exhibition of his versatility and

control. Welles not only "does everything" as a filmmaker, he "does everything" as an actor as well. Both as filmmaker and as actor, he marries theater and film, high culture and low, the elite and the popular. In playing
Charles Foster Kane at different ages and in vastly different circumstances,
Welles can be said to employ a number of distinct acting styles, from the
relative naturalism of the scenes where Kane is still a young idealist, to the
heightened formalism of the scenes depicting Kane's final years at Xanadu.
Adopting and adapting a long and varied heritage of acting, Welles fash-
ions from it an overwhelming presence, one made up, dialogically, of other
performances, other presences. His experience in theater and radio, and his
notoriety in both media, contribute significantly to this process.

Welles's cinematic "entrance," in fact, seems to allude immediately to his
fame as a radio actor. He "appears" initially as a mouth and a voice, a huge
mouth in extreme close-up which speaks the single word "rosebud" in a
slightly hoarse, closely miked, weary, scratchy old man's voice. Welles, the
"boy wonder," thus begins his film life as an old man. Here we seem to
have a further personal allusion, this time to Welles's theater work, where
playing old men (like the octogenarian Captain Shotover in Shaw's *Heart-
break House*) had already become something of a Welles specialty. This
opening also suggests the importance Welles gives to his voice as a principal instrument of performance; his voice, in a sense, "comes on" before the
rest of him, makes an entrance for him, prepares his way.

"Voice" figures importantly in the middle sequences of the film as well,
where Welles the orator relishes the speechmaking and uses his voice, with
its distinctive harmonies, together with gesture and movement, in such a
way as to re-create elements of a nineteenth-century romantic tradition of
acting, a tradition associated, as I have noted earlier, with Shakespearean
actor-managers. Ironically, however, Welles says nothing for much of the
first quarter of the film. In the "News on the March" newsreel, he appears,
necessarily, as a silent film actor: he cannot speak until the advent of synchronous sound recording, and then his first words are "Don't believe
everything you hear on the radio," simultaneously alluding to his "War of
the Worlds" broadcast, calling into question the status of discourse, especially public discourse, within the narrated world of *Kane*, and undermining the efficacy of speech in general. In the silent film sequences, he gives
a notably striking presentational performance: as Kane the political candi-
date, he imitates the supposed excesses ("hamminess") of silent film actors,
gesticulating broadly, acting with his entire body. The jerky movements of
these "silent film" sequences prefigure Welles's performance as the old

Kane, where he adopts the movement and behavior associated with the extremes of German expressionist film acting, finally becoming, in the scene where he destroys his wife's bedroom, a Golem-like robot, a virtual automaton.

Welles's self-consciousness as an actor in part contributes to the presentational, Brechtian texture of his performances. One seldom has the impression of Welles losing himself in a role. (The actor, Brecht wrote, must "make himself observed standing *between* the spectator and the text.")[19] In this context, his claim that he "really felt" the emotions that went into Kane's breaking up of Susan Alexander's bedroom becomes difficult to credit, since what we see on the screen seems almost inhumanly mechanical and calculated.[20] Indeed, Welles's self-consciousness sometimes works against the grain of a particular dramatic moment. When, for example, Kane is interviewed for the radio (in the newsreel), he wears the external manifestations of curmudgeonly old age uncomfortably. Similarly, in the scene of Kane's return from Europe, Welles's awkwardness and diffidence seem bizarrely out of key, unrelated to anything the scene has been constructed to express.

Most of the time, however, Welles's self-consciousness becomes a key element in his characterization of Kane. This is especially true in the early *Inquirer* sequences, where we see the young Kane take on his role of crusading publisher with at least some awareness of the distance between his experience and his ambition. We sense here an air of improvisation, as if all the principal characters—Kane, Leland, Bernstein—were trying out their new roles. Pauline Kael's suggestion that Welles appears "almost embarrassed to be exposed as so young"[21] correctly gauges the effect; both the writing and the performing points to an identity between the young Kane and the young Welles. In the confrontation between Kane and Thatcher, in particular, we can see Welles quite deliberately producing his own screen persona. Photographed in three-quarter right profile, Welles is favored by the camera throughout, his movement and the way he points his lines determining when and where the camera will move. In what is virtually a single take (actually, the scene is managed in two takes, a long one followed by a very short "payoff" take), Welles modulates between a variety of attitudes and tones, from commanding presence, to self-righteousness, self-conscious posturing, irascibility, exuberance, and wit. Carefully prepared for by all that has preceded it since the film began, this scene indelibly stamps the Orson Welles phenomenon on the consciousness of the moviegoing public.

Not surprisingly, given the themes and concerns of *Citizen Kane*, we frequently find ourselves unable to separate Welles's performance from the "performing" nature of Kane himself. Both as a public and a private figure, Kane frequently performs for a variety of audiences, so that much of the time Welles is performing as a performer, acting as an actor. This, too, of course, provides a Brechtian coloring to his interpretation of Kane. Thus, the Shakespearean, oratorical style that Welles adopts for the middle-aged Kane, appropriately focuses on a delineation of Kane's political career. The "Boss Jim Gettys" speech, a specifically public act, necessarily demands an oratorical, stentorian method, though Welles nicely combines this with an easygoing, low-key charm. Leaning forward toward his audience, he gestures broadly, waiting out, with perfect timing, the desired response from his listeners. The whole "performance" here, though totally convincing, seems at the same time insincere, calculated, unspontaneous. Even Kane's casual gesture of salute to his son asks to be read as premeditated. Does Kane mean what he says when he speaks of helping the working man and the slum dweller? Does Welles mean what Kane says? Clearly, both Kane and Welles are performing here, and we are thus left unable to determine precisely where sincerity ends and insincerity begins. In the "Love Nest" scene that immediately follows the political rally, Welles draws on the same resources and employs similar techniques, but the charm disappears, casting the meaning of the previous scene in even greater doubt. Kane, as Welles interprets him, is a public figure even in private: he uses his body and, especially, his voice to dominate, to intimidate, to take center stage. "Voice" now becomes a signifier of Kane's tyrannical hold on those around him, so that Welles's authority as a performer cannot be distinguished from Kane's authoritarian personality. Although he stands shadowed in the background during much of this scene, Welles/Kane totally controls its dynamics.

If Charles Foster Kane as a dramatic character never comes entirely into focus, as a number of viewers have felt, this is in part because we never see him except as a commentary on himself, a receptacle whose every action and emotion serves to reveal the judgment others, including Orson Welles, have made on him. Indeed, apart from the brief moment at the beginning of the film when he dies, Kane only exists in the context of another character's narration. At the same time, he is also always a subject of Welles's "narration," not only in Welles's role as enunciator, but in his role as actor as well. Considered as a totality, Welles's performance in *Citizen Kane* is tailored especially to express Kane's power, the sheer forcefulness of his personality and position. Many of the roles Welles has chosen to perform over the years, both in his own films and in films directed by others, exhibit a similar projection of power. Welles has himself commented on this tendency:"You know, in the old classic French theater, there were always some actors who played kings and others who did not. I'm one of those who play kings. I have to, because of my personality."[22] Even when not cast as the king, he finds a way to be king. In *Chimes at Midnight*, where he plays Falstaff to John Gielgud's King Henry IV, he manages both to "play" the king, briefly, and to dominate the film in a kingly fashion. Such "kingly" roles allow Welles the luxury to express outsized emotions, to give full play to the rhetorical, to be, in short, excessive.

It is in this sense of excess that we find what Brecht would call the "gestus" of Welles's performance as Kane. The gestus, for Brecht, meant more than gesture; it covers, as Martin Esslin explains it, "the whole range of the outward signs of social relationships, including 'deportment, intonation, facial expression.' "The gestus was thus a "clear and stylized expression of the social behavior of human beings towards each other."[23] In performing as Kane, Welles does not so much embody a set of psychological traits as construct a commentary on the shifting and varied aspects of Kane's life and career. Welles's performance becomes the primary conduit for a critique of the romantic myth of American capitalism.[24] Whereas the script allows for an ambivalent response which includes a residue of sympathy for Kane, Welles as actor thoroughly and unsentimentally judges Kane and all that he represents. Kane, as Welles interprets him, has no personality, no wholeness, no self. Just as there is no center to Kane apart from power, so there is no center to Welles's performance apart from the power with which he expresses himself and dominates the film image. Welles's performance—showy, eccentric, cunning, vigorous, versatile, precocious, fragmented, domineering—ironically reveals in its richness and plenitude the fundamental emptiness of Charles Foster Kane.

Welles's post-*Citizen Kane* performances were many and varied. One might, somewhat arbitrarily, group them into categories: Shakespearean clowns and kings (Macbeth, Othello, Falstaff, Lear on stage and television) and roles of "Shakespearean" weight (Tiresias in *Oedipus the King*, for example, or Ahab in his own stage adaptation of *Moby Dick* and Father Mapple in John Huston's film version); historical or pseudohistorical figures (Cardinal Wolsey, Benjamin Franklin, Cagliostro, Cesare Borgia, Winston Churchill, Robert Fulton, Louis XVIII, Jonathan Wilk, etc.); and a large gallery of more or less corrupt, frequently sinister figures of power and/or wealth (Franz Kindler, Harry Lime, Edward Rochester, Quinlan, Will Varner, Gregory Arkadin, Max Buda, Hastler, General Dreedle, and many others). To these groupings we must add those guest appearances, on television talk shows, variety programs, and commercials of all sorts, where Welles either plays some version of a character called "Orson Welles"—that is, a character who, though a fictional construct, nevertheless reflects aspects of the Orson Welles persona as it was constructed over the years— or where he literally plays "himself" in documentary films, in semifictional films, and in his own "essay films,"[25] *F for Fake* and *Filming Othello*. (And he continues to be a guest star of sorts after his death: witness his "cameo" in Tim Burton's *Ed Wood* [1994] or his haunting presence in Peter Jackson's *Heavenly Creatures* [1994].) Welles, of all film performers, was always both himself—that is, a recognizable "real" person, someone pre- or extra-filmically famous—and a theatrical construct; he was always someone who, even when (perhaps especially when) being "himself," was a performer, and who, even when most disguised in a role, most "performing," was most himself, most clearly "Orson Welles."

The appeal for an actor and the effect on an audience of the special guest appearances Welles so frequently made was explained by Welles himself in a discussion with Peter Bogdanovich apropos of Harry Lime in *The Third Man*:

> In theatre, you know, the old star actors never liked to come on until the end of the first act. *Mister Wu* is a classic example—I've played it once myself. All the other actors boil around the stage for about an hour shrieking, "What will happen when Mister Wu arrives?," "What is he like, this Mister Wu?," and so on. Finally a great gong is beaten, and slowly over a Chinese bridge comes Mister Wu himself in full mandarin robes. Peach Blossom (or whatever her name is) falls on her face and a lot of coolies yell, "Mister *Wu*!!!" The curtain comes down, the audience goes wild, and everybody says, "Isn't that guy playing Mr. Wu a great actor!" *That's* a star part for you! What matters in that kind of role is not how many lines you have, but how few.[26]

Although there are other reasons for the effectiveness of Welles's Harry Lime, the "Mr. Wu" factor, as Welles was quite aware, contributed significantly to the kinds of performances he was regularly called upon to give, and it was an effect he manipulated even in the films he directed himself, generally for sound narrative and dramatic reasons, most notably *Touch of Evil* and *The Trial*.

Although the phrase "guest star" seems to put as much emphasis on "star" as on "guest," Welles was not really a conventional star, if by that we mean primarily a romantic leading man, except for a brief period in the early to mid-1940s, roughly from *Citizen Kane* to *Tomorrow Is Forever* (1946); he was always more of what is popularly known as a character actor. The distinction between star and character actor, a vocabulary that is part of the Hollywood discourse but may not be entirely meaningful outside of it, is not clear-cut. A "star" is, presumably, not an "actor" at all, but centrally a performer who again and again plays him or her self, who is, in a sense, *expected* to play him or her self. As Edgar Morin has written, "The star is more than an actor incarnating characters, he incarnates *himself in them*, and they become incarnate in him."[27] A character actor, on the other hand, is first and foremost an actor: the "character" part of the phrase suggests a specific construction, or an infinite sequence of constructions—a character actor, by implication, plays something other than him or her self (i.e., plays a "character"), by which is meant not only a precisely delineated individual but also a role provided to the actor from the outside.

In practice, of course, this distinction is illusory, if not actually perverse. Some stars are character actors—Paul Muni, Dustin Hoffman—and many, if not most, character actors come to function very like stars, become adept at playing slight variations of a single persona, whether that persona be James Gleason or William Gargan or Brian Dennehy or J. T. Walsh. Welles, I would suggest, is a star as character actor, or a character actor as star. He constantly played "himself," quite literally when enacting some version of "Orson Welles," something he began to do quite early in his career, appearing as "guest star" on the Jack Benny or Fred Allen radio shows. He was a performer who brought to his roles a nexus of associations that went beyond, and had little to do with, the intertextual references stars ordinarily bring from the other roles they have played at other times. The relationship between the role Welles played in one film and the roles he had played in other films was not nearly as significant as the way his personality outside of the movies (or theater or radio) could be fed back into a specific performance. Starring as "Orson Welles" always gave Welles his best-known, most recognizable "role."

In one period of his career as a movie actor, Welles would sometimes be given star billing for what was essentially a guest performance. In *Prince of Foxes* (1949), for example, his billing is virtually equal to Tyrone Power's, even though he occupies far less screen time. But Welles gives the impression of being more central in part because he has a grand entrance at the beginning of the film and an equally impressive exit near the end. In his other moments on screen, he imbues the role of Cesare Borgia with extra-textual irony and with a flair and sweep that make this evil character quite attractive. Welles characteristically works against the grain of the script; he seems far too self-aware and to hold too ironic a view of life to be the cruel and vindictive despot the film wants him to be. Even the presence in the film of Everett Sloane, a longtime Mercury Theatre associate and cast member of *Citizen Kane, Journey into Fear,* and *Lady from Shanghai,* provides an extra frisson; it is to Sloane that Welles delivers his final line in the film: "Then your future's assured—depending on which one of us is hanged first." Here, for a brief but significant moment, we have the sense of two actors who have also been colleagues winking at each other, and some-thing of the "real" Orson Welles world—the Mercury Theater and all that—seems to have insinuated itself into the text.

The somewhat paradoxical nature of his billing versus his actual partic-ipation in *Prince of Foxes* reinforces the suggestion that Welles became a "guest star" because he was only marginally a "real" star, or, to put it another way, because his real stardom was essentially himself, his public persona. He was a guest because he had no "home" of his own, no stable place in which to locate himself; he was a guest because he had been a guest before, because his identity was that he was a guest, a "guest star," a specialty act. That Welles's performances are nearly always bracketed to one degree or another both allows us to make sense of an otherwise seemingly incoherent series of roles and appearances in what are often forgettable, and forgotten, films and at the same time goes a long way to explaining the decidedly mixed reception his career as a performer has inspired. Very much like a nonactor or amateur performer, Welles, even when playing himself—that is, when playing a character identified as "Orson Welles"—at times exhibits signs of self-consciousness and discomfort: he doesn't seem to know quite how to be himself, or to remember or reconstruct exactly what being himself might mean. Given the multiplicity of roles Welles has taken up, or been required to take up, in the course of his career, this is not entirely surprising. In *F for Fake* or *Filming Othello,* the effect can be disarming: what may, at some level, be merely unease projects itself as modesty, tentativeness, and self-deprecating humor.

Like the "witnesses" in Woody Allen's *Zelig,* Welles has also enacted more or less fraudulent versions of himself, as he notably does in the appro-priately titled *F for Fake.* Unlike the various celebrity "real people" of Allen's film, however, Welles's performance does not call forth the discomfort and even irritation we frequently experience when celebrities discuss fictional persons and events as if the latter were part of the same reality as the speakers. Welles's persona, his authority to speak, is always implicated in a good deal of fraudulence, of fakery, of sleight of hand. When Welles speaks authoritatively, that authority necessarily has an ironic component, an irony that has in part been constructed through his always ambiguous relationship to commodification and commercialization. Hence, his early authority as host (as well as producer, writer, star) of the radio program "First Person Singular," produced by CBS without a sponsor for its first season, was very quickly co-opted and compromised when Campbell Soups took over sponsorship at the beginning of the second season. Insofar, in other words, as he was a spokesman for Campbell soup—or, later, Lady Esther beauty products, American Airlines, Paul Masson wines, and so forth—his opinions and his ideas, together with his image and voice, were to a certain extent bought and paid for, even if, at times, he managed to subvert his role as salesman through ironic excess.[28]

In virtually all his performances, Welles's "real" identity as "Orson Welles" tends to overwhelm whatever identity he has as an actor. In particular, when Welles appears in his own films, especially in the later ones, we are just as aware of his function as the film's director as we are of his function as a specific character. We are familiar, of course, with the effect of a recognizable director like Alfred Hitchcock making an appearance in his own film; whatever the motive underlying that appearance, it breaks, if only for a moment, the fictional matrix and at the same time introduces material evidence of authorship. But even when the director is also an actor, as with Welles in most of his films, or with, say, Jerry Lewis or Woody Allen or Spike Lee, our knowledge that the performer and the director are one colors the scenes in which he appears. We are conscious of a peculiar "doubling" effect with characters like Hank Quinlan in *Touch of Evil* or Mookie in *Do the Right Thing*; what such characters say and do almost always takes on an authority that seems to speak simultaneously from inside and from somewhere outside the film.

If Welles's film performances call attention to themselves, it is in part because that is one effect of the "guest star" phenomenon and in part because Welles, as we have seen, deliberately sets himself against the dominant tonality of the film in which he appears by adopting a style that provides something in excess of, or at least different from, what the project or the role demands; he often interferes with or works at cross-purposes to, the norm of his context. This is not simply a matter of inflated ego, as if

Welles saw himself as essentially superior to the material and hence wanted to draw all attention to himself; it is more of a conspiracy with the audience, a conspiracy that seems to say, "you and I, together, can make this work, can salvage pleasure and even significance from what at first sight appears to be unpromising material indeed." He needs, in other words, to justify his presence and maintain his value, his guest star status.

In the thoroughly mediocre *Black Rose* (1950), for example, Welles's performance (as Bayan, a Mongol warrior!) is oddly inflected through the adoption of peculiar speech patterns and, more significantly, by his projection of the impression that the character he is playing possesses secrets not only unknown to the other characters but forever unknown to us as well; here, the peculiarity of Welles's performance is reinforced by the generally lackluster proceedings in which he finds himself. His eccentricities can be interpreted in part as the defensive maneuver of someone with energy and ideas but with no real control over the filmmaking process. By the same token, Welles can, in a more interesting film like *Compulsion*, produce something like the opposite effect. Given an overheated, slightly hysterical film style, he withdraws, closes in, and consequently calls attention to himself through restraint rather than histrionics.

On other occasions, Welles gives the appearance of having constructed a film's mise-en-scène around himself, even to have taken control of a film's narrative strategies. It is difficult to determine how much input Welles may or may not have had on a particular project (he was usually coy and inconsistent on this issue in interviews), so we can only speculate about specific instances. In Martin Ritt's *The Long Hot Summer*, for example, Welles's presence and persona nearly take over the film, or at the very least structure the sequences in which he appears, even though he has a subsidiary role. Although the writers have conceived Will Varner in wildly inconsistent terms—he begins as an overbearing, Tennesse Williams near-sadist, a cross between Big Daddy and Boss Finley, and ends the film as a "sentimental old fool"—Welles, all greasy makeup, sloppy appearance, and lines delivered in a calculated manner and inflected with a dubiously "southern" accent, gives the role a larger-than-life theatricality that balances out the hysterical Method "hot" of Anthony Franciosa as well as the self-conscious Method "cool" of Paul Newman. Indeed, Welles so dominates the concluding section of *Long Hot Summer* that the narrative appears to have been about him all along. In five successive scenes, bridged by shots of Will Varner tearing along the Mississippi countryside in his jeep, and each conceived quite differently in mood and tone, Welles interacts with each of the film's major characters, thereby becoming the crucial narrative link among them all, while giving the appearance of resolving the various strands of the film's loose narrative construction. At literally the last moment, Varner/Welles has simply taken control of the film and has provided it with meaning.

Welles's frequent appearances as "narrator," a role that defines as well as anything can his uniqueness as a performer, provides him with another way of seeming to shape material over which he had no real control. His easily recognizable, highly authoritive manner of speaking allowed him to be featured in films and television, as well as in the more obvious media of radio and sound recordings, as a voice only,[29] to such an extent that "Narrated by Orson Welles" became, depending on the context and occasion, a promise of a variety of specific moods or tones: importance, significance, seriousness; mystery, weirdness, the strange; false seriousness, comic portentousness, camp. In nearly all such vocal performances, Welles is not simply the narrator; he is very much a "guest star," and when the film or video is a documentary, his may be the name that appears first in the publicity material, the name used to sell the project. At its most "serious," the voice of Welles is the voice of God (literally, when he reads paraphrases from the gospels as voice-over for Nicholas Ray's *King of Kings*); at the other end of the scale, presumably, we have Welles as narrator of *Bugs Bunny Superstar*. But whether employed "straight" or for purposes of parody, each instance of narration depends for its effect on the *authority* of Welles's voice, its ability to transcend the mere materiality of the spoken word, to invest words with an excess of meaning, with, quite precisely, *resonance* in both its acoustic and its metaphoric sense.

Though it is perhaps inevitable to speak of Orson Welles as always playing himself, he has, of course, simultaneously played numerous small "character" parts along the way. He made a virtual career of appearing in a particular, and peculiar, genre, what we might call the International Coproduced Historical Spectacle—a genre that presents a number of featured actors from different countries, speaking in a variety of accents or dubbed into a language other than their own, playing historical or pseudohistorical personages in a few brief scenes or single, self-contained segments. A characteristic example would be Abel Gance's *Austerlitz* (aka *Battle of Austerlitz*, 1959), a French/Italian/Yugoslav/Lichtenstein coproduction which features, in addition to Welles, Jack Palance, Claudia Cardinale, Leslie Caron, Michel Simon, Rossano Brazzi, and Vittorio De Sica. The presence of more or less well-known performers in these films lends "color" and texture and a certain verisimilitude to the narrative, while the limited and often self-contained nature of their contributions conveniently keeps to a minimum their actual time on the payroll. In this genre, the recognizability of the performer becomes a guarantee for the historicity of the character. Our ability as viewers to recognize "Orson Welles" contributes to the aura surrounding "Benjamin Franklin" (*Si Versailles m'était conté* [*Royal Affairs in Versailles*], 1954, and *Lafayette*, 1963) or "Cardinal Wolsey" (*A Man For All Seasons*) or "Louis XVIII" (*Waterloo*, 1970), and entirely constructs the historical reality of lesser-known figures Welles enacted, like "Hudson Lowe" (*Napoleon*, 1954) or "Robert Fulton" (*Austerlitz*).

Welles's "Mr. Wu" anecdote not only illustrates the effect of a well-timed, delayed entrance; it also shows how a relatively small role can be given a weight and significance far in excess of the amount of time and space it actually occupies. If we think of "character" in film as a complex intertwining of a variety of discourses and signs including audience foreknowledge, appearance, speech (both by the character as well as what others say about the character), gesture, action, structure, and mise-en-scène,[30] the guest star in a brief or cameo appearance must necessarily rely more on some signs than on others. Audience foreknowledge—what the spectators already know about either the performer (star image, for example, but also, in the case of nonactors, fame in general) or the character (historical figures or types), or both, together with such pointers as what others say about the character—will be among the most useful ingredients in the construction of a cameo, whereas matters of structure, action, and mise-en-scène will, of necessity, be relatively less important.

As a cameo or guest performer, Welles was thus very likely to play already constructed characters: there is little opportunity, in a cameo, to develop the character through narrative action or even to suggest the possibility of change. Such characters are, in a sense, prefabricated, characters who need to be met, to some degree or other, on their own terms; there is nothing to discover about them: he or she is simply there. Their words and actions are preordained because already known, always already known. What else can Louis XVIII do but leave Paris at the news of Napoleon's approach (*Waterloo*)? He has always left Paris. Welles, in his two brief scenes (one of which he plays with the Marshall Ney of Dan O'Herlihy, his 1948 Macduff), lends an element of pathos and comic irony to the king's departure; beyond this, however, there is little he can or needs to give to the role—he simply, for a brief moment, *is* Louis XVIII, though, at the same time, the king simply *is* Orson Welles.

Even when playing historical characters, however, Welles does not merely inhabit them—his performances almost always provide us with something in excess of or apart from the character he plays, and that something might be described precisely as that which defines Welles as a star, that part of Welles that resists assimilation into the character he is playing. Welles's performance style in film might be said to provide us with a denial of the so-called Kuleshov effect. That famous experiment, as related by V. I. Pudovkin,[31] was meant to demonstrate that the meaning we read into a performer's expression is almost entirely a matter of the context created by montage, by editing. Juxtapose a shot of an actor's face with a funeral, and his expression is interpreted as sad, but instead show a laughing baby, and that very same expression will be read as happy. Welles's acting style, however, is a mise-en-scène style, not a montage style. It is nearly impossible to read anything *into* Welles's physical image, impossible for the filmmaker to manipulate the meaning of that image: Welles give us more than the film's editing strategies can possibly reveal. It is not the context provided by other shots that supply the significance of his performance; rather, it is what is intrinsic to the performance that provides meaning to the surrounding shots.

Over a period of half a century and more which saw dramatic shifts in modes of narrative and the rapid development of new media, Welles always found a way both to be himself—to insist, that is, on his uniqueness as a public persona—and at the same time to parlay the various aspects of his public persona and public activities into performance, into a wide variety of roles that provided him with the material means to work on his own projects. As star, guest star, narrator, host, cameo, or specialty act, among other incarnations, Welles was quite literally a *marginal* performer for most of his post-*Citizen Kane* career, a figure almost always in brackets of one kind or another—part joke, part savant, part fraud, part highbrow, part sideshow freak, part carny huckster, and—an aspect of Welles perhaps too seldom on view—part a witty, commonsensical, insightful commentator on virtually any topic under the sun. Perhaps only in his final screen appearance, in Henry Jaglom's *Someone to Love*, released in 1988, more than two years after Welles's death, does Welles seem nakedly "himself," a wise, witty, somewhat avuncular but never pretentious sage/raconteur. With a characteristic mixture of domineering ego and self-deprecating irony ("I'm speaking from the cheap seats, not from Mt. Sinai"), he gives the impression of having injected himself into the film retrospectively, directing himself, as it were, from the grave, shaping his scenes into a tribute to Orson Welles: the film only ends after Welles himself says "Cut.

It may have been self-serving for Welles, at around the age of twenty-five, to claim that "the theatre is nothing except an actor." He went on, however, to make a more complicated claim, one that seems to forecast his whole performing career. After asserting that "there is nothing in the theatre of great moment but Shakespeare," he adds that "audiences don't need Shakespeare, but the actor does. . . . When acting becomes good enough, it is a substitute for a good play."[32] By the end of his life, if not long before, Welles's "real" self had become impossible to distinguish from his acting personality, a personality shaped and sustained by an internalizing of his understanding of Shakespeare. So that even—indeed, especially—when playing himself, Welles was a Shakespearean actor who "put some artistry into the act of showing," who remained to the end imbued with the wit and ceremonious manner, the sense of fun and the need to teach, that for Brecht defined the height of the actor's art.[33]

Epilogue

In retrospect, we can now see that Welles's Shakespeare activities could not, in themselves, restore Shakespeare to his nineteenth-century eminence. For one thing, American culture had itself changed and nothing could bring back the model Lawrence Levine reconstructs in *Highbrow/Lowbrow* (Levine's model itself is not above revisionist modification),[1] except in extremely local and particular ways. Insofar as Welles was able to be a "Shakespearean" at all, it was, more often than not, precisely when the quotation marks were in evidence. Shakespeare was acceptable when bracketed in some fashion, as part of something else, one item on a varied menu. In this sense, perhaps, Welles's activities were not that far removed from those famous Mark Twain hucksters to whom I have already referred, the King and the Duke. Like them, though not quite to the same extent, Welles was willing to play fast and loose with the works of the immortal bard, to ladle out his Shakespeare in dribs and drabs. He was, as we have seen, at certain times and in certain circumstances heir to the "purple passage" school of Shakespeare presentation prevalent at the turn of the century. His television appearances and recitations fit here, but, in fact, he was doing pretty much the same type of thing on the radio, on the lecture circuit, in Las Vegas, and wherever and whenever the opportunity presented itself throughout his career.

Many of Welles's projects aimed at demystifying Shakespeare, at bringing him to the level of a popular, commercial artist. He clearly had a mission both to educate his public and to make Shakespeare accessible and entertaining. In Michael Denning's words, "Welles, like other Popular Front popularizers, wanted to use the new mass media to democratize elite culture, expropriating the cultural wealth of the past for the working classes."[2] Welles was not, of course, the first, nor would he be the last, of Shakespeare popularizers. We have seen how his implicit (and, at times, explicit) rivalry with Laurence Olivier became part of the discourse of Shakespeare as popular entertainer in the forties and fifties. In the 1950s, in particular, Shakespeare entered popular culture via a variety of new venues, from comic books (Classics Illustrated, most visibly, sold versions of *Hamlet*, *Macbeth*, and *Julius Caesar*) to television. Indeed, just as radio had wanted to establish its cultural credentials in the 1930s, so television was going out of its way to demonstrate an allegiance to culture in the early to mid-1950s.

Welles, as we saw in chapter 2, made his own contribution to Shakespeare on television, but, in part because he was in European exile during most of this period, he remained marginal to the medium. Maurice Evans, an erstwhile rival and object of Welles's scorn, appeared on television in productions of *Hamlet*, *Richard II*, *Taming of the Shrew*, and *Macbeth*,[3] and there were a number of other Shakespeare adaptations on both the CBS and NBC networks. Hollywood, for its part, though it shied away from more or less "straight" Shakespeare films throughout most of the forties, fifties, and sixties (MGM's 1953 *Julius Caesar* was the exception), released a number of films with Shakespearean connections, from *Kiss Me Kate* (1953) to *West Side Story* (1961), from *A Double Life* (1947) to *Prince of Players* (1955) to *Forbidden Planet* (1956). Most of this was far removed from Welles's at once more direct and more subversive approach to Shakespeare.

Ironically, it could be argued that what I have defined as Welles's project—bringing Shakespeare back to something like his nineteenth-century familiarity—was doomed from the start in part because the very means by which Shakespeare and other cultural productions have been transmitted in the twentieth century mitigate against, indeed make impossible, the conditions of reception necessary for the creation of a popular culture in the first place. What made the culture of nineteenth-century America—including the plays of Shakespeare—at all "popular" was the interaction between production and reception, actor and audience, speaker and listener. By definition, of course, radio, recordings, television, the movies, and all other forms of mass communication are antithetical to such a relationship. Not only is there no genuine interaction between sender and receiver, but there is precious little interaction among the various "receivers" themselves. The whole notion of popular culture, when the term is used in a positive sense, nearly ceases to have meaning in the twentieth century. For most people most of the time, the consumption of culture is an individual, private experience. Without attempting to make too absolute a distinction, it might be suggested that a rock concert is an instance of popular culture, a rock video is not. A production of Shakespeare in front of a spirited, engaged audience of two hundred is (or can be) popular culture; a television transmission of a Time-Life/BBC Shakespeare play viewed by five million people, each watching his or her own receiver, can in no way be thought of as "popular" in this sense.

Welles, nonetheless, can be shown to have had a significant impact on the reception of Shakespeare's plays, and his efforts would make him, arguably, the premier American Shakespearean of the twentieth century. Perhaps his greatest success was in the schools: his emphasis on theatricality and showmanship, on treating Shakespeare as a living dramatist, contributed to changing the way Shakespeare came to be taught in the secondary schools and in colleges and universities throughout America. If Welles was not finally able to revivify Shakespeare's nineteenth-century status, he nonetheless succeeded, with such projects as *Everybody's Shakespeare* and the Mercury Text Records, in making Shakespeare's plays available, in a vivid, living form, to a wide, heterogeneous audience. Editions of Shakespeare would be increasingly inclined to incorporate commentary and illustrations emphasizing historical and theoretical modes and methods of staging. By the late 1960s, both the Marlowe Recording Society based at Cambridge University and Caedmon Records in New York would record, between them, all of Shakespeare's plays.

Welles's first theatrical success—the Federal Theatre *Macbeth*—took place within the context of government sponsorship, which helped to insure a popular reception for Shakespeare and the classics. The Mercury Theatre, founded by Welles and John Houseman, continued, on a more commercial footing, the populism of the Federal Theatre. The Mercury *Julius Caesar*, in its flamboyant success, would be frequently imitated. Though Welles did not invent the fascist trappings, it was his 1937 production that would influence subsequent recastings of Shakespeare's Roman plays in contemporary settings. Both the first British (BBC, 1938) and first American (CBS, 1949) television broadcasts of *Julius Caesar* were in modern dress, and the 1953 MGM motion picture of *Julius Caesar*, though not updated in the same fashion, exhibits signs of Mercury influence: produced by Welles's former partner, John Houseman, it included in its cast several actors (Edmond O'Brien, John Hoyt, Tom Powers) who had appeared in either the original or the touring production of the play.[4]

From the 1930s on, technology and social conditions came together in a particularly fruitful way to support Welles's project. Via radio and sound recordings, he was able to reach a hitherto impossibly large audience. Again, *Everybody's Shakespeare* and the Mercury Text Records played a significant role here in constructing Shakespeare as a living dramatist whose plays only truly come to life on the stage, in production. Motion pictures and television expanded the reach of Welles's activities even further. His Shakespeare films, even if not commercially successful, were seen by hundreds of thousands of people who otherwise might have little or no exposure to theatrical versions of Shakespeare, and video distribution has given them an even larger audience for the future. Even Welles's personal hold on the popular imagination, his cult status, served the purpose of promoting Shakespeare: Welles's "cool" made Shakespeare "cool." Born in the American heartland (Kenosha, Wisconsin) and coming into artistic prominence during the Great Depression and at the height of the Popular Front era, Welles, in his lifelong love affair with Shakespeare, acted out of a very American conviction that art, whatever other needs it may serve, ought to have an educational function and serve a social purpose. This democratic ideal defines, as much as anything can, the role Orson Welles played in twentieth-century American culture.

1. Shakespeare in Las Vegas: Welles and American Culture

1. "Lucy Meets Orson Welles," *I Love Lucy*, CBS Television, October 15, 1956.

2. So Lucy does, for a moment, perform Shakespeare at Ricky's club with Welles. For Lucy's ability to upstage her guest stars, see Patricia Mellencamp, "Situation Comedy, Feminism, and Freud: Discourses of Gracie and Lucy," in Modleski, ed., *Studies in Entertainment*, 80–95 (quotation from 88).

3. John Mason Brown, "Knock, Knock, Knock!" *Saturday Review of Literature*, July 29, 1950, 22–24 (quotation from 24).

4. Letter to the editor, *Saturday Review*, September 2, 1950, 26.

5. Ibid.

6. Ibid.

7. For a discussion of censorship in relation to Shakespeare films in the early 'teens of the century, see William Uricchio and Roberta E. Pearson, *Reframing Culture: The Case of the Vitagraph Quality Films*, 87–95.

8. On this topic see Thomas Doherty, *Teenagers and Teenpics: The Juvenilization of American Movies in the 1950s*.

9. Sam Nathanson to Herbert J. Yates, March 7, 1950 (Correspondence File, Richard Wilson Papers, UCLA).

10. Lawrence W. Levine, *Highbrow/Lowbrow: The Emergence of Cultural Hierarchy in America*, 20.

11. Levine, *Highbrow/Lowbrow*, 23.

12. In this context, it seems particularly appropriate that in 1847 the well-known American circus impresario P. T. Barnum tried to purchase Shakespeare's birthplace. See Gary Taylor, *Reinventing Shakespeare*, 216.

13. Levine, *Highbrow/Lowbrow*, 31.

14. D. Richardson, quoted in Levine, *Highbrow/Lowbrow*, 33.

15. Levine, *Highbrow/Lowbrow*, 222–23.

16. For an interesting discussion of the Shakespearean elements in *My Darling Clementine*, see Scott Simon, "Concerning the Weary Legs of Wyatt Earp: The Classic Western According to Shakespeare," *Literature/Film Quarterly* 24, no. 2 (1996): 114–27.

17. Charles H. Shattuck, *Shakespeare on the American Stage* 1:31.

18. Shattuck, *Shakespeare on the American Stage* 1:55.

19. See *With Orson Welles: Stories from a Life on Film* (1990), Turner Network Television; reedited from *The Orson Welles Story* (BBC, 1980), directed and produced by Alan Yentob and Leslie Megahey.

20. Alva Johnston and Fred Smith, "How to Raise a Child: The Education of Orson Welles, Who Didn't Need It (Part 1)," *Saturday Evening Post*, January 20, 1940, 94.

21. "The Jello Program with Jack Benny," CBS Radio, March 17, 1940.

22. For a detailed study of Barrymore's Shakespearean activities, see Michael A. Morrison, *John Barrymore: Shakespearean Actor*.

23. *South Bank Show*, editor/presenter Melvyn Bragg, ITV, April 2, 1989

24. Joan Shelly Rubin, *The Making of Middlebrow Culture*.

25. Cf. François Truffaut's comment that "Orson Welles has made films with his right hand . . . and films with his left hand. . . . In the right-handed films there is always snow, and in the left-handed ones there are always gunshots." Truffaut, "Foreword" to André Bazin, *Orson Welles: A Critical View*, trans. Jonathan Rosenbaum, 26.

26. Interview in the *New York Post*, November 24, 1937 (Orson Welles Clipping Files, New York Public Library for the Performing Arts at Lincoln Center).

27. Michael Bristol, *Shakespeare's America, America's Shakespeare*, 1–2.

28. "Mercury Summer Theatre," September 13, 1946.

29. Michele Hilmes, *Hollywood and Broadcasting: From Radio to Cable*, 82.

30. See Welles to Diana Bourbon, October 12, 1939 (Welles Papers, Lilly Library, Bloomington, Ind., box 1).

31. Lawrence Levine, in *Highbrow/Lowbrow*, 85–104, shows how opera, like Shakespeare, was originally popular entertainment which became highbrow culture by the beginning of the twentieth century.

32. Barbara Leaming, *Orson Welles: A Biography*, 336–38.

33. As William Simon comments, "[In *Mr. Arkadin*] the low American colloquialisms clash with the traditional rituals and the high art of European civilization." Simon, "Welles: Bakhtin: Parody," *Quarterly Review of Film Studies* 12, nos. 1–2 (1990): 23–28 (quotation from 26).

34. These comments, written on preview cards, are reproduced, along with a number of others, in Orson Welles and Peter Bogdanovich, *This Is Orson Welles*, ed. Jonathan Rosenbaum, 116–18.

35. For a brief discussion of Welles's radio *Hamlet*, see Bernice W. Kliman, *Hamlet: Film, Television, and Audio Performance*, 285–88.

36. A few intriguing extracts—fragments of a partly faded work copy—from this film can be seen in the documentary *Orson Welles: The One Man Band* (dir., Vassili Silovic, 1995).

2. "Raise Hell with Everything": Shakespeare as Event

1. Michael Denning, *The Cultural Front: The Laboring of American Culture in the Twentieth Century*, 376; Denning provides an excellent discussion of Welles's politics in general. See also Peter Wollen, "Foreign Relations: Welles and *Touch of Evil*," *Sight and Sound*, n.s., 6, no. 10 (October 1996): 20.

2. Welles and Bogdanovich, *This Is Orson Welles*, ed. Rosenbaum, 207.

3. For the Gate Theatre see Richard Pine, with Richard Cave, *The Dublin Gate Theatre, 1928–1978*; and Bulmer Hobson, ed., *The Gate Theatre—Dublin*.

4. For a useful account of these movements, see J. L. Styan, *The Shakespeare Revolution: Criticism and Performance in the Twentieth Century*.

5. Statistics for the Cornell tour are taken from her article, "I Wanted to Be an Actress," as told to Ruth Woodbury Sedgwick, *Stage* 16 (January 1939): 43.

6. Charles H. Shattuck, *Shakespeare on the American Stage* 2:45–48.

7. Unpaginated notebook, Welles Papers (Lilly Library, box 5, file 2).

8. See John Houseman, *Run-Through: A Memoir*, 144–45, for a vivid description of the impact Welles's Tybalt had on him.

9. Claudia Cassidy, *Chicago Herald and Examiner*, July 27, 1934 (Gate Theatre Collection, Clipping File, Northwestern University).

10. Lloyd Lewis, *Chicago Daily News*, n.d., (Gate Theatre Collection, Clipping File, Northwestern University).

11. Simon Callow, *Orson Welles: The Road to Xanadu*, 171.

12. Michael Denning, in his important essay, "Towards a People's Theater: The Cultural Politics of the Mercury Theatre," goes even further, claiming, "with tongue in cheek," that "Welles is our Shakespeare, the Mercury our Globe" (26). This essay is recast in an expanded version in Denning, *The Cultural Front*.

13. Both productions are discussed in detail in Richard France, *The Theatre of Orson Welles*. Versions of the original playscripts, with introductions and notes, have been edited by France in *Orson Welles on Shakespeare: The WPA and Mercury Theatre Playscripts*. For a colorful insider's view, see John Houseman, *Run-Through*. See also John S. O'Connor, "But Was It 'Shakespeare'?: Welles's *Macbeth* and *Julius Caesar*," *Theatre Journal* 32, no. 3 (October 1980): 337–48; Andrea Nouryeh, "The Mercury Theatre: A History" (Ph.D. diss., New York University, 1987); and Bernice Kliman, *Shakespeare in Performance: Macbeth*.

14. See preceding note.

15. *Everybody's Shakespeare: Three Plays*, ed. Roger Hill and Orson Welles,

"Introduction," 26. (The three plays—*Julius Caesar, The Merchant of Venice,* and *Twelfth Night*—were also published in separate volumes.)

16. Richard France, "The 'Voodoo' Macbeth of Orson Welles," *Yale Theatre* 5, no. 3 (1974): 67.

17. France, "The 'Voodoo' Macbeth of Orson Welles," 68.

18. A transcription of a different typescript of the adaptation can be found in France, ed., *Orson Welles on Shakespeare.*

19. "Macbeth" typescript, Welles Papers (Lilly Library, box 5, file 13).

20. "The voodoo *Macbeth,* produced by the Negro unit in Harlem, was condemned as a capitulation to stereotypes, the primitive black men superstitious and afraid, and praised for the change it offered black men and women to perform Shakespeare." Rena Fraden, *Blueprints for a Black Federal Theatre, 1935–1939,* 16–17.

21. For an analysis of the contradictory effects of the production within the context of the racial politics of the Federal Theatre Project, see Zanthe Taylor, "Singing for Their Supper: The Negro Units of the Federal Theatre Project and Their Plays," *Theater* 27, nos. 2–3 (1997): 43–59.

22. *New York World Telegram,* April 15, 1936 (Orson Welles Clipping Files, New York Public Library for the Performing Arts at Lincoln Center).

23. Arthur Pollock, *Brooklyn Daily Eagle,* April 15, 1936 (Orson Welles Clipping Files, New York Public Library at Lincoln Center).

24. *New York Herald Tribune,* April 15, 1936 (Orson Welles Clipping Files, New York Public Library at Lincoln Center).

25. For a discussion of the voodoo *Macbeth* as an instance of the modernist project of associating Shakespeare with primitivism, see Richard Halpern, "Shakespeare in the Tropics: From High Modernism to New Historicism," *Representations* 45 (winter 1994): 1–21.

26. Not officially, at least; but Welles did manage to act in *Macbeth* nonetheless: "In Indianapolis, an event occurred that might have set back the cause of black theatre by many years. Maurice Ellis [who played Macbeth on tour] fell ill; his understudy too, was sick, nor did the new stage manager know the role. As if it was what he had been waiting for all along, Welles jumped onto the next plane and took over the role, playing it in blackface. This well-attested event is best contemplated in awed silence" (Callow, *Orson Welles: The Road to Xanadu,* 245).

27. For an illustration from the Delaware production, which was reviewed on February 11, 1937, see Ruth B. Kerns, "Color and Music and Movement," *Performing Arts Annual* 47 (1987): 52–77 (illustration is on 56).

28. Sidney Howard to John Houseman, Welles Papers (Lilly Library, box 1).

29. Harold J. Kennedy, *No Pickle, No Performance,* 25.

30. "The Student and *Julius Caesar*" (brochure) (in Orson Welles Clipping Files, New York Public Library at Lincoln Center).

31. Mercury Files (Lilly Library, box 5, file 28).

32. Houseman, quoted in the *Christian Science Monitor*, February 17, 1939, cited in France, ed., *Orson Welles on Shakespeare*, 171.

33. Frank Brady, *Citizen Welles: A Biography of Orson Welles*, 478.

34. It is part of the nature of television, according to Theodor Adorno, writing in 1954, to create genres that develop "into formulas which, to a certain degree, pre-established the attitudinal pattern of the spectator before he is confronted with any specific content and which largely determine the way in which any specific content is being perceived." Adorno, "How to Look at Television," in Bernstein, ed., *The Culture Industry*, 145.

35. Kenneth S. Rothwell makes a similar point: "The scrapping of the subplot with its redemptive thrust in the behaviour of Edgar, of Albany, and of Gloucester . . . almost guaranteed a victory of existentialism over essentialism." Rothwell, "Representing *King Lear* on Screen: From Metatheatre to 'Meta-Cinema,' " in Anthony Davies and Stanley Wells, eds., *Shakespeare and the Moving Image: The Plays on Film and Television*, 211–33 (quotation from 219).

36. George Rosen, "Orson Welles in U.S. Video Debut Scores Smashing 'King Lear' Triumph," *Variety* 192, October 21, 1953, 33.

37. Jack Gould, "Television Review: 'King Lear' Seen on 'Omnibus,' " *New York Times*, October 19, 1953, 28.

38. John Crosby, "Orson Welles' Lear," *New York Herald Tribune*, October 23, 1953, 17.

39. Marvin Rosenberg, "Shakespeare on TV: An Optimistic Survey," *Quarterly of Film, Radio, and Television* 9, no. 2 (1954): 166–74.

40. "King Lear," *Theatre Arts*, March 1956, 20.

41. Eric Bentley, "The Other Orson Welles," *New Republic*, April 30, 1956, 29.

42. Brooks Atkinson, " 'King Lear,' " *New York Times*, January 13, 1956, sec. 1, p. 17.

43. *Newsweek*, January 23, 1956, 57.

44. Henry Hewes, *Saturday Review*, January 28, 1956, 18.

45. Brooks Atkinson, " 'King Lear,' " *New York Times*, January 20, 1956, sec. 2, p. 1. (Atkinson wrote two articles on the production: see note 42, above.)

46. Richard Hayes, "The Stage," *Commonweal*, March 2, 1956, 568.

47. Alexander Leggatt, *Shakespeare in Performance: King Lear*, 98.

48. Orson Welles to Marc Blitzstein, December 4, 1955, Welles Papers (Lilly Library, box 1).

49. *New York Times*, January 8, 1956, sec. 2, p. 1.

50. See Leonard Lyons's column in the *New York Post*, December 1, 1955 (City Center Scrapbooks, New York Public Library at Lincoln Center).

51. *Collier's* magazine for October 14, 1955, published, on consecutive pages, photos of Laurence Olivier (in color) costumed as Richard III and Welles (in black and white) as himself, slightly disheveled and smoking a large cigar. Each photo is accompanied by a brief block of text. "Among English theater royalty," the

Olivier paragraphs begin, "Sir Laurence Olivier unquestionably wears the shiniest crown." Next to Welles's photo we read: "Wrapped in the usual haze of confusion that obscures most of Orson Welles's projects . . ." (*Collier's* 136, no. 8: 37 and 38).

52. Bentley, "The Other Orson Welles," 29.

3. "Cashing in on the Classics": *Everybody's Shakespeare* and the Mercury Text Records

1. For a good discussion of Hudson and Rolfe and their Shakespeare editions, see John Hampton Lauk II, "The Reception and Teaching of Shakespeare in Nineteenth and Early Twentieth-Century America."

2. Lauk, "The Reception and Teaching of Shakespeare," 189–90 and 372.

3. Arthur N. Applebee, *Tradition and Reform in the Teaching of English: A History*, 36, 50, 66, 125.

4. The Folger Shakespeare Library in Washington, D.C. had opened its doors in 1932, and Hill (who writes as if he had been there) takes enthusiastic note of the library's immense collection of Shakespeareana. The establishment of the Folger library was an important moment in the "Americanization" of Shakespeare in the twentieth century, a movement to which Welles's own activities also contributed. For the cultural significance of the Folger, see Michael Bristol, *Shakespeare's America, America's Shakespeare*, ch. 3.

5. *Everybody's Shakespeare: Three Plays*, ed. Roger Hill and Orson Welles, "Introduction," 8. (Page numbers cited in the text refer to this volume.)

6. For a good discussion of this movement, with special reference to British Shakespeare productions, see J. L. Styan, *The Shakespeare Revolution*. See also Cary M. Mazer, *Shakespeare Refashioned: Elizabethan Plays on Edwardian Stages*.

7. Hilton Edwards, quoted in Richard Pine, with Richard Cave, *The Dublin Gate Theatre, 1928–1978*, 73.

8. Charles Higham, *Orson Welles: The Rise and Fall of an American Genius*, 62.

9. At times, the verbal descriptions are elaborated with complementary drawings. At the beginning of act I, scene iii, we read:

> Olivia's House. This can be an interior, quite distinct from those other scenes similarly designated, though usually it is Olivia's garden, the most elaborate setting and one used several times in the play. Something of formality, terraces and marble balustrades, is usually to be found in the design. . . . Sir Toby is the Countess Olivia's Uncle, and, we may suppose, a cousin of some sort to Sir John Falstaff. He is a fun and liquor-loving old gentleman, very fat and very hearty. He swaggers in valorously hatted and gauntleted, carrying a whip.
>
> (*Everybody's Shakespeare*, "Twelfth Night," 9)

And so forth, in considerable detail.

10. *Everybody's Shakespeare*, "The Merchant of Venice," 11.

11. "Irving ended [the scene] with a piece of business which was perfectly original. There was a 'Very Quick' act drop, which rose again immediately with the applause. 'When it went up again the stage was empty, desolate, with no light but the pale moon, and all sounds of life at a great distance—and then over the bridge came the wearied figure of the Jew.' The drop fell as he was about to enter the house." Alan Hughes, *Henry Irving, Shakespearean*, 232.

12. *Everybody's Shakespeare*, "Introduction," 27.

13. *Everybody's Shakespeare*, "Twelfth Night," 23.

14. Ibid., 20.

15. *Everybody's Shakespeare*, "Introduction," 26.

16. Orson Welles and Roger Hill, "On the Teaching of Shakespeare and Other Great Literature," *English Journal* 27 (1938): 464–68 (quotation from 467).

17. Welles and Hill, "On the Teaching of Shakespeare," 465 and 468.

18. Samuel Weingarten, "The Use of Phonograph Recordings in Teaching Shakespeare," *College English* 1, no. 1 (October 1939): 45–61.

19. For a discussion of this issue, see Roberta E. Pearson and William Uricchio, "How Many Times Shall Caesar Bleed in Sport: Shakespeare and the Cultural Debate About Moving Pictures," *Screen* 31, no. 3 (autumn 1990): 252, 258. See also the extension of their argument in Uricchio and Pearson, *Reframing Culture*.

20. Lauk, "The Reception and Teaching of Shakespeare," 30.

21. Welles and Hill, eds., *The Mercury Shakespeare*, "Twelfth Night," 2.

22. Callow, *Orson Welles: The Road To Xanadu*, 337.

23. *Everybody's Shakespeare*, "Julius Caesar," 8.

24. Walter Ginsberg, "How Helpful Are Shakespeare Recordings?" *English Journal* 29 (1940): 289–300 (quotation from 291).

25. Ginsberg, "How Helpful Are Shakespeare Recordings?" 292, 293, 296.

26. A. H. Lass and C. S. Steingart, "Recordings and the English Classroom," quoted in the proof copy of a Harper and Brothers circular, "Announcing the Mercury Shakespeare," Welles Papers (Lilly Library, box 14, file 13). For a positive response to the Mercury *Macbeth*, see William Ladd, " 'Macbeth'—As a Reading Production," *English Journal* 33 (1944): 374–77.

27. In her influential *The Stage and the School*, Katharine Anne Ommanney writes of the Mercury project that "when you have completed a play by this aural method, you should feel that you have contacted Shakespeare himself, not as the literary genius, but as the great actor-playwright" (267).

28. As Jean-Christophe Agnew argues, however, the "assumption that the cultural interplay of commerciality and theatricality in contemporary mass culture [is] a peculiarly modern and peculiarly American phenomenon" cannot be seriously maintained. See his *Worlds Apart: The Market and the Theater in Anglo-American Thought, 1550–1750*, quotation from xiii.

29. "Mercury Text Records," unpaginated brochure, Welles Papers (Lilly Library, box 14, file 13).

30. "Tentative Outline of Columbia Phonograph's Campaign to Educate Its Own Distributors as to the possibilities of selling Mercury Text Records," Welles Papers (Lilly Library, box 14, file 13).

31. Mark Twain [Samuel L. Clemens], *Huckleberry Finn* (1884–85), ed. Leo Marx (Indianapolis, Ind.: Bobbs-Merrill, 1967): 162. Harriet Hawkins, writing with special reference to Shakespeare's place in popular culture, has noted that "the fact is that the forces and energies and impacts that account for the status and indeed the survival of an 'immortal' masterpiece are pretty much the same forces and energies and impacts that assure commercial success at the box office in any age." Hawkins, *Classics and Trash: Traditions and Taboos in High Literature and Popular Modern Genres*, 118.

32. "Cashing in on the Classics—4," Welles Papers (Lilly Library, box 14, file 13).

33. "Cashing in on the Classics—1," ibid.

4. Welles/Shakespeare/Film: An Overview

1. Theodor W. Adorno, "Culture and Administration," in Bernstein, ed., *The Culture Industry*, 102.

2. Levine, *Highbrow/Lowbrow*.

3. Roberta E. Pearson and William Uricchio, "How Many Times Shall Caesar Bleed in Sport," 248.

4. Ibid., 258.

5. Graham Holderness, "Radical Potentiality and Institutional Closure: Shakespeare in Film and Television," in Jonathan Dollimore and Alan Sinfield, eds., *Political Shakespeare: New Essays in Cultural Materialism*, 182.

6. "The movie was produced as a conscious exercise in prestige building, not necessarily with any cynical motive but rather as an attempt to consolidate Warner's reputation as a socially responsible company with both the public and the Hays Office." John Collick, *Shakespeare, Cinema, and Society*, 83.

7. Tad Mosel, with Gertrude Macy, *Leading Lady: The World and Theatre of Katharine Cornell*, 387–88.

8. So, for example, Roger Manvell writes that Shakespeare constructed "his plays in a manner which closely resembles the structure of a screenplay." Manvell, *Shakespeare and the Film*, 9.

9. In the Arden edition of *Antony and Cleopatra*, editor M. R. Ridley writes of the necessity of "becoming accustomed, in Shakespeare and other Elizabethan drama, to 'non-localised' scenes—some characters meet 'somewhere' to transact some necessary business of the play, and where the 'somewhere' is may often be of small importance" (xix).

10. Jorgens is here quoting from Arthur Knight, "Three Problems in Film Adaptation," *Saturday Review*, December 18, 1954, 26.

11. Jack J. Jorgens, *Shakespeare on Film*, 7–10.

12. Jorgens, *Shakespeare on Film*, 15.

13. Lorne M. Buchman, *Still in Movement: Shakespeare on Screen*, 6.

14. See James Naremore, "The Walking Shadow: Welles's Expressionist *Macbeth*," *Literature/Film Quarterly* 1, no. 4 (fall 1973): 360–66.

15. "Certainly every finished work of art is already predetermined in some way but art strives to overcome its own oppressive weight as an artefact through the force of its very construction. Mass culture on the other hand simply identifies with the curse of predetermination and joyfully fulfils it." Theodor W. Adorno, "The Schema of Mass Culture," in Bernstein, ed., *The Culture Industry*, 53–84 (quotation from 62). Welles's entire career could be read as a refusal to accept that predetermination.

16. See Roland Barthes, "The Reality Effect," in *The Rustle of Language*, trans. Richard Howard, 141–48.

17. Collick, *Shakespeare, Cinema, and Society*, 60.

18. See Ace G. Pilkington, "Zeffirelli's Shakespeare," in Davies and Wells, eds., *Shakespeare and the Moving Image*, 165–66.

19. This tendency has been carried on by Kenneth Branagh, especially in the lavishly illustrated screenplay book *Hamlet by William Shakespeare* (New York: Norton, 1996).

20. See Laurie E. Osborne, "Filming Shakespeare in a Cultural Thaw: Soviet Appropriations of Shakesperean Treacheries in 1955–6," *Textual Practice* 9, no. 2 (1995): 325–47.

21. Bruce Eder, liner notes, *Richard III*, dir. Laurence Olivier, 1955 (videodisk, Voyager, 1994). Kenneth Branagh's *Henry V* and *Much Ado About Nothing*, in part because of preselling to secondary markets like cable television and video, are exceptions to the rule that Shakespeare films can't make money; Branagh's *Hamlet*, on the other hand, cost $24 million and only grossed $11.3.

22. Patricia Parker, *Shakespeare from the Margins: Language, Culture, Context*, 15.

23. Michael Bristol, *Big-Time Shakespeare*, 61.

24. These examples are drawn from Julie Hankey, ed., *Othello: Plays in Performance*, 138, 91, and 237.

25. Virginia Mason Vaughan, *Othello: A Contextual History*, 200; Collick, *Shakespeare, Cinema, and Society*, 96; Peter S. Donaldson, *Shakesperean Films/Shakespearean Directors*, 124n18; Barbara Hodgdon, "Kiss Me Deadly; or, The Des/Demonized Spectacle," in Vaughan and Cartwright, eds., *Othello: New Perspectives*, 222.

26. Like the far more obviously "experimental" and "underground" Shakespeare films discussed by Graham Holderness ("Shakespeare Rewound," *Shakespeare Survey* 45 [1993]: 63–74), Welles's Shakespeare films, too, "can be used to

challenge traditional notions and to provoke debate about some central issues of both text and performance" (70).

27. Collick, *Shakespeare, Cinema, and Society*, 63, 73.

28. And thus they are relatively safe from the danger articulated by James C. Bulman: "Because film and video allow us repeated viewings of a single performance, they encourage us to assimilate that performance to the condition of a literary text—a stable artifact rather than a contingent, ephemeral experience." Bulman, "Introduction: Shakespeare and Performance Theory," in Bulman, ed., *Shakespeare, Theory, and Performance*, 2.

29. Dennis Kennedy, ed., *Foreign Shakespeare: Contemporary Performance*, 6.

30. Dennis Kennedy, *Looking at Shakespeare: A Visual History of Twentieth-Century Performances*, 302.

31. Kennedy, ed., *Foreign Shakespeare*, 10.

32. Henri LeMaitre, "Shakespeare, the Imaginary Cinema and the Pre-cinema," in Charles W. Eckert, ed., *Focus on Shakespearean Films*, 36.

33. Robin Wood, "Welles, Shakespeare, and Webster," *Personal Views*, 136–52 (quotations from 136–37 and 152).

34. Gary Taylor, *Reinventing Shakespeare*, 384.

35. James Naremore, "The Walking Shadow" and *The Magic World of Orson Welles*, ch. 5; Anthony Davies, *Filming Shakespeare's Plays*, ch. 5; Jorgens, *Shakespeare on Film*, ch. 12; Peter Donaldson, *Shakesperean Films/Shakespearean Directors*, ch. 4; Buchman, *Still in Movement*, ch. 7; Joseph McBride, *Orson Welles*, ch. 12; Samuel Crowl, "The Long Goodbye: Welles and Falstaff," *Shakespeare Quarterly* 31 (autumn 1980): 369–80, reprinted in *Shakespeare Observed: Studies in Performance on Stage and Screen*, ch. 3.

36. Kliman, *Shakespeare in Performance: Macbeth*; Barbara Hodgdon, *Shakespeare in Performance: Henry IV, Part II*.

37. Terence Hawkes, "Bardbiz," *London Review of Books*, February 22, 1990, 11–13.

38. Bristol, *Big-Time Shakespeare*, 109.

5. Shakespeare Rides Again: The Republic *Macbeth*

1. *Daily Variety*, September 15, 1948, 2.

2. *Daily Variety*, September 8, 1948, 2.

3. Copy of cable, Orson Welles to Herbert Yates, September 9, 1948 (Correspondence File, Richard Wilson Papers, UCLA).

4. *Life*, March 15, 1948, 117–27 (quotations from 118).

5. *Life* May 20, 1946 (quotations from 38, 39).

6. *Life*, November 24, 1947 (quotations from 19, 20).

7. John Kobler, "Sir Laurence Olivier," *Life*, October 18, 1948, 129.

8. *Life*, October 11, 1948 (quotations from 107).

9. *Life*, March 14, 1949 (quotations from 50, 45).

10. *Life*, September 13, 1948 (quotations from 133, 131).

11. *Variety*, October 13, 1948, 11; *Hollywood Reporter*, October 11, 1948, 3.

12. Elinor Hughes, in the *Boston Herald*, begins her review in this fashion: "Methought I heard a voice that cried, 'Sleep no more, for Welles doth murder Shakespeare, and therefore "Macbeth" shall be no more, and "Hamlet" shall reign supreme' " (October 5, 1948, 53); the *Hamlet* reference, of course, is to Olivier's film, then in the eighth week of its Boston run. Marjory Adams, in the *Boston Globe*, was more balanced; she missed "splendor and royal pomp" in the banquet scene, but she liked the battle sequence and the movement of Birnam Wood: "When you see 'Macbeth' you may find other scenes which will please and gratify you," she concludes, "despite the production's failure to make the imposing and artistic success we have a right to expect" (October 8, 1948, 36).

13. *Newsweek*, October 18, 1948, 109–10.

14. *Time*, November 1, 1948, 90.

15. *Good Housekeeping*, January 1949, 100.

16. Richard Wilson to Orson Welles, undated draft of memorandum, late April–early May 1949 (Correspondence File, Richard Wilson Papers, UCLA).

17. Interoffice memorandum, November 1, 1948 (Correspondence File, Richard Wilson Papers, UCLA).

18. Interoffice memorandum, May 10, 1949 (Correspondence File, Richard Wilson Papers, UCLA).

19. Richard Wilson to Orson Welles, November 29, 1947 (Correspondence File, Richard Wilson Papers, UCLA).

20. Herbert J. Yates to Orson Welles, July 18, 1947 (Correspondence File, Richard Wilson Papers, UCLA).

21. Richard Wilson, " 'Macbeth' on Film," *Theatre Arts*, June 1949, 55.

22. These figures, which may not be 100 percent accurate but which, I believe, give a fair picture of the situation, are from the Richard Wilson Papers, UCLA.

23. "In Welles's *Macbeth*," Anthony Davies writes, "there are no familiar places. The spatial context for the drama has the disorienting properties of an endless elusiveness of form together with the suggestions of an unstable organism. The spatial substance, in some affinitive way, takes on the involuntary biochemistry of Macbeth. Its cavernous walls exude drops of moisture just as Macbeth's skin glistens with the torrid sweat of panic" (*Filming Shakespeare's Plays*, 89).

24. "[Shakespeare's] method seems to have been to work in short, swift scenes dominated by the great protagonist, interspersed with other scenes of slower movement." J. Munro, *The London Shakespeare* 6:1091 (1958), cited in Geoffrey Bullough, ed., *Narrative and Dramatic Sources of Shakespeare* 7:455.

25. Roger Hill and Orson Welles, eds., *Everybody's Shakespeare: Three Plays*, "Introduction," 26.

26. Cocteau, "Profile of Orson Welles," in Bazin, *Orson Welles: A Critical View*, 28–32, trans. Jonathan Rosenbaum (quotation from 29: Cocteau's phrase is here translated as "dreamlike subway").

27. Claude Beylie, "*Macbeth* our la Magie des Profondeurs," *Études Ciné-matographiques* 24–25 (1963): 86–89, trans. Charles Eckert and reprinted in Eckert, ed., *Focus on Shakespearean Films*, 72–75 (quotation from 72).

28. Bazin, *Orson Welles: A Critical View*, 101.

29. Ibid., 29.

30. Bertolt Brecht, *The Messingkauf Dialogues*, trans. John Willett, 84.

31. For a view of Shakespeare's play inflected by a full awareness of the Holocaust, see Jan Kott, "Macbeth or Death-infected," in *Shakespeare Our Contemporary*, trans. Boleslaw Taborski, 85–97. Maurice Bessy writes that Welles's film "reflects the bloody horror the world had just been through: the war, the concentrations camps; in this way, the individual pasts of Welles's characters participate in the collective past, and point toward an apocalyptic future" (*Orson Welles*, trans. Ciba Vaughan, 43).

32. In *Filming Othello* (1978), Welles discusses the similarity between the sets of the two productions. Bernice Kliman sees the two productions as very closely related, as indeed they are: "With all their differences, the Voodoo and film productions are remarkably similar in method and intent" (*Shakespeare in Performance: Macbeth*, 97).

33. Kott, *Shakespeare Our Contemporary* (quotations from 92 and 89).

34. Anthony Davies (*Filming Shakespeare's Plays*, 92), who otherwise comments on the film with some sensitivity, makes the extraordinary claim that there is very little camera movement in the film, and he isolates the England scene (Shakespeare's IV.iii) as an example of the immobile camera. But the England scene, filmed in a single take, exhibits in fact virtually continuous camera movement, as Welles constantly reframes in order to follow the dramatic rhythm of the scene. Davies' misreading exemplifies how unaccustomed critics are to interpret or even to read the long-take style. Here Welles is giving us Shakespeare more or less straight, and yet the effect is not, as a number of critics have suggested, "theatrical" or static—the mobile frame provides us with a specifically cinematic experience in no way comparable to what we would experience in a stage production.

35. For a useful survey comparing the two versions, see Bernice Kliman, "Welles's *Macbeth*: A Textual Parable," in Michael Skovmand, ed., *Screen Shakespeare*, 25–37. Kliman actually writes of *three* versions of Welles's film, on the assumption that the "restored" version is not identical to the original release, at least when it is compared to a cutting continuity in the Wilson papers; although she is undoubtedly right, it should be noted that the cutting continuity itself does not appear to be final.

36. As Bernice Kliman notes (*Shakespeare in Performance: Macbeth*, 7), the language of Shakespeare's play is difficult to comprehend at best, and the speeches of Macbeth himself are notably "difficult, convoluted, even tortured."

37. In an essay entitled "Imagining the Sound(s) of Shakespeare: Film Sound and Adaptation" (in Altman, ed., *Sound Theory/Sound Practice*, 204–16 and 269n3),

Mary Pat Klimek, writing specifically about *Macbeth*, notes that "in Welles' world, sound and space are not linked. We can't confidently expect sound signature to function as a spacial indicator" (212). Her comments are based on the 1950 release version of the film. In a note, she claims that the restored version "smooths over many of the 'bad' sound qualities I discuss here. . . . In general, the restoration transforms the often jarring sound I heard in the unrestored version to closer approximations of standard Hollywood sound" (270).

I would argue, however, that the differences between the two are more complex than these comments would indicate; in any case, the restored version incorporates Welles's original sound design (the sound track used for the restoration came from a nitrate duplicate negative of Welles's original cut which was discovered in England; see "UCLA Archivist Reconstructs Orson Welles's Original 'Macbeth'," *Variety*, May 7, 1980, 144), which, as my discussion suggests, was already quite unusual by normal Hollywood standards. As Fred Camper has noted, "The sound tracks of Orson Welles's films often seem to take on a life of their own, . . . his sound has a palpable, physical presence that is a perfect extension of the extreme physicality of his shooting style." Camper, "Sound and Silence in Narrative and Nonnarrative Cinema," in Elizabeth Weis and John Belton, eds., *Film Sound: Theory and Practice*, 374.

38. Typed memorandum signed "Orson Welles," no date or addressee, p. 2; emphasis in the original (Correspondence File, Richard Wilson Papers, UCLA).

39. Robert Hatch (review), *The New Republic*, January 15, 1951, 30.

40. John McCarten (review), *The New Yorker*, December 30, 1950, 57.

41. Orson Welles, "The Third Audience," *Sight and Sound* 23 (January–March 1954): 120–22 (quotation from 122).

42. Arthur Knight (review), *Saturday Review*, February 3, 1951, 25.

43. *Scholastic*, October 27, 1948, 29.

44. See John Ashworth, "Olivier, Freud, and Hamlet," *Atlantic Monthly* 183 (May 1949): 30–33.

45. Parker Tyler, "*Hamlet* and Documentary," *Kenyon Review* 11 (1949): 527–32.

46. *Life*, October 11, 1948, 107.

47. Charles K. Feldman to Richard Wilson, May 5, 1949 (Correspondence File, Richard Wilson Papers, UCLA).

48. With *Macbeth*, according to François Truffaut, "Welles rediscovered freedom, poverty and his own genius, all intact." Truffaut, "Foreword," in Bazin, *Orson Welles: A Critical View*, 15.

6. The Texts of *Othello*

1. Davies, *Filming Shakespeare's Plays*, xi.

2. See Walter Benjamin, "The Work of Art in the Age of Mechanical Reproduction," in *Illuminations*, ed. Hannah Arendt, trans. Harry Zohn, 217–51.

3. See Jonathan Rosenbaum, "Orson Welles's Essay Films and Documentary Fictions: A Two-Part Speculation," *Cinematograph* 4 (1991): 169–79. See also Phillip Lopate, "In Search of the Centaur: The Essay-Film," in Charles Warren, ed., *Beyond Document: Essays on Nonfiction Film*, 243–70.

4. For some skeptical observations concerning what Welles calls his "round, unvarnished tale," see Gérard Legrand, "Strange Sense of Eternity . . . (Filming Othello)," *Positif* 231 (June 1980): 66–68. Cf. Rosenbaum, "Orson Welles's Essay Films": "Creatively misquoting his own film at the same time that he misquotes his critics, Welles thus continues his projects of candid concealment and continuous revision which have already made his filmmaking career as labyrinthine and as mysterious as it is" (173).

5. Jorgens, *Shakespeare on Film*, 179.

6. As André Bazin has observed, "In *Macbeth* Welles chose to recreate a universe that was artificial in every particular, a world closed in on its own incompleteness, like a grotto. In *Othello* the artifice is in the open and recreated from entirely natural materials." Bazin, *Orson Welles: A Critical View*, 114.

7. Charles Higham sees the contrast in complementary, if somewhat different, terms: "Physically, while *Macbeth* is a film of dark interiors, of a cramped and rain-swept world of crags and man-made stone labyrinths, *Othello* is its opposite: full of sun-drenched, wind-lashed exteriors, of settings that are extravaganzas of baroque, a chiaroscuro of whipping flags, sky-piercing turrets, bristling spears, and lashing foam, a world in which the sea and the clouds are eternally present." Higham, *The Films of Orson Welles*, 138.

8. The line numbering here follows the Signet *Othello*, ed. Alvin Kernan (New York: New American Library, 1963).

9. "Both he [Hilton Edwards] and O. [Welles] believe that the more you cut out of a play the better it is, and I suggest, not without bitterness, that they would be better employed in Atomic Bomb Factory than in theatre." Michael MacLiammoir, *Put Money in Thy Purse: The Filming of Orson Welles' "Othello,"* 211.

10. Response to a question at Orson Welles Theatre, Cambridge, Mass., January 8, 1976.

11. Lorne Buchman describes the sequence in somewhat different terms: "Indeed, when one sees the processional image again at the end of *Othello*, one recognizes how the rhythm of time has been broken and restored through the course of the tragedy." Buchman, *Still in Movement*, 127.

12. Jorgens, *Shakespeare on Film*, 178–85.

13. Buchman, who is interested in Welles's manipulation of time in *Othello*, notes that Welles exploits the cinema's unique capacity to perform scenes in motion, and the effect of his presentation is to create the feeling that Iago, the manipulator of time, works best on the move (*Still in Movement*, 141).

14. Samuel Crowl finds that "Welles was the first great postmodern reader of

Shakespeare, straddling like a colossus the territory between Twain's King and Duke and Derrida" (*Shakespeare Observed*, 52).

15. Vaughan, *Othello: A Contextual History*, 199; Donaldson, *Shakespeare Films/Shakespeare Directors*, 97.

16. Julie Hankey, ed. *Plays in Performance: Othello*, 38.

17. Ibid., 67.

18. See Geoffrey Tillotson, " 'Othello' and 'The Alchemist' at Oxford in 1610," *Times Literary Supplement*, July 20, 1933, 494, cited in *Othello*, ed. Norman Saunders, 38.

19. Cf. Hugh Grady: "The small amount of evidence that exists on the reactions of early audiences to the play supports the supposition that Othello's skin colour was not necessarily his most important characteristic for the audience" (*Shakespeare's Universal Wolf: Studies in Early Modern Reification*, 115).

20. Vaughan, *Othello: A Contextual History*, 65.

21. At the same time, as Michael Bristol has suggested, "To present Othello with a black face, as opposed to presenting him as a black man, would confront the audience with a comic spectacle of abjection rather than with the grand opera of misdirected passion" (*Big-Time Shakespeare*, 186).

22. Richard Wilson to Orson Welles, March 8, 1948 (Correspondence File, Richard Wilson Papers, UCLA). On March 24, Wilson sent Welles the relevant passage from the Production Code: "Miscegenation (sex relationship between the white and black races) is forbidden."

23. Naremore, *The Magic World of Orson Welles*, 182.

24. Jorgens, *Shakespeare on Film*, 188.

25. Eric Bentley, "Theatre," *New Republic*, October 3, 1955, 22.

26. Quoted in Vaughan, *Othello: A Contextual History*, 171.

27. See Ruth Cowig, "Actors, Black and Tawny, in the Role of Othello—and Their Critics," *Theatre Research International* 4, no. 2 (February 1979): 133–46.

28. *Newsweek*, May 23, 1955, 120.

29. Philip Hamburger (review), *New Yorker*, September 17, 1955, 141–43; Bentley (review), *New Republic*, October 3, 1955, 22; Bosley Crowther (review), *New York Times*, September 13, 1955, 27 (Crowther wrote a follow-up piece for the Sunday *Times* as well [September 18, 1955, sec. 2, p. 1]).

30. Robert Hatch (review), *The Nation*, October 1, 1955, 290.

31. Hamburger, *New Yorker*, September 17, 1955, 141.

32. Cf. director Martin Scorsese, who has admitted to deliberately leaving scenes in his films out of sync: "Sometimes I do four takes, and I like how one line sounds better in the third take but I like the visuals of the first take. When I take the soundtrack from the third take and put it onto images of the first take, it doesn't sync up as well. And colleagues have said to me, 'See his mouth?' My answer is 'If they're looking at his mouth at this point in the picture, we might as well just stop working and go home.' " In "Roughing Up the Surface: Simon Schama and

Martin Scorsese Talk About How They Make History," *Civilization* 5 (February-March 1998): 82–89 (quotation from 84).

33. The restorers, perhaps disturbed by the graininess of Welles's blowup, or because there is a clear smudgelike flaw on the negative, have gone back to the original shot to make a less extreme enlargement.

34. For discussions of the restored *Othello*, see the two essays by Jonathan Rosenbaum, "Improving Mr. Welles," *Sight and Sound*, n.s., 12, no. 6 (October 1992): 28–30, and "Othello Goes Hollywood," *Chicago Reader* 10 (April 10, 1992): 12, 36–37, 39; David Impastato, "Orson Welles's *Othello* and the Welles-Smith Restoration: Definitive Version?" *Shakespeare Bulletin* 10, no. 4 (fall 1992): 38–41; and Philippe Elhem, "Avatars de la restauration: à propos d'*Othello* et *Don Quichotte* d'Orson Welles," *24 Images*, nos. 62–63 (September-October 1992): 42–43. The technical aspects of the restoration are discussed in Brooke Comer, "Carving Out the Couplets," *American Cinematographer* 73 (July 1992): 74–76.

35. Orson Welles to Richard Wilson, undated (March ?, 1951), p. 2 (Correspondence File, Richard Wilson Papers, UCLA). Welles adds that "Coote wont be of any help by way of explanation because this cistern business was invented after he left the picture."

36. Ibid.

37. See note 33.

38. Impastato, "Orson Welles's *Othello* and the Welles-Smith Restoration," 40.

39. One of the restorers, Arnie Saks, claims that the main objective of the restorations "was not to use any nonoriginal dialogue. We didn't bring actors in to do any more dubbing. That would have made the film more understandable, but then we'd be tampering with something that should not be tampered with. You can't do that with a master like Welles." Brooke Comer, "Restoring the 'Dusky Moor': Welles' *Othello*," *American Cinematographer* 73 (July 1992): 66–71 (quotation from 70). In an article that came to my attention after I had completed this chapter, François Thomas provides a detailed account of the many arbitrary changes the restorers made to Welles's sound track ("La tragédie d' 'Othello'," *Positif* 424 [June 1996]: 70–76).

40. Victor Paul Squitieri, "The Twofold Corpus of Orson Welles's 'Othello.'" Ph.D. diss., University of California at Berkeley, 1993 (see *Dissertation Abstracts International* 55 [1995]: 1721A).

41. Rosenbaum, "Improving Mr. Welles," 28–30.

42. See main text at note 1 above, and Davies, *Filming Shakespeare's Plays*, xi.

43. *The Criterion Collection: A Comprehensive Guide*, ed. Elizabeth Collumb (1994 Voyager catalog), 37.

44. Orson Welles to Hilton Edwards and Michael MacLiammoir, undated letter (Gate Theatre Collection, Correspondence Files, Northwestern University).

45. Dawson, quoted in "Restoration Team Resurrects 'Othello,' " *Millimeter* 20 (February 1992): 35.

46. Penelope Mesic, "Improving on Genius," *Chicago* 41, no. 2 (February 1992): 43–44 (quotations from 44).

7. *Chimes at Midnight*: Rhetoric and History

1. For a brief discussion of the relationship between Van Sant's film and Shakespeare (and, secondarily, Welles), see Robert F. Willson, Jr., "Recontextualizing Shakespeare on Film: *My Own Private Idaho, Men of Respect, Prospero's Books*," *Shakespeare Bulletin* 10, no. 3 (summer 1992): 34–37.

2. As David Cairns has noted, "Boito, by a brilliant piece of literary surgery, restored the original, the true Falstaff. The libretto is strengthened, again and again, by graftings from the two parts of *Henry IV*" (Giuseppe Verdi, *Falstaff: National Opera Guides 10*, ed. Nicholas John, 19).

3. Juan Cobos and Miguel Rubio, 'Welles and Falstaff," *Sight and Sound* 35 (autumn 1966): 158–63 (quotation from 159).

4. Bridget Gellert Lyons, ed., *Films in Print: Chimes at Midnight*, 5.

5. For useful descriptions and discussions of *Five Kings*, see Richard France, *The Theater of Orson Welles*, and Simon Callow, *Orson Welles: The Road to Xanadu*, 423–53; a version of the playscript is reproduced in Richard France, ed., *Orson Welles on Shakespeare*, 174–289.

6. For an excellent discussion of the relationship between the two stage productions and the film, see Robert Hapgood, " 'Chimes at Midnight' from Stage to Screen: The Art of Adaptation," *Shakespeare Survey* 39 (1987): 39–52. For a thorough and painstaking attempt to reconstruct the stage production, see Aleksandra Jovicevic Tatomirovic, "The Theatre of Orson Welles, 1946–1960," 629–834.

7. See, for example, Joseph McBride, *Orson Welles*; James Naremore, *The Magic World of Orson Welles*; Samuel Crowl, "The Long Goodbye: Welles and Falstaff," 369–80; and the comments by David Bordwell ("Citizen Kane," *Film Comment* 7 [1971]: 38–47) and Brian Henderson ("The Long Take," ibid., 6–11): both have been reprinted in Bill Nichols, ed., *Movies and Methods*.

8. Most of the negative points are summarized by Jack Jorgens in *Shakespeare on Film*; Jorgens, however, provides a generally positive analysis. See also Higham, *The Films of Orson Welles*; Higham writes of Welles's "impatience with detail and finalization that, combined with [his] tragic perennial lack of funds, have left the work just short of the triumph it should have been" (177).

9. "If Falstaff had made films," Scott McMillin writes, "he would have made something like this one" (*Shakespeare in Performance: Henry IV, Part I*, 95).

10. The language here is paraphrased from Hugh Grady, *Modernist Shakespeare*, 228–29.

11. I am using the term *deconstruct* in its narrow, Derridean sense, the sense well summarized by Jonathan Culler: "To deconstruct a discourse is to show how it

undermines the philosophy it asserts, or the hierarchical oppositions on which it relies, by identifying in the text the rhetorical operations that produce the supposed ground of the argument, the key concept or premise" (*On Deconstruction*, 86).

12. For a discussion of some of these adaptations, see Hodgdon, *Shakespeare in Performance: Henry IV, Part II.*

13. In conflating the two parts into a single play, Welles may have, ironically, fashioned something close to the single play version that some scholars believe Shakespeare to have originally written, before revising it into two plays. See Shakespeare, *The Second Part of King Henry IV*, ed. Giorgio Melchiori, 9–13.

14. Samuel Crowl convincingly demonstrates that "Welles's overriding visual and structural emphasis is to signal farewell, to say a long goodbye to Falstaff, rather than to celebrate Hal's homecoming to princely right reason and responsible rule" ("The Long Goodbye," 373).

15. Grady, *Modernist Shakespeare*, 128–48.

16. Quoting one passage, Grady comments: "It might justly be said of this, and similar passages, that we are a single step short of deconstruction" (ibid., 135).

17. For a sensitive discussion of Hal's role in Welles's film, see Leland Poague, " 'Reading' the Prince: Shakespeare, Welles, and Some Aspects of *Chimes at Midnight*," *Iowa State Journal of Research*, 56, no. 1 (August 1981): 57–65.

18. Cobos and Rubio, "Welles and Falstaff," 159.

19. Naremore, *The Magic World of Orson Welles*, 217.

20. Welles and Bogdanovich, *This Is Orson Welles*, ed. Rosenbaum, 261.

21. Richard Lanham, *The Motives of Eloquence: Literary Rhetoric in the Renaissance*, 206–207.

22. Huston, "Power and Dis-Integration in the Films of Orson Welles," *Film Quarterly* 35 (summer 1982): 2–12 (quotation from 2).

23. Dudley Andrew's comments on the nature of Welles's sound track in *Chimes at Midnight* and in other films closely parallel my own observations (see *Film in the Aura of Art*, 164–68). See also Mary Pat Klimek, "Imagining the Sound(s) of Shakespeare: Film Sound and Adaptation," in Altman, ed., *Sound Theory/Sound Practice*, 204–216: "In *Falstaff*, quality of voice takes precedence over sound/image match even more so than in *Macbeth*. . . . A rare instance of sound/space fidelity . . . is saved for the climactic moment when Falstaff yells to the now-king Henry V in the midst of the royal procession. Falstaff's voice echoes off the high stone walls, contrasting dramatically with Henry's silent, cold reception of him. Only such an echo could convey the futility of Falstaff's dreams" (213–14).

24. As Keith Baxter, Welles's Hal, remarks: "Most directors either move the actors or the camera. Orson would move both at the same time, and that is tricky" (Lyons, ed., *Chimes at Midnight*, 270).

25. "What is likely to strike us first about Welles's film is the peculiarly objec-

tified quality of its language—the apparent divorce between words and expression. . . . Shakespeare's dialogue is broken into fragments, dispersed in space so that we cannot connect it with the countenance of the speaker or with the reaction of whoever hears." Terry Comito, "Notes on Panofsky, Cassirer, and the 'Medium of the Movies,' " *Philosophy and Literature* 4, no. 2 (fall 1980): 229–41 (quotation from 238).

26. Keith Baxter, who ought to know, claims that "there isn't a word of the film that was shot in direct sound" (Lyons, ed., *Chimes at Midnight*, 278). Although this may be an exaggeration (I suspect, for example, that King Henry's sleep soliloquy was recorded and photographed at the same time), the extensive postrecording contributes to the tension between word and image throughout the film.

27. Welles even goes so far as to have Falstaff's admission of how he has "misused the King's press" spoken directly to the Earl of Westmoreland.

28. "Ungratified sexuality is a substratum which lies beneath all the relationships in the film" (Davies, *Filming Shakespeare's Plays*, 131). Leonard F. Dean makes a similar point: "here is the young man of honor in training, brushing aside his wife, his mind on the big meet" (Dean, "Comedy, Cultural Poetics, and *Chimes at Midnight*," *Sewanee Review* 102, no. 3 [1994]: 451–455; quotation from 453).

29. Daniel Seltzer, "Shakespeare's Texts and Modern Productions," in Norman Rabkin, ed., *Reinterpretations of Elizabethan Drama*, 108.

30. The battle sequence, Bridget Gellert Lyons writes, "reflects not only [Welles's] personal horror of war, but also the changed perspective of the 1960s, when antiwar feeling and representations of all war as absurd were common" (*Chimes at Midnight*, 14).

31. Naremore, *The Magic World of Orson Welles*, 229. For a description by Welles's cinematographer of how this sequence was constructed, see Jean-Pierre Berthomé and François Thomas, "Sept années en noir et blanc," *Positif* 378 (July-August 1992): 36–48.

32. John Gielgud later recalled that "we never did the scene at all. On the last day Orson said, 'There's a close-up I have to do of you, just look down there, that's Hotspur's body, now look up at me.' " Gyles Brandreth, *John Gielgud: A Celebration*, 152.

33. Some critics—Davies, Pilkington, Gus Van Sant (by implication at least), and Peter Cowie (*A Ribbon of Dreams: The Cinema of Orson Welles*)—have noted the presence of a gay subtext in the scenes between Hal and Poins (not to mention Hal and Falstaff), as well as in the Justice Shallow scenes. Sylvan Barnet goes so far as to describe Hal as "an effeminate bisexual, probably the lover of Poins" on, as far as I can see, very little evidence (Barnet, "Henry IV, Part One on Stage and Screen," in Shakespeare, *Henry IV, Part I*, ed. Maynard Mack, 282).

34. Lyons, ed., *Chimes at Midnight*, 7.

35. Shakespeare, *Henry IV, Part II* (Arden Edition), ed. A. R. Humphries, V.v.85–86 and 89–90.

36. Stanley S. Rubin discusses Welles's use of Holinshed as a narrative device in "Welles/Falstaff/Shakespeare/Welles: The Narrative Structure of *Chimes at Midnight*," *Film Criticism* 2 (winter/spring 1978): 66–71.

37. By the end of Welles's film, Andrew McLean notes, "an epoch has passed, a world view has altered, and a new historical consciousness has been born" ("Orson Welles and Shakespeare: History and Consciousness in *Chimes at Midnight*," *Literature/Film Quarterly* 11 (1983): 197–202; quotation from 202); see also Richard Marienstras who comments on the way the ending of *Chimes* presents us with a greatly diminished world ("Orson Welles, interprète et continuateur de Shakespeare," *Positif* 167 [March, 1975]: 36–44).

38. Welles and Bogdanovich, *This is Orson Welles*, ed. Rosenbaum, 100.

39. Davies, *Filming Shakespeare's Plays*, 133.

40. Bosley Crowther, "Falstaff," *New York Times*, March 20, 1967, sec. 2, p. 26.

41. Kael, *The New Republic*, June 24, 1967; the review is reprinted in Pauline Kael, *Kiss Kiss Bang Bang*, 245–48.

42. Rosenbaum, "Improving Mr. Welles," 29.

43. Jorgens, *Shakespeare on Film*, 111–12.

44. Perhaps more to the point is Anthony Davies' observation that in the Falstaff plays, "Welles found the center of his Shakespearian interest: the tussle between child and adult, between nostalgia for the past and the demand to adjust to coming age" (*Filming Shakespeare's Plays*, 121).

45. Hapgood, " 'Chimes at Midnight' from Stage to Screen," 41.

46. See France, ed., *Orson Welles on Shakespeare* (illustrations between 168–69).

47. Quoted in France, *The Theater of Orson Welles*, 167.

48. Garry O'Connor, *Ralph Richardson: An Actor's Life*, 125.

49. For a full description of this significant theatrical event, see John Dover Wilson and Thomas C. Worsley, *Shakespeare's Histories at Stratford 1951*.

50. "THE DEATH OF HOTSPUR IS MORE THAN A MERE CLIMAX . . . It introduces the note of tragedy. . . . It represents the death of the chivalric idea." Orson Welles to Hilton Edwards, undated letter (Gate Theatre Collection, Correspondence Files, Northwestern University).

51. Ackland, quoted in an interview with Jack Tinker, *What's On in London*, June 4, 1982; cited by Hodgdon, *Shakespeare in Performance: Henry IV, Part II*, 99.

52. Hodgdon, ibid., 84. See also Hodgdon, " 'Heir Apparent': Photography, History, and the Theatrical Unconscious," in *Textual and Theatrical Shakespeare: Questions of Evidence* (Iowa City: University of Iowa Press, 1996), who, after describing a moment in Terry Hands's production of *Henry IV, Part II*, comments: "Falstaff . . . starts to walk slowly toward the dead branches on the back wall and an upstage center exit. Falstaff's upstage move cites, raids, and pays homage to Orson Welles' 1965 film, *Chimes at Midnight (Falstaff)*" (201n21).

8. Welles as Performer: From Shakespeare to Brecht

1. The major exception is Joseph McBride's *Orson Welles: Actor and Director*. McBride, however, provides little more than a hurried, film-by-film survey of Welles's film acting career.

2. James Naremore's *Acting in the Cinema* provides an excellent beginning toward a *poetics* of film acting. See also Naremore's essay, "The Director as Actor," in Morris Beja, ed., *Perspectives on Orson Welles*, 273–80. Charles Affron's *Star Acting*, though not explicity theoretical, contains sensitive analyses of specific performances. A useful collection of essays can be found in Carole Zucker, ed., *Making Visible the Invisible*.

3. As early as 1946, the *Harvard Lampoon* awarded Welles its "Worst Single Performance—Male" award for *The Stranger*. See Cobbett Steinberg, *Reel Facts: The Movie Book of Records*, 333.

4. The success Christopher Plummer had playing John Barrymore on Broadway in the late 1990s represents a self-reflective revival of this tradition.

5. Richard Dyer, *Stars*, 89.

6. Wexman, *Creating the Couple: Love, Marriage, and Hollywood Performance*, 17–18.

7. Pearson, *Eloquent Gestures: The Transformation of Performance Style in the Griffith Biograph Films*, 38–51 and passim.

8. "Orson Welles, as Darrow, Defends Leopold, Loeb," *Life*, April 13, 1959, 60.

9. Bertolt Brecht, *Brecht on Theatre*, ed. and trans. John Willett (quotations from 138 and 126). (Page numbers cited in the text refer to this volume.)

10. Benjamin, "What Is Epic Theater?" in *Illuminations*, 150.

11. William K. Wimsatt Jr. and Cleanth Brooks, *Literary Criticism: A Short History*, 5.

12. Cf. Truffaut: "What has always interested Orson Welles isn't psychology or thrillers or the romances and adventure stories that have been made since the cinema began; no, what interests him are stories in the form of tales, fables, allegories." Truffaut, "Foreword," in Bazin, *Orson Welles: A Critical View*, 22.

13. McBride, *Orson Welles: Actor and Director*, 45.

14. Naremore, *Acting in the Cinema*, 75.

15. Brecht, *Brecht on Theatre*, 139.

16. Leaming, *Orson Welles: A Biography*, 336.

17. See James K. Lyon, *Bertolt Brecht in America*, 179. See also Brecht's letter to Berthold Viertel dated June(?) 1946: "Have you seen Orson Welles's review? Wilson, his manager, will probably get you tickets if you mention me" (John Willett, ed., *Bertolt Brecht Letters*, trans. Ralph Manheim, 406).

18. On December 28, 1941, Brecht recorded the following comment in his journal apropos of *Citizen Kane*: "they [some friends] find the hearst film *Citizen*

Kane eclectic and uneven in style. i find that it is unfair to apply the word eclectic to techniques, and modern to use a variety of different styles for a variety of different functions. they are critical of orson welles's showmanship. but he shows things that are interesting from a social point of view, though it may be that as an actor he has not yet turned his showmanship into a stylistic element. Of course the soil here is not conducive to developing talent" (capitalization per the original). John Willett, ed., *Bertolt Brecht Journals*, trans. Hugh Rorrison, 186.

19. Brecht, quoted in John Willett, *The Theatre of Bertold Brecht*, 3d ed. (London: Methuen, 1979), 174.

20. McBride, *Orson Welles: Actor and Director*, 38.

21. Pauline Kael, ed., *The Citizen Kane Book*, 55.

22. Welles, quoted in Terry Comito, ed., *Films in Print: Touch of Evil*, 205.

23. Martin Esslin, *Brecht: The Man and His Work*, 143.

24. For recent evaluations of *Kane* as political statement, see Laura Mulvey, *Citizen Kane*, and Sidney Gottlieb, "*Citizen Kane*: American Heroes and Witnesses," *North Dakota Quarterly* 60, no. 4 (fall 1992): 105–115.

25. The term is borrowed from Jonathan Rosenbaum, "Orson Welles's Essay Films and Documentary Fictions," 169–79.

26. Welles and Bogdanovich, *This Is Orson Welles*, ed. Rosenbaum, 220–21.

27. Edgar Morin, *The Stars*, trans. Richard Howard (New York: Grove Press, 1961).

28. For Welles's role as huckster for Campbell's soup, see Michele Hilmes, *Radio Voices: American Broadcasting, 1922–1952*, 224–27. As Hilmes notes, "It was a role from which Welles would increasingly distance himself" (224).

29. As an actor, Welles's first Hollywood film was not *Citizen Kane* (1941), but *Swiss Family Robinson* (1940), for which he speaks the opening narration, albeit uncredited.

30. These categories are drawn from Dyer, *Stars*, 121–32.

31. V. I. Pudovkin, *Film Technique and Film Acting*, 168–69.

32. "The New Actor," typescript notes for a lecture, c. 1940, p. 2 (Welles Papers, Lilly Library, box 4, file 26).

33. Brecht, *Brecht on Theatre*, 194.

Epilogue

1. See Uricchio and Pearson, *Reframing Culture*: "Our evidence suggests a greater continuity of Shakespeare's presence among all social formations, as well as a greater complexity in the social uses of Shakespeare, than Levine acknowledges" (67).

2. Denning, *The Cultural Front*, 371.

3. For a discussion of the Maurice Evans productions, see Bernice Kliman, "The Setting in Early Television: Maurice Evans' Shakespeare Productions," in J.

C. Bulman and H. R. Coursen, eds., *Shakespeare on Televison: An Anthology of Essays and Reviews* (Hanover and London: University Press of New England, 1988), 91–101. As Kliman notes, Evans was essentially an old-fashioned Shakespearean actor: "Evan's mannered and declamatory style . . . may have been, even in 1953, an exaggerated and outmoded 'Shakespearean' acting technique" (94).

4. During his American exile, Brecht had considered making a film tentatively titled *Caesar's Last Days*, in a manner reminiscent of the Mercury production: "the industry isn't making costume films," he noted. "it is wary of the nightshirts the meiningers clothed the romans in. in actual fact you could dye the tunics dark colours and have them elegantly cut. the plebs could wear trousers and shirts. the public would come to see this kind of thing since its interest in history and large-scale politics has been awakened" (capitalization per the original). Willett, ed., *Bertolt Brecht Journals*, trans. Rorrison, 219.s

Adorno, Theodor W. "Culture and Administration." In Bernstein, ed., *The Culture Industry*, 93–113.

———. "How to Look at Television." In Bernstein, ed., *The Culture Industry*, 136–53. Originally published in the *Quarterly of Film, Radio, and Television* 8, no. 3 (1954): 213–35.

———. "The Schema of Mass Culture." in Bernstein, ed., *The Culture Industry*, 53–84.

Affron, Charles. *Star Acting*. New York: Dutton, 1977.

Agnew, Jean-Christophe. *Worlds Apart: The Market and the Theater in Anglo-American Thought, 1550–1750*. Cambridge: Cambridge University Press, 1986.

Altman, Rick, ed. *Sound Theory/Sound Practice*. New York: Routledge, 1992.

Andrew, Dudley. *Film in the Aura of Art*. Princeton: Princeton University Press, 1984.

Applebee, Arthur N. *Tradition and Reform in the Teaching of English: A History*. Urbana, Ill.: National Council of Teachers of English, 1974.

Ashworth, John. "Olivier, Freud, and Hamlet." *Atlantic Monthly* 183 (May 1949): 30–33.

Barasch, Frances K. "Revisionist Art: *Macbeth* on Film." *University of Dayton Review* 14 (1979–1980): 15–20.

Barthes, Roland. "The Reality Effect." In *The Rustle of Language*. Translated by Richard Howard. New York: Hill and Wang, 1986.

Bazin, André. *Orson Welles: A Critical View*. With a Foreword by François Truffaut. Translated by Jonathan Rosenbaum. New York: Harper and Row, 1978.

Beja, Morris, ed. *Perspectives on Orson Welles*. New York: G. K. Hall, 1995.

Benjamin, Walter. *Illuminations*. Edited by Hannah Arendt. Translated by Harry Zohn. New York: Schocken, 1969.

Bennett, Susan. *Performing Nostalgia: Shifting Shakespeare and the Contemporary Past.* London: Routledge, 1996.

Bentley, Eric. "The Other Orson Welles." *New Republic,* April 30, 1956, 29.

Bernstein, J. M., ed. *The Culture Industry: Selected Essays on Mass Culture.* London: Routledge, 1991.

Berthomé, Jean-Pierre and François Thomas. "Sept années en noir et blanc." *Positif* 378 (July-August 1992): 36–48.

Bessy, Maurice. *Orson Welles.* Translated by Ciba Vaughan. New York: Crown, 1971.

Boose, Lynda E. and Richard Burt, eds. *Shakespeare, the Movie: Popularizing the Plays on Film, TV, and Video.* London and New York: Routledge, 1997.

Brady, Frank. *Citizen Welles: A Biography of Orson Welles.* New York: Scribner's, 1989.

Brandreth, Gyles. *John Gielgud: A Celebration.* Boston: Little, Brown, 1984.

Brecht, Bertolt. *Brecht on Theatre.* Edited and translated by John Willett. 2d ed. New York: Hill and Wang, 1974.

——. *The Messingkauf Dialogues.* Translated by John Willett. London: Eyre Methuen, 1965.

Bristol, Michael. *Big-Time Shakespeare.* London: Routledge, 1996.

——. *Shakespeare's America, America's Shakespeare.* London: Routledge, 1990.

Brown, John Mason. "Knock, Knock, Knock!" *Saturday Review,* July 29, 1950, 22–24.

Buchman, Lorne M. *Still in Movement: Shakespeare on Screen.* New York: Oxford University Press, 1991.

Bullough, Geoffrey, ed. *Narrative and Dramatic Sources of Shakespeare.* Vol. 7, *Major Tragedies: Hamlet, Othello, King Lear, Macbeth.* London: Routledge and Kegan Paul, 1973; New York: Columbia University Press, 1973.

Bulman, James C., ed. *Shakespeare, Theory, and Performance.* London and New York: Routledge, 1996.

Callow, Simon. *Orson Welles: The Road to Xanadu.* New York: Viking, 1995.

Cobos, Juan and Esteve Riambau. *Orson Welles.* Vol. 1, *Una España Immortal,* vol. 2, *España Como Obsesión.* Valencia: Filmoteca de la Generalitat Valenciana, 1993.

Cobos, Juan and Miguel Rubio. 'Welles and Falstaff." *Sight and Sound* 35 (autumn 1966): 158–63.

Collick, John. *Shakespeare, Cinema, and Society.* Manchester and New York: Manchester University Press, 1989.

Collumb, Elizabeth, ed. *The Criterion Collection: A Comprehensive Guide* (1994 Voyager catalog).

Comer, Brooke. "Carving Out the Couplets." *American Cinematographer* 73 (July 1992): 74–76.

———. "Restoring the 'Dusky Moor': Welles' *Othello*." *American Cinematographer* 73 (July 1992): 66–71.

Comito, Terry. "Notes on Panofsky, Cassirer, and the 'Medium of the Movies.' " *Philosophy and Literature* 4, no. 2 (fall 1980): 229–41.

———, ed. *Films in Print: Touch of Evil*. New Brunswick, N.J.: Rutgers University Press, 1985.

Cornell, Katharine, as told to Ruth Woodbury Sedgwick. "I Wanted to Be an Actress." *Stage* 16 (January 1939): 43.

Cowie, Peter. *A Ribbon of Dreams: The Cinema of Orson Welles*. South Brunswick and New York: A. S. Barnes, 1973.

Cowig, Ruth. "Actors, Black and Tawny, in the Role of Othello—and Their Critics." *Theatre Research International* 4, no. 2 (February 1979): 133–46.

Crowl, Samuel. "The Long Goodbye: Welles and Falstaff." *Shakespeare Quarterly* 31 (autumn 1980): 369–80.

———. *Shakespeare Observed: Studies in Performance on Stage and Screen*. Athens: Ohio University Press, 1992.

Culler, Jonathan. *On Deconstruction*. Ithaca, N.Y.: Cornell University Press, 1982.

Davies, Anthony. *Filming Shakespeare's Plays*. Cambridge: Cambridge University Press, 1988.

Davies, Anthony and Stanley Wells, eds. *Shakespeare and the Moving Image: The Plays on Film and Television*. Cambridge: Cambridge University Press, 1994.

Dean, Leonard F. "Comedy, Cultural Poetics, and *Chimes at Midnight*." *Sewanee Review* 102, no. 3 (1994): 451–55.

Denning, Michael. *The Cultural Front: The Laboring of American Culture in the Twentieth Century*. London and New York: Verso, 1996.

———. "Towards a People's Theater: The Cultural Politics of the Mercury Theatre." *Persistence of Vision* 7 (1989): 24–38.

Doherty, Thomas. *Teenagers and Teenpics: The Juvenilization of American Movies in the 1950s*. Boston: Unwin Hyman, 1988.

Dollimore, Jonathan and Alan Sinfield, eds. *Political Shakespeare: New Essays in Cultural Materialism*. Ithaca and London: Cornell University Press, 1985.

Donaldson, Peter S. *Shakespearean Films/Shakespearean Directors*. Boston: Unwin Hyman, 1990.

Dyer, Richard. *Stars*. London: British Film Institute, 1979.

Eckert, Charles W., ed. *Focus on Shakespearean Films*. Englewood Cliffs, N.J.: Prentice-Hall, 1972.

Eder, Bruce. Liner notes for *Richard III*. Laurence Olivier, dir., 1955. Videodisk. Voyager, 1994.

Elhem, Philippe. "Avatars de la restauration: à propos d'*Othello* et *Don Quichotte* d'Orson Welles." *24 Images*, nos. 62–63 (September-October 1992): 42–43.

Esslin, Martin. *Brecht: The Man and His Work.* Garden City, N.Y.: Doubleday, 1960.

Fraden, Rena. *Blueprints for a Black Federal Theatre, 1935–1939.* Cambridge: Cambridge University Press, 1994.

France, Richard. *The Theatre of Orson Welles.* Lewisburg, Penn., and London: Bucknell University Press, 1977.

———. "The 'Voodoo' Macbeth of Orson Welles." *Yale Theatre* 5, no. 3 (1974): 67.

———, ed. *Orson Welles on Shakespeare: The W.P.A. and Mercury Theatre Playscripts.* New York: Greenwood, 1990.

Ginsberg, Walter. "How Helpful Are Shakespeare Recordings?" *English Journal* 29 (1940): 289–300.

Gottlieb, Sidney. "*Citizen Kane*: American Heroes and Witnesses." *North Dakota Quarterly* 60, no. 4 (fall 1992): 105–115.

Grady, Hugh. *Modernist Shakespeare.* Oxford: Clarendon Press, 1991.

———. *Shakespeare's Universal Wolf: Studies in Early Modern Reification.* Oxford: Clarendon Press, 1996.

Halpern, Richard. "Shakespeare in the Tropics: From High Modernism to New Historicism." *Representations* 45 (winter 1994): 1–21.

Hankey, Julie, ed. *Othello: Plays in Performance.* Bristol, Eng.: Bristol Classics Press, 1987.

Hapgood, Robert. " 'Chimes at Midnight' from Stage to Screen: The Art of Adaptation." *Shakespeare Survey* 39 (1987): 39–52.

Harper, Wendy Rogers. "Polanski vs. Welles on *Macbeth*: Character or Fate?" *Literature/Film Quarterly* 14, no. 4 (1986): 203–210.

Hawkes, Terence. "Bardbiz." *London Review of Books*, February 22, 1990, 11–13.

Hawkins, Harriett. *Classics and Trash: Traditions and Taboos in High Literature and Popular Modern Genres.* Toronto: University of Toronto Press, 1990.

Higham, Charles. *The Films of Orson Welles.* Berkeley: University of California Press, 1970.

———. *Orson Welles: The Rise and Fall of an American Genius.* New York: St. Martin's, 1985.

Hill, Roger, and Orson Welles, eds. *Everybody's Shakespeare: Three Plays.* Woodstock, Ill.: Todd Press, 1934.

Hilmes, Michele. *Hollywood and Broadcasting: From Radio to Cable.* Urbana and Chicago: University of Illinois Press, 1990.

———. *Radio Voices: American Broadcasting, 1922–1952.* Minneapolis: University of Minnesota Press, 1997.

Hobson, Bulmer, ed. *The Gate Theatre—Dublin.* Dublin: Gate Theatre, 1934.

Hodgdon, Barbara. *Shakespeare in Performance: Henry IV, Part II.* Manchester and New York: Manchester University Press, 1993.

Holderness, Graham. "Radical Potentiality and Institutional Closure: Shakespeare in Film and Television." In Dollimore and Sinfield, eds., *Political Shakespeare*, 182–201.

———. "Shakespeare Rewound." *Shakespeare Survey* 45 (1993): 63–74.

Houseman, John. *Run-Through: A Memoir*. New York: Simon and Schuster, 1972.

Houston, Beverle. "Power and Dis-Integration in the Films of Orson Welles." *Film Quarterly* 35 (summer 1982): 2–12

Hughes, Alan. *Henry Irving, Shakespearean*. Cambridge: Cambridge University Press, 1981.

Impastato, David. "Orson Welles's *Othello* and the Welles-Smith Restoration: Definitive Version?" *Shakespeare Bulletin: A Journal of Performance Criticism and Scholarship* 10, no. 4 (fall 1992): 38–41.

"Jello Program with Jack Benny." CBS Radio, March 17, 1940.

Johnston, Alva and Fred Smith. "How to Raise a Child: The Education of Orson Welles, Who Didn't Need It." *Saturday Evening Post* (Part 1, January 20, 1940; Part 2, January 27, 1940; Part 3, February 3, 1940).

Jorgens, Jack J. *Shakespeare on Film*. Bloomington: Indiana University Press, 1977.

Kael, Pauline. *Kiss Kiss Bang Bang*. Boston: Little, Brown, 1968.

———, ed. *The Citizen Kane Book*. Boston: Little, Brown, 1971.

Kennedy, Dennis. *Looking at Shakespeare: A Visual History of Twentieth-Century Performance*. Cambridge: Cambridge University Press, 1993.

———, ed. *Foreign Shakespeare: Contemporary Performance*. Cambridge: Cambridge University Press, 1993.

Kennedy, Harold J. *No Pickle, No Performance*. Garden City, N.Y.: Doubleday, 1978.

Kerns, Ruth B. "Color and Music and Movement." *Performing Arts Annual* 47 (1987): 52–77.

Kliman, Bernice W. *Hamlet: Film, Television, and Audio Performance*. Rutherford, N.J.: Fairleigh Dickinson University Press, 1988.

———. *Shakespeare in Performance: Macbeth*. Manchester and New York: Manchester University Press, 1992.

Kott, Jan. *Shakespeare Our Contemporary*. Translated by Boleslaw Taborski, Garden City, N.Y.: Anchor Books, 1966.

Lanham, Richard. *The Motives of Eloquence: Literary Rhetoric in the Renaissance*. New Haven: Yale University Press, 1976.

Lauk, John Hampton II. "The Reception and Teaching of Shakespeare in Nineteenth and Early Twentieth-Century America." Ph. D. diss., Univerity of Illinois, 1991.

Leaming, Barbara. *Orson Welles: A Biography*. New York: Viking, 1985.

Leggatt, Alexander. *Shakespeare in Performance: King Lear*. Manchester, Eng.: Manchester University Press, 1991.

Legrand, Gérard. "Strange Sense of Eternity . . . (Filming Othello)." *Positif* 231 (June 1980): 66–68.

Leonard, Harold. "Notes on Macbeth." *Sight and Sound* 19 (March 1950): 15–17.

Leonard, William Torbert. *Masquerade in Black*. Metuchen, NJ: The Scarecrow Press, Inc., 1986.

Levine, Lawrence W. *Highbrow/Lowbrow: The Emergence of Cultural Hierarchy in America*. Cambridge: Harvard University Press, 1988.

Lopate, Phillip. "In Search of the Centaur: The Essay-Film." In Charles Warren, ed. *Beyond Document: Essays on Nonfiction Film*, 243–70. Hanover and London: Wesleyan University Press, 1996.

Lyon, James K. *Bertolt Brecht in America*. Princeton: Princeton University Press, 1980.

Lyons, Bridget Gellert, ed. *Films in Print: Chimes at Midnight*. New Brunswick, N.J.: Rutgers University Press, 1988.

MacLiammoir, Michael. *Put Money in Thy Purse: The Filming of Orson Welles' "Othello."* London: Eyre Methuen, 1952.

Manvell, Roger. *Shakespeare and the Film*. New York: Praeger, 1971.

Marienstras, Richard. "Orson Welles, interprète et continuateur de Shakespeare." *Positif* 167 (March 1975): 36–44.

Marowitz, Charles. *The Marowitz Shakespeare*. New York: Drama Book Specialists, 1978.

Mazer, Cary M. *Shakespeare Refashioned: Elizabethan Plays on Edwardian Stages*. Ann Arbor, Mich.: UMI Research Press, 1981.

McBride, Joseph. *Orson Welles*. New York: Viking, 1972.

——. *Orson Welles: Actor and Director*. New York: Harcourt Brace, 1977.

McLean, Andrew. "Orson Welles and Shakespeare: History and Consciousness in *Chimes at Midnight*." *Literature/Film Quarterly* 11 (1983): 197–202.

McMillin, Scott. *Shakespeare in Performance: Henry IV, Part I*. Manchester: Manchester University Press, 1991.

Mellencamp, Patricia. "Situation Comedy, Feminism, and Freud: Discourses of Gracie and Lucy." In Tania Modleski, ed., *Studies in Entertainment*. Bloomington: Indiana University Press, 1986.

Mesic, Penelope. "Improving on Genius." *Chicago* 41, no. 2 (February 1992): 43–44.

Morrison, Michael A. *John Barrymore: Shakespearean Actor*. Cambridge: Cambridge University Press, 1997.

Mosel, Tad, with Gertrude Macy. *Leading Lady: The World and Theatre of Katharine Cornell*. Boston: Little, Brown, 1978.

Mulvey, Laura. *Citizen Kane*. BFI Film Classics. London: British Film Institute, 1992.

Naremore, James. *Acting in the Cinema*. Berkeley: University of California Press, 1988.

——. "The Director as Actor." In Beja, ed., *Perspectives on Orson Welles*, 273–80.

———. *The Magic World of Orson Welles.* New and revised edn. Dallas, Texas: Southern Methodist University Press, 1989.

———. "The Walking Shadow: Welles's Expressionist *Macbeth.*" *Literature/Film Quarterly* 1, no. 4 (fall 1973): 360–66.

Nichols, Bill, ed. *Movies and Methods.* Berkeley and Los Angeles: University of California Press, 1976.

Nouryeh, Andrea. "The Mercury Theatre: A History." Ph. D. diss., New York University, 1987.

O'Connor, Garry. *Ralph Richardson: An Actor's Life.* Revised and updated ed. London: Hodder and Stoughton, 1986.

O'Connor, John S. "But Was It 'Shakespeare'?: Welles's *Macbeth* and *Julius Caesar.*" *Theatre Journal* 32, no. 3 (October 1980): 337–48.

Ommanney, Katharine Anne. *The Stage and the School.* 2d ed. New York: Harper, 1939.

Orson Welles Clipping Files, New York Public Library for the Performing Arts.

Orson Welles: The One Man Band. Directed by Vassili Silovic, 1995.

Orson Welles on the Air: The Radio Years. New York: Museum of Broadcasting, 1988.

Osborne, Laurie E. "Filming Shakespeare in a Cultural Thaw: Soviet Appropriations of Shakesperean Treacheries in 1955–6." *Textual Practice* 9, no. 2 (1995): 325–47.

Parker, Patricia. *Shakespeare from the Margins: Language, Culture, Context.* Chicago and London: University of Chicago Press, 1996.

Pearson, Roberta. *Eloquent Gestures: The Transformation of Performance Style in the Griffith Biograph Films.* Berkeley: University of California Press, 1992.

Pearson, Roberta E. and William Uricchio. "How Many Times Shall Caesar Bleed in Sport: Shakespeare and the Cultural Debate About Moving Pictures." *Screen* 31, no. 3 (autumn 1990): 252, 258.

Pechter, Edward. *Textual and Theatrical Shakespeare: Questions of Evidence.* Iowa City: University of Iowa Press, 1996.

Pilkington, Ace G. *Screening Shakespeare from "Richard II" to "Henry V."* Newark: University of Delaware Press, 1991.

Pine, Richard, with Richard Cave. *The Dublin Gate Theatre, 1928–1978.* Cambridge and Teaneck, N.J.: Chadwyck-Healy, 1984.

Poague, Leland. " 'Reading' the Prince: Shakespeare, Welles, and Some Aspects of *Chimes at Midnight.*" *Iowa State Journal of Research* 56, no. 1 (August 1981): 57–65.

Pudovkin, V. I. *Film Technique and Film Acting.* Translated and edited by Ivor Montagu. New York: Grove Press, 1970.

Rabkin, Norman, ed. *Reinterpretations of Elizabethan Drama.* New York: Columbia University Press, 1969.

"Restoration Team Resurrects 'Othello.' " *Millimeter* 20 (February 1992): 35.

Richard Wilson Papers. UCLA Special Collections, University of California Library, Los Angeles.

Rosenbaum, Jonathan. "Improving Mr. Welles." *Sight and Sound*, n.s., 12, no. 6 (October 1992): 28–30.

———. "Orson Welles's Essay Films and Documentary Fictions: A Two-Part Speculation." *Cinematograph* 4 (1991): 169–79.

———. "Othello Goes Hollywood." *Chicago Reader* 10 (April 10, 1992): 12, 36–37, 39.

Rosenberg, Marvin. "Shakespere on TV: An Optimistic Survey." *The Quarterly Review of Film and Television* 9, no. 2 (1954): 166–174.

Rosenberg, Marvin. *The Masks of Macbeth*. Berkeley: University of California Press, 1978.

———. *The Masks of Othello*. Berkeley: University of California Press, 1971.

Rubin, Joan Shelly. *The Making of Middlebrow Culture*. Chapel Hill and London: University of North Carolina Press, 1992.

Rubin, Stanley S. "Welles/Falstaff/Shakespeare/Welles: The Narrative Structure of *Chimes at Midnight*." *Film Criticism* 2 (winter / spring 1978): 66–71.

Shakespeare, William. *Antony and Cleopatra*. Edited by M. R. Ridley. Cambridge: Harvard University Press, 1954.

———. *Henry IV, Part I*. Edited by Maynard Mack. Rev. Signet ed. New York: Penguin Books, 1986.

———. *Henry IV, Part II* (Arden Edition). Edited by A. R. Humphries. London: Metheun, 1966.

———. *Othello*. Edited by Alvin Kernan. New York: New American Library, 1963.

———. *Othello*. Edited by Norman Saunders. Cambridge: Cambridge University Press, 1984.

———. *The Second Part of King Henry IV*. Edited by Giorgio Melchiori. Cambridge: Cambridge University Press, 1989.

Shattuck, Charles H. *Shakespeare on the American Stage*. 2 vols. Vol. 1, *From the Hallams to Edwin Booth*; vol. 2, *From Booth and Barrett to Sothern and Marlowe*. Washington, D.C.: Folger Shakespeare Library, 1976, 1987.

Simon, Scott. "Concerning the Weary Legs of Wyatt Earp: The Classic Western According to Shakespeare." *Literature / Film Quarterly* 24, no. 2 (1996): 114–27.

Simon, William. "Welles: Bakhtin: Parody." *Quarterly Review of Film and Video* 12, nos. 1–2 (1990): 23–28.

Skoller, Donald S. "Problems of Transformation in the Adaptation of Shakespeare's Tragedies from Play-Script to Cinema." Ph. D. diss., New York University, 1968.

Skovmand, Michael, ed. *Screen Shakespeare*. Aarhus, Denmark: Aarhus University Press, 1994.

Smeets, Marcel. "*Macbeth*: Une adaptation cinématographique d'Orson Welles." *Revue des Langues Vivantes* 17 (1951): 58–62.

South Bank Show. Editor/presenter Melvyn Bragg, ITV, April 2, 1989.

Steinberg, Cobbett. *Reel Facts: The Movie Book of Records.* Updated ed. New York: Vintage, 1982.

Styan, J. L. *The Shakespeare Revolution: Criticism and Performance in the Twentieth Century.* London: Cambridge University Press, 1977.

Tatomirovic, Aleksandra Jovicevic. "The Theatre of Orson Welles, 1946–1960." Ph.D. diss., New York University, 1990.

Taylor, Gary. *Reinventing Shakespeare.* New York: Weidenfeld and Nicolson, 1989.

Taylor, Zanthe. "Singing for Their Supper: The Negro Units of the Federal Theatre Project and Their Plays." *Theater* 27, nos. 2–3 (1997): 43–59.

Thomas, François. "La tragédie d' 'Othello.' " *Positif,* 424 (June 1996): 70–76.

Thomson, David. *Rosebud: The Story of Orson Welles.* New York: Knopf, 1996.

Tyler, Parker. "*Hamlet* and Documentary." *Kenyon Review* 11 (1949): 527–32.

Ulbricht, Walter. "Orson Welles' Macbeth: Archetype and Symbol." *University of Dayton Review* 14 (1979–1980): 21–27.

Uricchio, William and Roberta E. Pearson. *Reframing Culture: The Case of the Vitagraph Quality Films.* Princeton: Princeton University Press, 1993.

Vaughan, Virginia Mason. *Othello: A Contextual History.* Cambridge: Cambridge University Press, 1994.

Vaughan, Virginia Mason and Kent Cartwright, eds. *Othello: New Perspectives.* Rutherford, N.J.: Fairleigh Dickinson University Press, 1991.

Verdi, Giuseppe. *Falstaff: National Opera Guides 10.* Edited by Nicholas John. London: John Calder, 1982.

Weingarten, Samuel. "The Use of Phonograph Recordings in Teaching Shakespeare." *College English* 1, no. 1 (October 1939): 45–61

Weis, Elizabeth and John Belton, eds. *Film Sound: Theory and Practice.* New York: Columbia University Press, 1985.

Weiss, Steven Marc. "The Rise of Directorial Influence in Broadway Shakesperean Production: 1920–1950." Ph.D. diss, Ohio State University, 1994.

Welles, Orson. Mercury Theatre Collection. Lilly Library, Bloomington, Ind.

——. "The Third Audience." *Sight and Sound* 23 (January-March 1954): 120–22.

Welles, Orson and Peter Bogdanovich. *This Is Orson Welles.* Edited by Jonathan Rosenbaum. New York: HarperCollins, 1992.

Welles, Orson and Roger Hill. "On the Teaching of Shakespeare and Other Great Literature." *English Journal* 27 (1938): 464–68.

Welles, Orson and Roger Hill, eds. *The Mercury Shakespeare.* New York: Harper, 1939.

Wexman, Virginia Wright. *Creating the Couple: Love, Marriage, and Hollywood Performance.* Princeton: Princeton University Press, 1993.

Willett, John. *The Theatre of Bertolt Brecht.* 2d ed. London: Methuen, 1960.

——, ed. *Bertolt Brecht Journals*. Translated by Hugh Rorrison. New York: Routledge, 1993.

——, ed. *Bertolt Brecht Letters*. Translated by Ralph Manheim. New York: Routledge, 1990.

Willson, Robert F., Jr. "Recontextualizing Shakespeare on Film: *My Own Private Idaho, Men of Respect, Prospero's Books*." *Shakespeare Bulletin* 10, no. 3 (summer 1992): 34–37.

Wilson, John Dover and Thomas C. Worsley. *Shakespeare's Histories at Stratford 1951*. New York: Theatre Arts Books, 1952.

Wilson, Richard. *See* Richard Wilson Papers.

Wimsatt, William K. Jr. and Cleanth Brooks. *Literary Criticism: A Short History*. New York: Knopf, 1957.

Winge, John H. "*Macbeth*: Directed by Orson Welles." *Records of the Film*, no. 20. London: British Film Institute, n.d.

With Orson Welles: Stories from a Life on Film (1990), Turner Network Television; reedited from *The Orson Welles Story* (BBC, 1980), directed and produced by Alan Yentob and Leslie Megahey.

Wollen, Peter. "Foreign Relations: Welles and *Touch of Evil*." *Sight and Sound*, n.s., 6, no. 10 (October 1996): 20.

Wood, Robin. *Personal Views*. London: Gordon Fraser, 1976.

Zucker, Carole, ed. *Making Visible the Invisible*. Metuchen, N.J.: Scarecrow, 1990.

INDEX

—

—